# IN GRANITE
## OR **INGRAINED?**

# IN GRANITE
## OR INGRAINED?

What the Old and New Covenants Reveal
about the Gospel, the Law, and the Sabbath

Skip MacCarty

Andrews
University Press

Berrien Springs, Michigan

Andrews University Press
Sutherland House
8360 W. Campus Circle Dr.
Berrien Springs, MI 49104-1700
Telephone: 269-471-6134
Fax: 269-471-6224
Email: aupo@andrews.edu
Website: http://universitypress.andrews.edu

ISBN 978-1-883925-57-4

Printed in the United States of America
16   15   14   13   12          8   7   6   5   4

Library of Congress Cataloging-in-Publication Data

MacCarty, Skip.
  In granite or ingrained? : what the Old and New Covenants reveal about the Gospel, the Law, and the Sabbath / Skip MacCarty.
    p. cm.
  Includes bibliographical references and index.
  ISBN 978-1-883925-57-4 (pbk. : alk. paper)  1. Covenant theology. 2. Sabbath--Biblical teaching. 3. Covenants--Religious aspects--Seventh-day Adventists. 4. Seventh-day Adventists--Doctrines. I. Title.

BT155.M23 2007
231.7'6--dc22
                          2006038830

    All scripture quotations, unless otherwise indicated, are taken from the HOLY BIBLE, NEW INTERNATIONAL VERSION®. NIV®. Copyright ©1973, 1978, 1984 by International Bible Society. Used by permission of Zondervan. All rights reserved.
    Scripture quotations marked "ASV" are taken from the American Standard Version.
    Scripture quotations marked "ESV" are taken from The Holy Bible, English Standard Version, copyright © 2001 by Crossway Bibles, a division of Good News Publishers. Used by permission. All rights reserved.
    Scripture quotations marked "KJV" are taken from the King James Version.
    Scripture quotations marked "NASB" are taken from the New American Standard Bible®, Copyright © 1960, 1962, 1963, 1968, 1971, 1972, 1973, 1975, 1977, 1995 by The Lockman Foundation. Used by permission. (www.Lockman.org)
    Scripture quotations marked "NJPS" are taken from the Jewish Study Bible. Jewish Publication Society Tanakh Translation, © Copyright 1985, 1999.
    Scripture quotations marked "NKJV" are taken from the New King James Version. Copyright © 1982 by Thomas Nelson, Inc. Used by permission. All rights reserved.
    Scripture quotations marked "NRSV" are taken from the New Revised Standard Version Bible, copyright 1989, Division of Christian Education of the National Council of the Churches of Christ in the United States of America. Used by permission. All rights reserved.

|  |  |
|---|---|
| Project Director | Ronald Alan Knott |
| Project Editor | Deborah L. Everhart |
| Line Editor | Kenneth Wade |
| Copy Editor | Denise McAllister |
| Typesetter | Thomas Toews |
| Text and Cover Designer | Robert N. Mason |

Typeset: 10.5/16 Adobe Caslon Pro

**Dedicated to**
Dwight K. Nelson
Boss, Colleague, Mentor, Friend
for twenty years and counting

# Table of Contents

# Acknowledgments

I prayed early in my study that God would guide me to the resources that could give me a depth of understanding about the covenants. At the time, I primarily had in mind written resources. But the help God provided primarily came through people. At critical times in my study, He sent people into my life who encouraged me, challenged me, and directed me to further resources at just the time they were needed.

My boss and senior pastor, Dwight K. Nelson, both encouraged me in this study and provided me with the title of this book. Professor Woodrow Whidden heard of my interest in the covenants and asked me to teach a two-hour session on the covenants for one of his religion classes at Andrews University, and later became a reader and constructive critic of an edited copy of the manuscript.

In the spring of 2003, I was asked to make a one-hour presentation on my study of the covenants to an ad hoc group, the "Gospel Study Committee" that, unknown to me, had been studying this subject for two years.[1] Its members subsequently asked me to write the opening chapter of a manuscript they were jointly writing on the covenants. When I submitted my first edition of a proposed chapter, they suggested that I expand it into a book manuscript in its own right. Their detailed critiques of that manuscript and its subsequent editions proved invaluable. Written critiques by Fred Bischoff and Seventh-day Adventist Theological Seminary professors Jon Paulien, Jerry Moon, and Roy Gane proved especially helpful. Dr. Gane's syllabus on "The Covenants, Law and Sabbath" also gave me great help early in my study. Jerry Finneman helped me with a critical point in appendix B, "'Under Law' vs. 'Under Grace.'"

One member of that committee took me under his wing and gave me invaluable encouragement, guidance, and support throughout the preparation of this manuscript—Richard Davidson, chair of the Seventh-day Adventist Theological Seminary Old Testament Department. Without his help, this book would never have gotten published.

George Knight gave me valuable help by critiquing an early edition of this manuscript and then rereading it after I had worked on his suggestions. Bruce Wrenn, professor of marketing at the South Bend, Indiana, campus of Indiana University, and a member of a small group I have been in for several years, gave me stylistic suggestions. Bryan von Dorpowski, another member of that small group and a close friend, endured the ups and downs I experienced during the most intense months of my study into this subject and still treated me as though I was normal.

I gained valuable insights from the questions and feedback I received from various groups to which I have presented seminars on the old and new covenants—members of the Pioneer Memorial Church Community Bible Class who allowed me to teach this subject over a period of several months as I was organizing a couple of years of study material; conference leaders and ministers of the Oregon Conference at their Fall, 2004, Worker's Retreat; members of the Jackson Seventh-day Adventist Church who were wrestling with the issues involved in this subject; and the Southern Adventist University religion professors and students at the Fall, 2005, Robert H. Pierson Lectureship Series.

I thank the Scholarly Publications and Andrews University Press Board for their faith in the manuscript; Ronald Knott, director of Andrews University Press, and Kenneth Wade whose editorial assistance made this a tighter, better manuscript; and Deborah Everhart, in-house editor at Andrews University Press, who guided the project through the editorial process and provided meticulous proofreading.

I'm especially grateful for my wife Lyn's patience, understanding, and loving support during several years in which my latest discoveries from my study of the covenants kept intruding into our conversations on more personal issues.

## Notes

1. Members of this group included Fred Bischoff, P. Gerard Damsteegt, Richard Davidson, Skip Dodson, Jerry Finneman, Roy Gane, R. J. Gravell, Lloyd Knecht, Jerry Moon, Jon Paulien, Paul Penno, John Peters, Brian Schwartz, and Peter Van Bemmelen.

# Introduction

Does the Bible have contradictory conceptions about God's law? Serious Bible students soon notice that God's law and commandments are described in these positive ways: "for your own good" (Deut. 10:13); "intended to bring life" (Rom. 7:10); written by God in the hearts of His children (Deut. 30:10–14; Heb. 8:10);[1] "perfect" (Ps. 19:7); "converting the soul" (Ps. 19:7 NKJV); "freedom" (Ps. 119:44–45; James 2:8–12); established by faith (Rom. 3:31); "holy…righteous…good…spiritual" (Ps. 119:172; Rom. 7:12, 14); fulfilled in the life of one who walks according to the Spirit (Rom. 8:14); that which reveals sin that sinners might be led to Christ (Gal. 3:23–24; Rom. 3:20; 7:13).

But the law and commandments are also described in the negative: as engraved on stone rather than in the heart (2 Cor. 3:7); the power of sin (1 Cor. 15:56); a letter that kills (Rom. 7:10–11; 2 Cor. 3:6); "the ministry that brought death" (2 Cor. 3:7); "the ministry that condemns men" (2 Cor. 3:9); something we must die to in order to be married to Christ and receive salvation (Rom. 7:1–4; Gal. 2:19); not based on faith (Gal. 3:12); a curse from which Jesus redeemed us (Gal. 3:13); that which will prevent those who try to live by it from ever sharing in the inheritance of the saints (Gal. 4:30); that which imprisons us (Gal. 3:23); that which produces slave children (Gal. 4:24–25, 30–31); no longer needed as a tutor once we've been converted and come to Christ (Gal. 3:24–25).[2]

How does the honest seeker of truth sort out these apparently conflicting biblical references regarding God's law?

## What Drew Me to This Study

On my way to a ministerial conference in August of 2000, I stopped by a Christian bookstore and bought a book someone had recommended dealing with the gospel, the Sabbath, and the old and new covenants. It focused heavily on texts from the second list above, texts that appear to disparage God's law. It portrayed the old covenant as the covenant God made with Israel at Sinai, though more broadly involving the entire Old Testament. It implied that the Old Testament covenant, especially the covenant and laws God gave His people at Sinai, was applicable only to Israel, and that Jesus abolished it when He instituted the new covenant. The author based this claim in part on Moses's statement concerning the Sinai covenant that "it was not with our fathers that the LORD made this covenant" (Deut. 5:3), coupled with God's own statement that the new covenant "will not be like the covenant I made with their fathers when I took them by the hand to lead them out of Egypt" (Jer. 31:31; Heb. 8:9). The new covenant, according to this author, reduced the many Old Testament laws to the simpler New Testament law of love with a few ethical principles added to show how love applies. Graphically depicted, this model looks like this:

| Abrahamic Covenant | Sinai Covenant | New Covenant |
|---|---|---|
| Promise/Faith | Law/Obedience | Promise/Faith<br>Holy Spirit/Love |
| | Not like the covenant made with their fathers.<br>Deuteronomy 5:3 | Not like the covenant made with those redeemed from Egypt.<br>Hebrews 8:8–9 |

According to this argument, the seventh-day Sabbath was exclusively a Sinaitic old covenant institution intended only for the nation of Israel. No one under the new covenant has been commanded to keep it, and in fact it has been repealed directly by New Testament texts such as Romans 14:5, Galatians 4:10, and Colossians 2:16. So, of course, God doesn't intend for the Sabbath to be applicable to new covenant Christians.

This book also highlighted the wonderful liberty experienced by new covenant believers who are converted, know God, are motivated by love, and are guided by the Holy Spirit in contrast to those who were in bondage to the old covenant, were "born of flesh," did not know God personally, and labored "in slavery" under the law God gave to Israel.

Reading this book stimulated me to a new study of the old and new covenants. It proved to be a most challenging and rewarding study. Many times the meaning of certain scriptural passages baffled me. Most commentaries didn't help much, and some just added to my confusion. I often had to pray my way toward an understanding of Bible passages that appeared to contradict each other. The conclusions I reached in the process often came with wonderful insights and glimpses into God's character that I long for and pray for regularly, but might never have gained except through the discipline, focus, and prayer required by this study.

## A Preview of What I Found

I found that God's covenant with humankind originated with the covenant that existed among the Trinity from the beginning. God's everlasting covenant that embraces the whole of His creation includes humankind, both before and after the entrance of sin. Though God's covenant is universal in its reach, it has been revealed progressively through the ages in a variety of covenants that He made with people whom He entrusted with His message to the world.

Sometimes when the Bible refers to the old and new covenants, it is referring to the historical epochs represented by the Old and New Testament eras. But more often the terms have an experiential connotation representing contrasting responses to God's gift of salvation. A "new covenant experience" refers to the response of faith and the consequent obedience of faith that results from God's writing His law on the heart, while an "old covenant experience" involves outright rejection of God's appeal and a perversion of true religion into legalistic, external obedience on the part of someone whose heart continues in rebellion. An old covenant experience may look like the real thing on the surface, but it isn't. It is essential to understand these issues related to the covenants if any confusion over the importance of faith, obedience, and God's laws, including the Sabbath, is to be resolved.

I considered presenting my conclusions in a quick, easy-to-read format—sort of a "covenant-lite" study. But the seriousness and depth of the questions raised by biblical passages demanded a more detailed exposition. While parts of this presentation are a bit heavy, I've tried to make a complex subject as easy to understand as possible. To do this, I've relegated some of the more technical material to footnotes.

I'm convinced that at the heart of this complex study lies a simple truth: God is love. God loves His entire creation and asks for its full devotion in return. This is the message of God's everlasting covenant: God loves people. The human race is sick and will die eternally if they do not get healed. God offers to heal them and appeals for them to devote themselves to Him and trust Him to do so. The old and new covenants progressively express God's everlasting love, adapted to the universal needs of the human race.

When God's love is responded to with faith, it produces a *new covenant experience*, which results in loving obedience. But if God is responded to with legalistic obedience (or with no obedience), it results in an *old covenant experience*. That's the significance of the old and new covenants in summary.

In the following chapters we will examine how such a complex subject can fairly be summarized in this astoundingly simple way. Chapter 1 defines "covenant" and looks at God's various covenants within the overarching framework and thematic continuity of His everlasting covenant/everlasting gospel. Chapter 2 establishes that God's covenants with individuals and Israel were never meant for them alone, but were always intended for the whole world. In chapters 3 and 4 we'll examine the "DNA characteristics" of the new covenant and note how they are embedded in all of God's covenants with humanity. Specific attention will be given to the Sinai covenant which many biblical teachers portray as being at odds with the new covenant. Chapter 5 focuses on how the historical new covenant differs from previous covenants. Chapters 6 and 7 establish the critical distinction between the historical and experiential dimensions of the covenants, exploring the momentous implications that this distinction makes for the interpretation of hotly debated New Testament passages on the covenants and God's law. Chapter 8 dispels a misconception held by many that the Old Testament emphasizes law while the New Testament emphasizes love. Chapter 9 examines the significance of the three covenant signs—the rainbow, circumcision, and the Sabbath. Chapter 10 turns to an important passage in Hebrews that focuses on the goal of the covenants and examines the significance and role of the Sabbath in achieving that goal. Chapter 11 distills this entire study into ten timeless, universal truths relative to human salvation, purpose, and destiny. Chapter 12 applies the implications of this study to daily life.

## Notes

1. Cf. Ps. 40:8; Isa. 51:7; Jer. 31:33; Rom. 2:12–16; Heb. 8:10.

2. Commenting on Paul's statement in Romans 5:20a—"The law was added so that the trespass might increase"—Douglas Moo states, "Paul describes the law as an instigator of sin." Moo further characterizes the law as possessing "sin-provoking," "sin-inducing," "sin-producing" power (Douglas J. Moo, "The Law of Christ as the Fulfillment of the Law of Moses," in *Five Views on Law and Gospel*, ed. Stanley N. Gundry [Grand Rapids, MI: Zondervan, 1993], 333, 336).

# Chapter 1

# The Core Truth of the Covenant(s)

The Hebrew word for covenant, *berit*, refers to "a legally binding relationship contracted between two parties."[1] This word appears nearly 250 times in the Old Testament. Most usages apply to God's covenant(s)[2] with humankind—primarily Adam, Noah, Abraham, Israel, and David, with 159 references to the covenant God made with Israel at Sinai.[3]

## The Definition and Nature of the Covenant(s)

Covenants differ in nature. Some covenants are legal stipulations, either mutually agreed on, such as a business contract, or unilaterally determined, such as a will. When writing of God's covenants with humanity, the New Testament authors chose not to use the Greek term for a mutually negotiated agreement, *syntheke*, but rather the one used for a will, *diatheke*. In some respects the divine covenant does indeed resemble a will in that its terms are defined by God rather than mutually negotiated (Gal. 3:15; Heb. 9:13–18ff.). But John Murray points out that God's covenant prescribes a divinely-initiated, grace-based relationship rather than a business contract or even a will, as it aims to direct humanity toward "the crown and goal of the whole process of religion, namely, union and communion with God."[4] Robert Rayburn states: "Covenant is a relational concept. The word does not so much mean laws or stipulations. The Abrahamic and Sinaitic covenants are not laws, they are rather a relationship between God and people, a relationship

conceived and ordered in a certain way. This is covenant in the Old Testament and the New."[5]

There are various kinds of covenantal relationships. In a master/slave relationship the slave is obligated to carry out the will of the master or suffer punishment. The Bible often refers to God's covenant recipients (including the Messiah Jesus Himself) as slaves/servants, though always in the context of God as a loving, benevolent, though not indulgent, Master (Gen. 26:24; Rom. 1:1).[6] The Bible places even greater emphasis on the covenant bonds between parent and child to illustrate the nature of God's covenant with humanity (Jer. 31:9, 20; Matt. 6:9; 7:9–11; 1 John 3:1). It even dares to liken the divine covenant with humanity to a marriage covenant between husband and wife, in which each promises wholehearted devotion to the other. God Himself likened His covenant with Israel at Sinai to such a covenant: "I was a husband to them" (Jer. 31:32).[7] Some biblical scholars have equated the divine covenant with divine promise.[8]

Thus, the biblical idea of God's covenant with humanity differs from that of human contracts. In the latter, each party to the contract tries to gain the most benefits for the least cost, or the superior party threatens severe penalties should the inferior party fail to live up to the demands made of them (as in penalties imposed for failure to pay taxes on time or for a late payment on a credit card) and offers rewards for superior performance (a bonus for getting the job done early). But in God's covenant with humankind, God promises His wholehearted, whole-souled commitment, even to the death if need be, for human welfare (e.g., Gen. 3:15),[9] and He requires that same wholehearted devotion from humanity in return (Rev. 12:11).[10] That is indeed the definition and nature of God's covenant with human beings. "The basic idea of the covenant is that of relationship with God,"[11] a relationship characterized by love, trust, and wholehearted commitment.

At no time was the divine covenant ever reduced merely to a list of legal stipulations with promised rewards for obedience and punishments threatened for disobedience. The true nature of the covenant was rather a loving relationship of wholehearted devotion to one another in which God pledged Himself to the death for the sake of humankind and asked for our reciprocal, wholehearted pledge of love, devotion, and obedience. The disciplinary rewards and punishments associated with the stipulations of God's covenant with humanity were built into the very nature of the relationship itself[12] and were always to be understood within the context of parental or marital love in which God the parent/husband provided the promise, protective boundaries,

> At no time was the divine covenant ever reduced merely to a list of legal stipulations with promised rewards for obedience and punishments threatened for disobedience.

and corrective action necessary to ensure that His covenant members, His believing and faithful children/wife, would mature in holiness and receive their eternal inheritance in the kingdom of God (Leviticus 26; Deut. 11:22–32; Eph. 5:23–32; Heb. 12:5–11).

## The Everlasting Covenant

Imagine yourself traveling back to the very beginning of time, back past the moment when God brought angels into being, past the time when the entire process of creation itself began, back to a time before "all things were created: things in heaven and on earth, visible and invisible, whether thrones or powers or rulers or authorities" (Col. 1:16). What would be there before the cosmic creation itself existed? The closer you got to that time, the more you would notice that the darkness of the cosmos was giving way to light, until the darkness became wholly swallowed by the light. That light is altogether "unapproachable" (1 Tim. 6:16) on the one hand, and yet it has a marvelous attraction that draws you toward it. And suddenly you realize that the light is God Himself (1 John 1:5; cf. John 8:12). Back in that primeval deep-space time, before anything else existed, before time itself existed, God—the everlasting, Trinitarian God: Father, Son and Holy Spirit—existed.

If we had been able to observe God for a time before the creation itself existed—to watch Father, Son, and Holy Spirit interacting—we likely would have had the remarkable experience of noting how they regarded one another with utmost honor and respect. We could have heard it in the words they spoke, noted it in their body language,[13] seen it in the way they treated one another, how supremely they valued one another. When one speaks, the others listen as though their very lives depended on the speaker's words, as though for the first time gaining some new depth of understanding and insight into the beauty and character of the speaker. Their words and actions display kindness, thoughtfulness, and courtesy. Nothing in their relationship resembles what we would recognize as rudeness or self-seeking. Rather, their relationship is characterized by genuine humility and a compelling desire to serve one another in practical expressions of love and affirmation. The trust levels among them seem to be without boundaries. Their other-centered relationship constitutes a veritable circle of beneficence. The longer we observe, the more practical evidences we see of the true meaning of the Bible's primary revelation of the nature and character of God: "God is love" (1 John 4:8). This wholehearted, whole-souled commitment in love that binds Father, Son, and Holy Spirit into one God, indivisible in character, is *covenant*.

If you have children, you no doubt love them to the point that you would die for them if necessary. But you probably have never told them either that you are in a "covenant" with them or have made a "covenant commitment" to them. And yet you are and you have. Likewise, the Father, Son, and Holy Spirit have always loved one another in covenant relationship.[14] The Trinitarian covenant of love reveals itself in each treating the others as He would want to be treated were their roles reversed. This is perhaps why Jesus identified the so-called "golden rule" as the essence of the law and the prophets (Matt. 7:12)[15] and taught that love to God and neighbor was the great law on which "all the law and the prophets hang" (Matt. 22:36–40). The "golden rule" (Matt. 7:12) plumbs the depths of God's commitment inwardly within the Trinity and outwardly to His entire creation. Herein lies the essence of God's covenant: it's an everlasting covenant of love.

John Ortberg illustrates this kind of covenant love with a story about his family. When his daughter was a baby, he and his wife would calm her by holding her and repeating over and over, "Honey, honey, honey...I know, I know." When she got a little older, they noticed her calming herself by saying, "Honey, honey, honey...I know, I know," just as they had done. But as soon as they would appear, her little arms would fly up along with her plaintive cry, "Hold you me." Ortberg makes the application to Trinity love and covenant:

> Even an infant being held knows, with an understanding deeper than words, that what is being expressed with the body is in fact the decision of the soul: to hold another person in one's heart. *I will seek your good; I will share your joy and hurt; we will know a kind of oneness, you and I.* It is the brief enactment of a covenant. It is a promise of self-giving love.
>
> The life of the Trinity is an unceasing offering and receiving of self-giving love. The Father holds the Son in his heart, and the Son does the same with the Father. "The Father is in me and I am in the Father," Jesus says, and the Spirit holds and is held as well. "Hold you me"—offering themselves to one another in ceaseless, joy-filled, mutually submissive, generous, creative, self-giving love—is what the Trinity has been doing from before the beginning of time.[16]

Before creation existed, God existed, love existed, covenant existed— everlasting God, everlasting love, everlasting covenant. This everlasting covenant expresses the heart of the everlasting God manifested in the sacrificial love that existed among the Trinity before the beginning of time. The term "everlasting covenant" can never be invoked without calling to mind the love bonds that existed from eternity past within the divine, triune heavenly council, each seeking the happiness of the other.

Every covenant God ever made with His creation has its roots in this everlasting, Trinitarian covenant of love. Each divinely initiated covenant with humankind is its own masterfully crafted and unique expression of the greater, original "everlasting covenant." Most books about covenants miss this important point. But the true nature, the organic unity, and the interdependence of the individual covenants becomes clear only when it is realized that they are all based on the one archetypal covenant of love.

There was a time when I assembled electronic kits called Heath Kits. A person could be completely ignorant about electronics and yet assemble a beautiful stereo system by following the directions ("solder the red transistor [see picture on p. 3] to electronic board A," etc.). While assembling my first Heath Kit, I learned how to solder. Using a soldering iron I was able to fuse multiple wires into a single strand, making a permanent unity of what had been separate strands.

The covenant love of Father, Son, and Holy Spirit is the solder that fuses together the individual, divinely-initiated covenants of the Bible into a single covenant. That's why the term "covenant(s)" is useful as a reminder that all God's individual covenants (plural) were manifestations of the one everlasting covenant (singular).

> Each divinely initiated covenant with humankind is its own masterfully crafted and unique expression of the greater, original "everlasting covenant."

All divinely initiated covenants are unique expressions of God's everlasting covenant of love adapted to the specific needs of those to whom they were addressed. Each bears the divine fingerprint of the everlasting covenant and is a locally applied adaptation of that greater covenant. In every time and place, God, true to His own nature, has treated His creation as He would want to be treated were His role and ours reversed. It's the natural, heart-felt response of God to His creation's call, "Hold You me." This core truth of the everlasting covenant is the core truth of every covenant God has ever made. "I the LORD do not change" (Mal. 3:6). "Jesus Christ is the same yesterday and today and forever" (Heb. 13:8).

## "An Everlasting Covenant"

The term "everlasting covenant" (Hebrew, *berith olam*; Greek, *ionios diatheke*) occurs sixteen times in Scripture. Thirteen times the English translation, "*an* everlasting covenant," is applied to the specific covenants God made with Abraham (Gen. 17:3–7, 13, 19), Israel at Sinai,[17] and David (2 Sam. 23:5). (See table 1 on pages 291–293 in appendix D for a brief, partial list and description of the covenants.) These covenants are each called "*an* everlasting covenant" because they are all expressions of the greater, primordial everlasting covenant of love that existed from eternity past within the Trinity and from the Trinity toward all creation. While each had its own unique fingerprint, each bore the essential nature of the archetypical everlasting covenant. Each was an expression of the everlasting covenant perfectly adapted to the needs of the people to which it was addressed. And embedded in each can be seen the eternal truths that God was progressively revealing throughout history.[18]

## "The Everlasting Covenant"

The remaining three times the phrase *berith olam / ionios diatheke* is found in Scripture, most English translations present it as "*the* everlasting covenant" based on the context in which it occurs.[19] In these three cases "the everlasting covenant" is said to include:

- the whole of God's creation on earth. "Whenever the rainbow appears in the clouds, I will see it and remember *the everlasting covenant* between God and all living creatures of every kind on the earth" (Gen. 9:16, italics added).

- His law for all humankind which they have all disobeyed: "The earth is defiled by its people; they have disobeyed the laws, violated the statutes, and broken *the everlasting covenant*" (Isa. 24:5, italics added).
- Jesus Christ's own once-for-all blood sacrifice as the atonement for the sins of the whole world, a sacrifice that while made in human history was potentiated from time immemorial, from everlasting: "May the God of peace, who through the blood of *the eternal covenant* brought back from the dead our Lord Jesus, that great Shepherd of the sheep, equip you with everything good for doing his will" (Heb. 13:20, italics added; cf. 1 John 2:2; Rev. 13:8).

These characteristics are specifically identified in Scripture, are comprehensive in their reach, and have been embedded in every covenant God initiated with humanity. Through them God acted on our behalf as He would have wanted us to act on His behalf were our role and His reversed.

## The Everlasting Gospel

Revelation speaks of "the everlasting gospel" (Rev. 14:6 NKJV), which is the good news of God's saving grace toward humanity. The reference to "the everlasting gospel" in Revelation 14:6–7 is specifically addressed to an end-time generation which is called to fear the creator God and give Him glory for "the hour of his judgment has come." God's final message to the end-time generation includes "the everlasting gospel" first announced in Genesis 3:15 and progressively revealed throughout Scripture. It is that which Paul contended for as the one and only true gospel (Gal. 1:6–9).

This good news runs like a golden, unifying thread throughout human history from Adam's fall to the second coming of Jesus. The everlasting gospel constitutes the core truth of the covenant of redemption—God's everlasting covenant crafted to meet humanity in its sinful condition, reconcile us to God, and restore our inheritance in God's eternal kingdom. This is the one and only gospel God ordained to be preached to all who dwell on the earth (Rev. 14:6). This is the same gospel that was preached through promise, symbols, and anticipation to Adam (Gen. 3:15), to Abraham (Gal. 3:8), to Israel in the wilderness (Heb. 3:7–4:2), to those in Isaiah's day (Isa. 52:7), and to all in the Old Testament era: "But they have not all obeyed the gospel" (Rom. 10:10–16 NKJV). It is also the same gospel that was preached by all New Testament authors, who had the privilege of looking back on Christ's sacrificial death as an accomplished fact.

Thus, to reiterate, the gospel preached in the Old Testament era, which looked forward to the coming Messiah, and the gospel preached in the New Testament era, which looked back on the Messiah's atoning death and resurrection, were the very same gospel. The author of Hebrews writes: "We [in the New Testament era] also have had the gospel preached to us, just as they [in the Old Testament era] did" (Heb. 4:2). In context, the "they" referred to in this verse was those to whom God had given His covenant on Sinai, but it has broader application to all those who lived in the Old Testament era.[20] Paul pronounced a curse upon anyone, even an angel from heaven, who dared preach "a different gospel" (Gal. 1:6–9).

Whatever else may be said about the covenants, it can never be said that any covenant ever initiated by God was based on, or was an expression of, anything other than the everlasting gospel He ordained to be preached "to every nation, tribe, language, and people" (Rev. 14:6). This is a foundational, core truth that must be affirmed and constantly kept in mind in any study of the covenants.

## Summary

Covenant has its origins in the relationship of love that has existed among God the Father, Son, and Holy Spirit from all eternity. Trinity love constitutes the "everlasting covenant" of which every divinely initiated covenant in human history is a unique adaptation to specific time and place. Thus the term "covenant(s)" may be used to signify that no divinely initiated covenant stands alone, but represents a specific expression of the archetype everlasting covenant love that exists within the Trinity. God's covenants with humanity may be defined generally as His whole-souled commitment in love to their ultimate welfare and happiness, with expectations of their whole-souled commitment in love, loyalty, and obedience to Him in return. God's sacrificial commitment during the reign of sin (from the fall of Adam to the second coming of Jesus) to restore humanity to an eternal hope may be termed "the covenant of redemption" or "the everlasting gospel." The "covenant of redemption"/ "everlasting gospel"—God's plan of salvation for the eternal salvation of human beings—is timeless and universal, having existed in the heart of God before time began, and having never changed since its implementation at the fall of Adam.

> The gospel preached in the Old Testament era, and the gospel preached in the New Testament era, were the very same gospel.

## Notes

1. Hasel and Hasel provide an elaborated definition specifically of the divine covenants: "a divinely initiated and sovereign-ordained relationship between God and man in which God as superior Lord graciously discloses, confirms, and fulfills the covenant promise," and "man, as beneficiary of the divine covenant gifts, freely accepts the enduring relationship and renders obedience to the divine obligations (commandments, statues, laws, or ordinances) by the assisting and enabling grace provided by God" (Gerhard F. Hasel and Michael G. Hasel, *The Promise: God's Everlasting Covenant* [Nampa, ID: Pacific Press Publishing Association, 2002], 18). Many other definitions could be included, but these would not add substantially to our study at this point without considerable elaboration.

2. The term "covenant(s)" is used in this book to signify that a discussion of the various individualized, divinely-initiated covenants always bears in mind the greater everlasting

covenant from which each was adapted and which binds them together in an essential unity.

3. Edward Heppenstall, "The Covenants and the Law," *Our Firm Foundation*, vol. 1 (Washington, DC: Review and Herald Publishing Association, 1953), 446.

4. John Murray, *The Covenant of Grace* (Phillipsburg, NJ: Presbyterian and Reformed Publishing, 1953), 31.

5. Robert Rayburn, "The Contrast Between the Old and New Covenants in the New Testament" (PhD thesis, University of Aberdeen, 1978), 164–165.

6. Cf. Exod. 14:31; Jer. 31:3; Isa. 42:1; Matt. 25:21–23; Phil. 2:7.

7. Cf. Isa. 54:5–10; Ezek. 16:1–14; 2 Cor. 11:2; Eph. 5:31.

8. E.g., Thomas Edward McComiskey, *The Covenants of Promise: A Theology of the Old Testament Covenants* (Grand Rapids, MI: Baker Book House, 1985), 229: "The unity of the people of God in all ages is more than a simple commonality in the way of salvation. It is an organic unity fashioned by the one promise covenant that is their common heritage.…The blessings of the inheritance promised to the remnant in the Old Testament are blessings shared by the church.…We share the same faith—the same hope—as the believing Jews of the old era."

9. Cf. Isaiah 53; Rom. 8:32; 2 Cor. 5:19.

10. Cf. Deut. 6:5; 11:1; 30:6, 16; John 14:21; Heb. 11:35–39; 2 John 5–6.

11. Rayburn, "The Contrast Between the Old and New Covenants in the New Testament," 227. Cf. Jon L. Dybdahl, *A Strange Place for Grace: Discovering a Loving God in the Old Testament* (Nampa, ID: Pacific Press Publishing Association, 2006), 68: "The best synonym [for God's covenants] is *relationships*. A covenant is a defined relationship between God and His people."

12. God's drawing, forgiving, empowering, promising, protecting covenant love is intent on saving every sinner, and will embrace forever all those who respond to Him in faith, setting their hearts on loving and obeying Him (Exod. 20:6; 34:7; John 14:21). But those people or that nation (even though it be God's own covenant bride, Israel) who, though they may show signs of an outward devotion to Him, have in reality rejected or divorced Him in their hearts, God will give up to the treacherous "protection" of the alternate lovers they have chosen (Isa. 1:10–20; 29:13; 50:1; Jer. 3:8; 16:10–13; Ezek. 16:8, 23–27, 39–43, 58–59; Hosea 11:7–8; Matt. 23:37–39; Rom. 1:21, 24, 26, 28). And those sinners who thus willfully reject God's every effort to save them He will ultimately and grievingly "give up" to the "second death" (Isa. 1:18–20; Ezek. 18:32, Rev. 2:11; 21:6–8). The rewards and penalties, including eternal life or its forfeiture, connected to the covenant can thus be viewed as the logical and natural consequence of one's acceptance or rejection of God's promises to those who are in covenant relationship with Him (1 John 5:11–12).

13. "God is spirit" and therefore not limited to a body (John 4:24). And yet God manifested Himself in bodily form (as a traveling visitor to Abraham [Gen. 18:2, 13, 17, 20, 22, 26, 30], as an angel to Israel [Judg. 2:1–2]), for the purpose of communicating with them. Therefore it is not unscriptural to use personified terms for the purpose of communicating a truth about God. The descriptions given in this paragraph are reasonable deductions based on the scriptural revelation that the almighty, all-powerful God of Scripture is a God who "is love" (1 John 4:8; cf. 1 Cor. 13:4–7), is "compassionate and gracious" (Exod. 34:6), and has the nature of a humble servant (Phil. 2:5–8; Matt. 20:28).

14. Cf. Luke 22:29: "I confer on you a kingdom, just as my Father conferred one on me." The Greek term for "confer" in this text is the verb form of the Greek word for "covenant,"

which Jesus used to refer directly to the covenant between Himself and the Father. Cf. John 17:24 where Jesus acknowledges in prayer to the Father, "you loved me before the creation of the world."

15. "So in everything, do to others what you would have them do to you, for this sums up the Law and the Prophets." In Matthew 7:9–11 Jesus asked His audience rhetorical questions regarding their treatment of their own children, pointing out that if they, being evil, would treat their children in love and concern for their welfare, how much more would their heavenly Father do the same to them. Then He said, "So [Greek, οὖν, 'therefore'], in everything do to others what you would have them do to you [i.e., treat one another as your perfect heavenly Father treats you], for this sums up the Law and the Prophets." The New Living Translation renders it, "This is a summary of all that is taught in the Law and the Prophets."

16. John Ortberg, *Everybody's Normal Till You Get to Know Them* (Grand Rapids, MI: Zondervan, 2003), 35–37.

17. Exod. 31:16 (the Sabbath, the sign of the covenant with Israel); Lev. 24:8 (the shewbread / bread of the Presence, a component of the temple which in this instance represents the Sinai covenant itself); 1 Chron. 16:14–18 (with Jacob/Israel).

18. "It is fair to say that there is a single covenant tradition in the Old Testament. It is developed in various dimensions and over a long period of time, but always it is rooted in the saving relationship God has established with his people. While there are several covenants, each in its own way fills in only a part of the whole picture of God's covenant with Israel and each of these theological covenants partakes of the same essential character." Rayburn, "The Contrast Between the Old and New Covenants," 27.

19. E.g., KJV, NKJV, NRSV, NIV, NASB.

20. Rayburn, "The Contrast Between the Old and New Covenants," 182, referencing others as well, notes the significance recognized by others in the unusual ordering of "we" and "they" in Hebrews 4:2: "While we would be more inclined to say 'they too,' the author of Hebrews writes 'we too,' almost as if he had to prove that Christians really had heard the gospel, whereas no one would dispute that the Israelites of old had heard it" (A. T. Hanson, *Jesus Christ in the Old Testament* [London: SPCK, 1965], 58). Of this inversion Geerhardus Vos writes: "No more striking proof than this could be afforded of the fact, that he regarded the same spiritual world with the same powers and blessings as having evoked the religious experience of the Old and New Testament alike" (Gerhardus Vos, "The Epistle of the Diatheke," *PTR*, 14, 19). Cf. Jon Paulien's comment on one of Paul's references to Deuteronomy, the primary covenant book of the Old Testament: "Romans 10:8: 'But what does it say?' 'The word is near you; it is in your mouth and in your heart,' that is the word of faith we are proclaiming,' what does Paul quote here? It is a passage from Deuteronomy, but not just any part of the book—it is Deuteronomy 30, the part about the blessings and the curses. Paul here quotes from *the* covenant, not from some new and different covenant. And he claims that the gospel he is preaching is one and the same with the covenant God gave to Moses in Old Testament times." Paulien, *Meet God Again for the First Time* (Hagerstown, MD: Review and Herald Publishing Association, 2003), 103.

# Chapter 2

# The Universality of the Covenant(s)

The covenants have been presented by some as a kind of exclusive deal God makes with a select (elect) group of people, singling them out for special favors. While there is some truth in that concept, it doesn't portray the whole picture. God did select (elect) certain individuals and make covenants with them and their descendants. These covenants not only included significant blessings but heightened responsibilities as well. God intended for His gospel of salvation to be shared, not hoarded. The covenants were designed to be inclusive, not exclusive. God's covenants with humanity are all grace-based, gospel-bearing, and mission-directed.

In at least one place in Scripture, the divine covenant is likened to a will (Heb. 9:16ff.). An executor of a will is responsible to inform those named in the will regarding their portion of the inheritance and to oversee the distribution of the estate to the beneficiaries. Using this metaphor, we may think of God's covenant as the will of His estate. His estate includes eternal salvation, as well as any temporal blessings and responsibilities that may be specified. Thus, we may think of those with whom God made His covenant (e.g., Adam, Noah, Abraham, Israel, David) not as exclusive beneficiaries of God's estate but rather as executors themselves, commissioned to notify the entire world that all nations of the earth have been listed as beneficiaries of this marvelous will—the gospel, resulting in life that glorifies God and lasts forever. It is

a gospel conceived and offered by grace, to be received according to the terms and conditions specified. The terms and conditions are simple and profound: faith, through which God works His inner transformation of heart and mind to produce love and obedience to His commandments.

The everlasting gospel of grace, expressing God's everlasting covenant promise and commitment to sinful human beings, has always been universal in its application.[1] It was always God's purpose that the recipients of the individualized, differentiated covenants would share the gospel with the entire world. The gospel would reveal to the world that God's law had been given for their benefit (Deut. 10:13), to bring life, but that the world had broken this law (1 Kings 8:46; Isa. 24:5; Rom. 3:23) and that God had kept His promise to send His Son to take away the sin of the world (Gen. 3:15; Isa. 53:4, 6; 1 Pet. 1:18–19; Gen. 22:8, 17; John 1:29; Heb. 13:20).

## The Universality and Mission-Directed Purpose of the Covenant(s)

God's covenants with Adam, Noah, Abraham, Israel, David, and new covenant believers were never intended to be for them alone, but for everyone who would accept God's appeal in the everlasting gospel through their witness, for "my house will be called a house of prayer for all nations" (Isa. 56:7). As Dallas Willard notes, "God not only interacts with every individual human being (John 1:9; Acts 10:30–31; 14:17; Rom. 1:14–15), but also establishes a *public* presence in human history through a covenant people in which he is tangibly manifest to everyone on earth who wants to find him."[2]

With the intent that His covenants would be applied universally, God designed them to groom, equip, and commission the people He chose to carry out this missionary purpose.[3] This insight is crucial for a proper understanding of the covenants.

A thorough study of the Scriptures will demonstrate the mission-directed purpose of God's covenant(s) and the awareness that His faithful followers in every historical era have had of their divinely appointed mission to share the gospel with the nations.

At creation, God's everlasting covenant of love and peace embraced the whole of His created order.[4] In the creation story, even the animals did not prey on one another but, like human beings, were given a plant-based diet (Gen. 1:29–30). Had Adam been faithful to God, all humankind would have benefited from the unending blessings of God's covenant of creation.

## The Universality and Mission-Directed Purpose of God's Covenant(s) Throughout the Old Testament Era

God's remarks to the serpent in Eden (Gen. 3:15) were an implicit covenant promise to Adam and all humankind that the woman's seed, the Messiah, would ultimately destroy Satan and the suffering Satan had imposed on them through the sin of Adam.[5] This grace-based, gospel-bearing covenant promise was mission-directed, and Adam was to pass it on to his descendants, providing them with hope.

God's covenant with Noah was a "renewal" of His grace-based, gospel-bearing covenant made previously with Adam and his descendants (Gen. 6:18).[6] That the Noahic covenant was indeed a gospel-bearing covenant is evident from the sanctifying effect it had on Noah who "became an heir of the righteousness that comes by faith" (Heb. 11:7). In addition, this covenant anticipated the impending flood and offered protection to Noah and his family. By strong implication, God's gracious offer of

> A thorough study of the Scriptures will demonstrate the mission-directed purpose of God's covenant(s) and the awareness that His faithful followers have had of their mission to share the gospel with the nations.

righteousness by faith and protection from the flood was extended to the entire world, for God's covenant with Noah had ordained and equipped him as "a preacher of righteousness" (2 Pet. 2:5).[7] After the flood, God's covenant with Noah was expanded further to include the universal sign of the rainbow to remind all people everywhere of "the everlasting covenant between God and *all living creatures* of every kind on the earth" in which God "swore that the waters of Noah would never again cover the earth" (Gen. 9:16, italics added; Isa. 54:9).

God's covenant with Abraham and his descendants envisioned that "*all peoples on earth* will be blessed through you." "Your descendants will be like the dust of the earth, and you will spread out to the west and to the east, to the north and to the south. *All peoples on earth* will be blessed through you and your offspring" (Gen. 12:3; 28:14, italics added). God envisioned Abraham's descendants spreading throughout the world carrying the gospel to every nation, tribe, tongue, and people. Ellet Waggoner suggests that the altars Abraham built were an evangelistic witness to the peoples around him: "When Abraham built an altar, he 'called upon the name of the Lord.' Gen. 12:8; 13:4….When Abraham erected the family altar, he not only taught his immediate family but he proclaimed the name of the Lord to all around him. Like Noah, Abraham was a preacher of righteousness. As God preached the Gospel to Abraham, so Abraham preached the Gospel to others."[8]

Meredith Kline likewise sees the altars built by Abraham and his descendants, including the nation of Israel prior to the conquest of Canaan, as "a missionary-evangelistic witness" to the nations they sojourned among:

> [Their altars] were a summons to repentant turning from the worship of idols and a call to reconciliation with the God of Abraham, Isaac, and Jacob, the Creator of heaven and earth. They were a missionary-evangelistic witness….In their function of summoning to covenantal commitment to the Lord of redemptive promise, these altars afforded an intimation of a coming day when the reconciling call of the altar

of Calvary would be heard in all the earth, when the gospel of Christ would go forth in the power of the Spirit to the Gentiles and the promise would be fulfilled that in Abraham's seed all the nations would be blessed with the salvation of God.[9]

God's covenant with Israel at Sinai called the entire nation to become a "kingdom of priests" through whom "'*the nations* will know that I am the LORD,' declares the Sovereign LORD, 'when I show myself holy through you before their eyes'" (Exod. 19:5–6; Ezek. 36:23, italics added). The believing Israelites perceived the universal scope of God's purpose for them as bearers of the everlasting gospel of salvation and prayed: "May God be gracious to us and bless us and make his face shine upon us, that your ways may be known on earth, *your salvation among all nations*" (Ps. 67:1–2, italics added). Through Israel's witness, God intended that "the law will go out from me; my justice will become a light to the nations" (Isa. 51:4). However, realizing the magnitude of Israel's failure to fulfill its God-given mission of evangelizing the nations with the everlasting gospel, Isaiah confessed on Israel's behalf: "We have not brought salvation to the earth; we have not given birth to people of the world" (Isa. 26:18). Stating that God's covenant at Sinai was "made with the nation of Israel *only*," some imply that God created conditions that made it difficult for outsiders to get in and share the blessings of the covenant.[10] Such a portrayal misrepresents God's heart and intent with regard to this, or any other covenant He has made. His covenants always bore the whole of humankind in mind, were always for humankind's benefit, and were designed to promulgate the gospel of eternal salvation worldwide.

It was clear also to David that God's "everlasting covenant" with him followed the precedent set in the earlier covenants made with his forefathers in that it intended for David to lead his people to "make known *among the nations* what he [God] has done," to "declare his glory among *the nations*, his marvelous deeds among *all peoples*" (2 Sam. 23:5; 1 Chron. 16:7–33; Isa. 55:3–5, italics added).

God often reiterated the timeless universal mission purpose of His covenants to His covenant people. In a scriptural passage that blends the proclaimed mission of Israel with the prophesied mission of the Messiah into what has sometimes been called "the Great Commission of the Old Testament,"[11] God said through Isaiah: "You are my servant, Israel, in whom I will display my splendor [NKJV: in whom I will be glorified]....It is too small a thing for you to be my servant to restore the tribes of Jacob and bring back those of Israel I have kept. I will also make you a light for the Gentiles, that you may bring my salvation to the ends of the earth" (Isa. 49:3, 6).

> Stating that God's covenant at Sinai was "made with the nation of Israel only," some imply that God created conditions that made it difficult for outsiders to get in and share the blessings of the covenant.

When Paul and Barnabas defended their own mission to preach the gospel to the Gentiles in the new covenant historical era, they quoted from this very passage in Isaiah, as if to say that they were fulfilling the commission God gave to His covenant people from the beginning (Acts 13:46–47).

Indeed, throughout the entire old covenant historical era, God's covenants with His chosen people commissioned them to extend His everlasting covenant/gospel invitation to the entire world: "Turn to me and be saved, *all you ends of the earth*" (Isa. 45:22, italics added). "For God is the king of all the earth; sing to him a psalm of praise. God reigns over the nations; God is seated on his holy throne. The nobles of the nations assemble as the people of the God of Abraham, for the kings of the earth belong to God; he is greatly exalted" (Ps. 47:7–9).

## The Universality and Mission-Directed Purpose of God's Covenant in the New Testament Era

Jesus instructed His followers that they were "the salt of the earth" and "the light of the world": "Let your light shine before men, that they may see your good deeds and praise your father in heaven" (Matt. 5:13–16). He adhered to the tradition of the everlasting covenant commission when He admonished New Testament believers, "Therefore go and make disciples of *all nations*" (Matt. 28:19–20, italics added). The book of Acts records the explosive growth of the church throughout the world as believers adopted and applied the great commission. Paul stated a universal, timeless truth when he said to the pagan philosophers in Athens: "From one man he made every nation of men, that they should inhabit the whole earth, and he determined the times set for them and the exact places where they should live. God did this so that men would seek him and perhaps reach out for him and find him, though he is not far from each one of us" (Acts 17:26–27).

Similarly, Paul wrote to the blended congregation of Jews and Gentiles at Rome, "Is God the God of Jews only? Is he not the God of Gentiles too? Yes, of Gentiles too, since there is only one God, who will justify the circumcised by faith and the uncircumcised through that same faith" (Rom. 3:29–30).

## God's Universal Covenant of Redemption Encompasses All Creation

Paul even intimates that the earthly ministry and atoning act of Jesus, which was at the core of God's everlasting covenant with humankind, reached far beyond the nations of the earth and encompassed the entire universe in its scope: "For God was pleased to have all his fullness dwell in him, and through him *to reconcile to himself all things, whether things on earth or things in heaven*, by making peace through his blood, shed on the cross" (Col. 1:19–20; cf. Eph. 3:10, italics added). From this verse it appears that God's redemptive actions through Christ in human history may have also addressed residual issues from the primordial fallout in heaven (Ezek. 28:13–15; Luke 10:17–18; Rev. 12:3–10). His everlasting covenant commitment of love encompasses the entire universe which naturally includes all humankind.

## What Might Have Been[12]

Scripture provides tantalizing glimpses of what might have been if God's covenant people in the Old Testament era had by faith embraced the gospel of His covenant, allowing God to make them "a kingdom of priests and a holy nation" who would carry His gospel to the ends of the earth (Exod. 19:5–6; cf. Gen. 28:14; Lev. 20:7–8).

God would shower the covenant blessings on His people (Deut. 28:1–14; cf. Lev. 26:1–13). They would be such healthy (Deut. 7:15; cf. Exod. 15:26), happy (Deut. 28:2–8), holy (28:9), wise (4:6–7), morally enlightened (4:8), and prosperous (28:6–7; cf. Lev. 26:4–5, 10) people that they would become "the head, not the tail" (Deut. 28:13), above all the nations of the earth "in praise, fame and honor" (Deut. 26:19). All the people of other nations would see that they were "called by the name of the Lord" (28:10). God's praise and saving power would be proclaimed to the ends of the earth (Ps. 48:10; 57:9; 66:4; 67; 72:10–11; 126:2–3; 145:11–12). Other nations would gather to Jerusalem to worship the Lord (Ps. 86:9; 102:21–22).

An all too brief period of Solomon's era provided a fleeting glimpse of what might have been as "the whole world sought audience with Solomon to hear the wisdom God had put in his heart" (1 Kings 10:24), and the wealth of the world poured into his expanding empire (vv. 14–29).

However, on the whole, the history of God's chosen people betrayed its divinely envisioned potential. Yet God didn't abandon His people or His dream for them and the world. Even after God had to administer the ultimate covenant curse by disciplining His covenant people at the hands of their Babylonian captors, the prophets continued to convey God's ideal plan.

Moved by His everlasting covenant love, God would pardon His covenant people, cleanse them from their sins, put His Spirit in them, and cause them to walk in His laws (Ezek. 36:24–28; cf. Isa. 40:1–2; Jer. 31:31–34). Their ruined cities and temple would be rebuilt and the land of Israel renewed "like the garden of Eden" (Isa. 44:24–28; Ezek. 36:33–35). Other nations would know that the God of Israel had done this for them (Ezek. 36:36). The surrounding nations would see God's righteousness and glory reflected in His covenant people and call them blessed (Isa. 61:9; 62:1–2; Jer. 33:9; Mal. 3:12). God's people would be His witnesses, a light to the nations (Isa. 43:10; 44:8; 49:6; 51:4). They would proclaim to the nations the gospel as taught in God's law, extending His universal offer of salvation to all who come to Him in faith, and warning of judgment on all who would refuse His gracious offer (Isa. 2:2–3; 45:22; 51:4; 52:7; Mic. 4:1–2; Jonah; Isaiah 13–33).

In response, nations would come to the light (Isa. 60:3). They would run to Jerusalem and go up to the house of the Lord—"a house of prayer for all nations"—to seek the Lord and join themselves to Him (Isa. 2:2–3; 45:20; 49:6–22; 55:5; 56:7–8; Zech. 2:11; 8:20–33). These converted peoples from the nations of the earth would be fully incorporated as part of the covenant community (Isa. 56:1–8; Ezek. 47:22–23). "'And I will select some of them also to be priests and Levites,' says the Lord" (Isa. 66:18–21).

This inclusive spiritual community, made up of the redeemed from every nation, would be prepared to receive and honor the Messiah who would come into the world to "bear their iniquities" and make "intercession for the transgressors" (Isa. 53:11–12). Upon His resurrection, the Messiah would immediately (or eventually, the timing is unclear) take the throne of David and rule over a re-united Israel, including the redeemed from the nations of the earth (Ezek. 37:24–26; Isa. 9:6–7; Zech. 9:9–10). The borders of the "Promised Land" would expand to encompass the entire earth (Isa. 27:6; Amos 9:12).

The remaining enemies of the Lord would eventually launch a final attack on God and His people, resulting in the final destruction of the wicked and the end of sin forever (Isaiah 24; 26:20–21; 66:24; Ezekiel 38–39; Joel 3; Obadiah 16; Nah. 1:9; Zechariah 14). Thereupon, God creates a new heavens and earth (Isaiah 35; 65:17). "'From one New Moon to another and from one Sabbath to another, all mankind will come and bow down before me,' says the Lord" (Isa. 66:23).

The Old Testament repeatedly tells us what might have been. The New Testament assures us that God's ultimate purpose will yet be realized. Sin and death will be destroyed and God's spiritual covenant community from every historical era and every nation will live with Him forever in "a new heaven and a new earth, the home of the righteous" (2 Pet. 3:10–13; Revelation 20–22). At the same time, the New Testament repeatedly sounds the following warning to anyone who persists in unbelief and the disobedient fruit it produces: the glorious future promised to God's covenant people, and to which they were destined from the foundation of the world, will be simply and tragically only "what might have been" (Matt. 7:21–23; 8:10–12; 25:1–12; Gal. 5:19–21; Titus 1:2; Rev. 21:7–8; 22:14–15).

> The Old Testament repeatedly tells us what might have been. The New Testament assures us that God's ultimate purpose will yet be realized.

## Summary

God's covenant(s) with His chosen people throughout the Old Testament period were never intended exclusively for those who initially received them. They applied universally. God gave His covenants to His chosen people to be shared with all peoples of the world. God's covenant(s) which envisioned the whole world, and indeed the entire universe, within the embrace of the everlasting covenant were never intended as a private possession. They were always intended as the missionary stewardship of those to whom they were initially given. If God's covenant people had been faithful as bearers and sharers of the gospel proclaimed in the covenant(s) divinely entrusted to them, His desire as expressed in the following texts would have been fulfilled: "Then the nations will know that I am the Lord, declares the Sovereign Lord, when I show myself holy through you before their eyes" (Ezek. 36:23). "The law will go out from me; my justice will become a light to the nations" (Isa. 51:4). "Many nations will be joined with the Lord in that day and will become my people" (Zech. 2:11). "For my house will be called a house of prayer for all nations" (Isa. 56:7).

## Notes

1. God's everlasting covenant embraces all nations. Note the following representative examples:

**Ps. 47:6–9** "God is the King of all the earth....God reigns over the nations....The nobles of the nations assemble as the people of the God of Abraham, for the kings of the earth belong to God..."

**Ps. 65:2, 5** "O God our Savior, the hope of all the ends of the earth and of the farthest seas..."

**Ps. 67:1–7** "May the nations be glad and sing for joy, for you rule the peoples justly and guide the nations of the earth."

**Ps. 65:1–2** "Praise awaits you, O God in Zion...to you all men will come."

**Ps. 117:1–2** "Praise the Lord, all you nations..."

**Isa. 19:22–25** "In that day there will be an altar to the Lord in the heart of Egypt, and a monument to the Lord at its border. It will be a sign and witness to the Lord Almighty in the land of Egypt. When they cry out to the Lord because of their oppressors, he will send them a savior and defender, and he will rescue them. So the Lord will make himself known to the Egyptians, and in that day they will acknowledge the Lord. They will worship with sacrifices and grain offerings; they will make vows to the Lord and keep them. The Lord will strike Egypt with a plague; he will strike them and heal them. They will turn to the Lord, and he will respond to their pleas and heal them. In that day there will be a highway from Egypt to Assyria. The Assyrians will go to Egypt and the Egyptians to Assyria. The Egyptians and Assyrians will worship together. In that day Israel will be the third, along with Egypt and Assyria, a blessing on the earth. The Lord Almighty will bless them, saying 'Blessed be Egypt my people, Assyria my handiwork, and Israel my inheritance.'"

In **Isaiah 13–23**, God sends messages to Assyria, Philistia, Moab, Aram, Israel, Cush, Egypt, Babylon, Dumah (Edom), Arabia, the Valley of Vision (Jerusalem), and Tyre.

**Isa. 56:1–7** "My house will be called a house of prayer for all nations."

**Hab. 2:14** Habakkuk envisions the day when "the earth will be filled with the knowledge of the glory of the LORD as the waters cover the sea."

**Hos. 2:23** "I will show my love to the one I called 'Not my loved one.' I will say to those called 'Not my people,' 'You are my people'; and they will say, 'You are my God.'"

**Zeph. 3:8–9** God pronounces judgment on numerous nations: "I have decided to assemble the nations, to gather the kingdoms and to pour out my wrath on them—all my fierce anger. The whole world will be consumed by the fire of my jealous anger. Then will I purify the lips of the peoples, that all of them may call on the name of the LORD and serve him shoulder to shoulder."

2. Dallas Willard, *The Divine Conspiracy: Rediscovering Our Hidden Life in God* (San Francisco: Harper Collins, 1998), 333.

3. The missionary purpose of God's covenant(s) is evident from the following representative examples:

**Isa. 66:18–21** "'And I, because of their actions and their imaginations, am about to come and gather all nations and tongues, and they will come and see my glory. I will set a sign among them, and I will send some of those who survive to the nations—to Tarshish, to the Libyans and Lydians (famous as archers), to Tubal and Greece, and to the distant islands that have not heard of my fame or seen my glory. They will proclaim my glory among the nations. And they will bring all your brothers, from all the nations, to my holy mountain in Jerusalem as an offering to the LORD —on horses, in chariots and wagons, and on mules and camels,' says the LORD. 'They will bring them, as the Israelites bring their grain offerings, to the temple of the LORD in ceremonially clean vessels. And I will select some of them also to be priests and Levites,' says the LORD."

Many passages that define the Messiah's evangelistic role as "a light to the Gentiles" (Isa. 42:6; 49:3; cf. 9:2) were directed first to Israel. *NIV Study Bible* (1052) on Isaiah 26:18 says, "Israel was designed to be 'a light for the Gentiles.'"

**Isa. 55:3–7** "See, I have made him [David] a witness to the peoples, a leader and commander of the peoples. Surely you will summon nations you know not, and nations that do not know you will hasten to you, because of the LORD your God, the Holy One of Israel, for he has endowed you with splendor."

**Jer. 18:7–8** When God sent messages of doom to the nations, it was always in an effort to bring about repentance and to save them. It was Israel's missionary stewardship to deliver those messages to representatives of those nations. Israel was strategically located on a main trade route, so not only the prophets, but also the traders who did business with representatives from those nations could deliver those messages.

Jonah is sent with a message of judgment to Nineveh, the capital of Assyria. Nineveh repents. *NIV Study Bible*, "Introduction to Jonah" (Grand Rapids, MI: Zondervan, 1985), 1364, states:

"In this story of God's loving concern for all people, Nineveh, the great menace to Israel, is representative of the Gentiles. Correspondingly, stubbornly reluctant Jonah represents Israel's jealousy of her favored relationship with God and her unwillingness to share the Lord's compassion with the nations.

"The book depicts the larger scope of God's purpose for Israel: that she might rediscover the truth of his concern for the whole creation and that she might better understand her own role in carrying out that concern."

The book of Nahum delivered God's judgment against Assyria, represented by Nineveh. This time they did not repent of their cruelty. Withdrawn from God's protection, they were destroyed by their enemies.

**Ezek. 36:23** "I will show the holiness of my great name, which has been profaned among the nations, the name you have profaned among them. Then the nations will know that I am the LORD, declares the Sovereign LORD, when I show myself holy through you before their eyes."

**Zech. 2:10–11** "'Shout and be glad, O Daughter of Zion. For I am coming, and I will live among you,' declares the LORD. 'Many nations will be joined with the LORD in that day and will become my people. I will live among you and you will know that the LORD Almighty has sent me to you.'" This is what God wanted to accomplish through Israel, but they essentially failed, and so now He will accomplish it through the coming of the Messiah.

**Zech. 8:22–23** "'And many peoples and powerful nations will come to Jerusalem to seek the LORD Almighty and to entreat him.' This is what the LORD Almighty says: 'In those days ten men from all languages and nations will take firm hold of one Jew by the hem of this robe and say, "Let us go with you, because we have heard that God is with you."'"

4. The covenant of creation, assumed in the early chapters of the Bible, is implicitly noted in Jeremiah 33:20–26 where God refers to creation when He says, I "established my covenant with day and night and the fixed laws of heaven and earth." That this covenant involved a deep relationship commitment between God and Adam, reflective of the everlasting covenant God has with His entire creation, a covenant that can be broken, is evident in Hosea 6:7 where God says of unrepentant Israel, "Like Adam, they have broken the covenant—they were unfaithful to me there." Israel broke God's covenant with them even as Adam had broken God's covenant with him.

5. Though not explicitly called a covenant, God's assurances to sinful Adam that He would provide redemption for the fallen race through the Seed of the woman constitutes a covenant with Adam through which God made His first, embryonic revelation of the everlasting gospel. Note the following comments relative to the existence of a real "covenant with Adam":

"The first explicit scriptural reference to God's making a covenant appears in Genesis 6:18: 'With thee [Noah] will I establish my covenant; and thou shalt come into the ark....'

"The typical expression for the making of a covenant does not appear in this passage, namely, the one employed in eighty Old Testament instances—'to cut a covenant,' or in the typical and appropriate idiomatic expression in English, 'to make a covenant.' Here the term used is *to establish* (*heqim*). A careful investigation of this term in connection with covenant-making reveals the significance of 'to maintain' or 'to confirm' (compare Deuteronomy 9:5; 27:26; 1 Samuel 15:11; 2 Samuel 7:25; 2 Kings 23:3, 24; etc.). This discovery gives us the impression that God's establishment of His covenant implies a maintaining of a commitment to which God had pledged Himself earlier.

"Even though Genesis 6:18 is the earliest reference to a covenant in the Bible, the use of this particular Hebrew term in connection with it implies that God had previously made a covenant with humanity. In this sense, the covenant of God with Noah may be seen as a renewal of His covenant with Adam, to which the Bible points implicitly in Genesis 3:15" (Hasel and Hasel, *The Promise*, 28–29).

6. Ibid.

7. God's promise to Noah is often referred to in covenant literature as a "common grace" promise—providing for the temporal welfare of humankind and the animals—in contrast to a

saving grace intent on providing eternal salvation for sinners. However, in Scripture, all grace is salvation-intended. "The heavens [the sun, moon, stars, etc.] declare the glory of God; [and] their voice goes out into all the earth" (Ps. 19:1–6; cf. Rom. 10:18). And this universal witness of these "common grace" elements of nature are used by the Holy Spirit for the salvation-intended purpose of making God known to all of humankind: "Since what may be known about God is plain to them, because God has made it plain to them. For since the creation of the world God's invisible qualities—his eternal power and divine nature—have been clearly seen, being understood from what has been made, so that men are without excuse" (Rom. 1:19–20; cf. 2:14–16). Thus, even through the common grace elements of nature "the grace of God that brings salvation has appeared to all men" (Titus 2:11).

8. Ellet J. Waggoner, *The Everlasting Covenant: God's Promises to Us* (A series of forty-seven articles published in *The Present Truth* magazine [May 1896–May 1897], which preceded the publication of Waggoner's book, *The Everlasting Covenant*) (Berrien Springs, MI: Glad Tidings Publishers, 2002), 46–47.

9. Meredith G. Kline, *Kingdom Prologue: Genesis Foundations for a Covenantal Worldview* (Overland Park, KS: Two Age Press, 2000), 378.

10. E.g., Dale Ratzlaff, *Sabbath in Crisis* (Glendale, AR: Life Assurance Ministries, 1995), 43, 191.

11. *NIV Study Bible* (1088), note on Isaiah 49:3: "Together with Ge 12:1–3; Ex 19:5–6, this verse is sometimes called the 'great commission of the OT' and is quoted in part by Paul and Barnabas in Ac 13:47."

12. This section is based upon Richard M. Davidson, "Interpreting Old Testament Prophecy," in *Understanding Scripture: An Adventist Approach*, ed. George Reid (Silver Spring, MD: Biblical Research Institute, 2005), 193–195.

# Chapter 3

# How God Defined the New Covenant

We have seen thus far that any thorough study of the covenant(s) that God has made with humanity must begin with the primeval covenant that is as everlasting as God Himself. This everlasting covenant of love has always existed within the Trinity and extends out from the Trinity to embrace all of God's creation. The divine adaptation of this everlasting covenant to meet the human need created by sin has been variously termed the covenant of redemption, covenant of grace, and everlasting gospel. The covenants God made with His chosen people (e.g., Adam, Noah, Abraham, Israel) were expressions of this everlasting covenant or everlasting gospel. The blessings and stipulations of this covenant/gospel were never intended to be hoarded by their original recipients, but rather to be shared with the entire world.

We must now turn our attention to the basis of the debate over God's covenant(s). Jeremiah prophesied that God would make "a new covenant" with His people (Jer. 31:31–34). The New Testament took up this theme and for the first time spoke of an "old covenant." Many Bible students have interpreted the "old covenant" and "new covenant" as terms referring exclusively to the Old Testament and New Testament, or, even more narrowly, to the difference between the terms of the covenant God made with Israel at Sinai and the terms of the gospel proclaimed in the New Testament. There is a widespread belief that the terms of salvation proclaimed in the old covenant are qualitatively different from

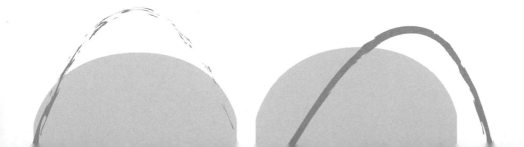

the terms of salvation proclaimed in the new covenant. Hence, when the New Testament speaks apparently disparaging words about the old covenant, some take this as evidence that God abandoned His old covenant and replaced it with the true gospel He presented in the New Testament. But is this the case? What, exactly, is the new covenant? It is clearly defined by God Himself in both the Old and New Testaments in nearly identical words. As expressed in Jeremiah, with very minor adaptations in Hebrews, the new covenant reads:

> "The time is coming," declares the LORD, "when I will make a new covenant with the house of Israel and with the house of Judah. It will not be like the covenant I made with their forefathers when I took them by the hand to lead them out of Egypt, because they broke my covenant, though I was a husband to them," declares the LORD. "This is the covenant I will make with the house of Israel after that time," declares the LORD. "I will put my law in their minds and write it on their hearts. I will be their God, and they will be my people. No longer will a man teach his neighbor, or a man his brother, saying, 'Know the LORD,' because they will all know me, from the least of them to the greatest," declares the LORD. "For I will forgive their wickedness and will remember their sins no more." (Jer. 31:31–34; cf. Heb. 8:8–12)

To understand the contrast between the old and new covenants, we must identify exactly what the new covenant is, then examine the scriptural passages that compare and contrast the two covenants.

## The DNA of the Everlasting Gospel Expressed in the New Covenant

When Saddam Hussein ruled Iraq, he protected himself from assassins by employing doubles who looked so much like him that no assassin would be sure whom he was killing. When Saddam was captured by American soldiers during the second Gulf War, no one could be sure it was really him until his DNA had been checked. Every human being's DNA is unique. When American scientists were able to match the DNA of the captured Iraqi with Saddam's, they knew they had the right man.

The new covenant contains specific DNA markers that enable us to detect its presence wherever it occurs in Scripture. In His own description of His new covenant, God imprinted these unique markers in His new covenant in the form of four specific promises or provisions He made to redeem human beings from sin and restore them to the eternal inheritance He planned for them at creation.

**Promise/Provision 1**: "I will put my law in their minds and write it on their hearts" (Jer. 31:33; Heb. 8:10). The theological term for this DNA marker is *sanctification*, a righteousness from God imparted to the believer by the Holy Spirit (Rom. 8:4). From the moment He created humankind in His image, God's goal for us has always been that we would be holy as He is holy, and we would reflect His character of love in all of our relationships (Lev. 20:7; Matt. 7:12; 1 Pet. 1:15–16). When God created Adam in His own image, He wrote His law in Adam's heart. Since God created him "very good," we can assume that Adam was naturally inclined toward love and obedience to God (Gen. 1:26–27, 31). Adam's sin subjected his descendants to sinful natures bent to sin and hostility toward God and His law, a condition they cannot change on their own (Rom. 5:12; 8:7; Jer. 13:23; Rom. 3:10–18).

> The new covenant contains specific DNA markers that enable us to detect its presence wherever it occurs in Scripture.

Human attempts to change this nature lead to an externalized religious experience, a legalistic compliance that is not born of faith or motivated by love. The resulting obedience may be carved into the granite of a stony heart, but it is not ingrained in the person's very nature. This results in the person "having a form of godliness but denying its power" (2 Tim. 3:5). But such formal religion is as much an expression of the sinful nature as is the most flagrant disobedience. Both are conditions we cannot change on our own. So when God commands, "Keep my decrees and follow them," He always includes the empowering promise, "I am the Lord, who makes you holy" (Lev. 20:8). Through the operation of His Spirit, God works to write His laws on our hearts that we might be "eager [and able] to do what is good," even as Adam once was (Ezek. 36:27; Phil. 2:13; Titus 2:14).

**Promise/Provision 2**: "I will be their God and they will be my people" (Jer. 31:33; Heb. 8:10). This provision expresses the bottom-line goal of every covenant God ever made with humanity—*reconciliation* with God. "At the center of covenant revelation as its constant refrain is the assurance 'I will be your God, and ye shall be my people.'"[1] What matters most to God is relationship—so much so that Jesus equated eternal life with knowing God (John 17:3).[2] He does not desire a universe filled with robots that do His will unthinkingly and dispassionately. He wants quality relationships. He created us so we could experience a relationship with Him based on love and trust and loyalty. Sin has estranged that relationship, and by sinning we have forfeited our rightful place in His eternal kingdom. "Be reconciled to God" constitutes the great appeal of the gospel and the sole requisite for eternal life (2 Cor. 5:20; cf. Isa. 45:22; 1 John 5:12).

**Promise/Provision 3**: "No longer will a man teach his neighbor or a man his brother, saying, 'Know the Lord,' because they will all know me, from the least of them to the greatest" (Jer. 33:34; Heb. 8:11). This provision highlights the forward-looking, eschatological nature of God's covenants with humanity.[3] They anticipate the return of Christ and the establishment of His eternal kingdom in which all will indeed have God's law written in their hearts; in which it finally can be said that "now the dwelling of God is with men, and he will live with them" and "they will be his people, and God himself will be with them and be their God" (Rev. 21:3); and in which indeed "all will know me, from the least of them to the greatest." We live in the "now—not yet" era in which the promises are in the process of being fulfilled. But the ultimate fulfillment awaits Christ's second coming and the establishment of His eternal kingdom. Until that day every believer is commissioned with "the everlasting gospel to preach to those who dwell on the earth" and is charged to participate in carrying out the great commission to "go and make disciples of all nations" (Rev. 14:6; Matt. 28:19–20).

This DNA marker of the new covenant constitutes the *mission* of all believers to seek and share the knowledge of God, whom to truly know is to have eternal life (Jer. 9:23–24; John 17:3). To a world that does not know Him (John 17:25), "God…through us spreads everywhere the fragrance of *the knowledge of him*…among those who are being saved and those who are perishing" (2 Cor. 2:14–15, italics added). It is not simply a list of religious truths, but "*the knowledge of Him*," that God's covenant people are commissioned to spread throughout the world. This calls for Christians to share more than intellectual knowledge of God. We must demonstrate God's everlasting love by deeds of sacrificial love: "He defended the cause of the poor and needy, and so all went well. Is that not what it means to know me?' declares the LORD" (Jer. 22:16).[4]

Many believe that while the old covenant was made with Israel, excluding Gentiles, the new covenant was made with Gentiles. But the texts in both Jeremiah and Hebrews are addressed to Israel: "'The time is coming,' declares the Lord, 'when I will make a new covenant with the house of Israel and with the house of Judah.…This is the covenant I will make with the house of Israel after that time,' declares the Lord" (Jer. 31:31, 33; Heb. 8:8, 10). In the New Testament era as in the Old, God entrusted His covenant to Israel, intending that they would share it with the world. When Gentiles became believers, they were no longer considered Gentiles but part of Israel. "Understand, then, that those who believe are children of Abraham.…If you belong to Christ, then you are Abraham's seed, and heirs according to the promise" (Gal. 3:7, 29). And it is precisely in this third promise/provision identity marker of His new covenant that God commissions His new covenant people with their evangelistic mission as "the fragrance of the knowledge of Him" until He comes—envisioning a day when God's covenant people will have completed their evangelistic mission, a day when this gospel of the kingdom will have been preached in the whole world and the end will have come (Matt. 24:14), a day indeed when "they will all know me, from the least of them to the greatest" in the restored kingdom of God.

**Promise/Provision 4**: "For I will forgive their wickedness and will remember their sins no more" (Jer. 31:34; Heb. 8:12). The theological term for this DNA marker of the new covenant is *justification*, God's gracious act in Christ to remove our sins and grant us a right standing before Him, imputing a righteousness to us that is not of our own making: the righteousness of Christ (Rom. 4:5–8; Phil. 3:8–9). Even before creation, when sin was only a possibility but not a reality, provision for forgiveness was already made in God's plan should the need arise—"This grace was given us in Christ Jesus before the beginning of time" (2 Tim. 1:9).[5] The atoning act that had long been anticipated through Old Testament types and prophecies came to fulfillment through Christ's passion and resurrection (Gen. 3:15; Isa. 53:5–10; Heb. 9:19–26).[6] "This is the blood of the covenant, which is poured out for many for the forgiveness of sins" (Matt. 26:28). In this single act of Christ, "through the blood of the everlasting covenant," all the covenants God ever made with humankind meet and merge as one with His great everlasting covenant of love (Heb. 13:20 NKJV).

## Why This Particular Order?

At this point, an important question naturally arises: why list sanctification as the first promise of the new covenant and justification as the last? Some may even be concerned that this ordering might somehow be a perversion of the gospel. But the answer is simple: for whatever reason, this is the very order God used in presenting the terms of the new covenant in Scripture.

It must be assumed that God either had no particular purpose in ordering them as He did, or that He started the list with the ultimate goal of His plan of salvation—the restoration of His image in the hearts, minds, and characters of His people—and then perhaps worked back through the steps that result in that final restoration.

In William Shea's commentary on Daniel, he discusses chapters 7-8-9 of Daniel in reverse order, 9-8-7. He explains this reversal this way: "One reason for the literary order has to do with Semitic thought processes. Modern western European thinking reasons from cause to effect; ancient Semitic people commonly reasoned from effect back to cause."[7]

Paul himself followed this pattern when he told the Corinthians, "But you were washed, you were sanctified, you were justified in the name of the Lord Jesus Christ and by the Spirit of our God" (1 Cor. 6:11).

## Tracing the New Covenant DNA Through Salvation History

These four explicitly stated promises/provisions—*sanctification*, *reconciliation*, *mission*, and *justification*—are the DNA markers of the new covenant, establishing it as a thoroughly grace-based, gospel-bearing, and mission-directed covenant. These identity markers constitute the everlasting gospel and are embedded in the everlasting covenant as it is expressed in the covenant of redemption. Once this is recognized, God's various covenants with humankind can be examined in a search for these DNA markers. Any covenant in which they might be found would certainly be invested with the same grace-based salvation principles that characterize the original covenant of our God who does not change.

As we will see, a careful study of God's covenant(s) reveals that every covenant God made with humanity bears the imprint of the new covenant DNA. In the covenants with Adam and Noah the evidence is strongly implied. With all the others it is explicitly evident. Moreover, the Old Testament is saturated with clusters of the four promises/provisions of the new covenant/everlasting gospel, with all four provisions grouped within a few verses or chapters of each other, or within thematically-related passages (see chart 1—"The DNA of the Covenant[s]"—on page 304 in appendix D).

With this foundation laid, we are now prepared to evaluate the divine covenant that has been most misunderstood and has received the most critical evaluation by many Bible students—the covenant God gave His people Israel at Sinai, referred to interchangeably by many as the Mosaic covenant, the Sinaitic covenant, and the old covenant.

> A careful study of God's covenant(s) reveals that every covenant God made with humanity bears the imprint of the new covenant DNA.

## Summary

As described by God Himself, the new covenant contains four specific promises/provisions that serve as DNA identity markers of the new covenant. The theological terms equivalent to these four new covenant promises/provisions are *sanctification*, *reconciliation*, *mission*, and *justification*. Once this has been ascertained, the groundwork has been laid for evaluating every covenant God initiated with humankind to determine its relation, by comparison or contrast, to the new covenant.

## Notes

1. Murray, *The Covenant of Grace*, 32.
2. The same word Jesus used in John 17:3 for "knowing" God is used in the Greek Septuagint of Genesis 4:1 referring to the intimacy Adam and Eve experienced that produced their first child.
3. Concerning the eschatological character of the covenant promises, O. Palmer Robertson writes, "Each of the successive covenants made with Adam, Noah, Abraham, Moses, and David finds its fulfillment in the new covenant....Indeed, the provisions of the new covenant shall receive a fuller realization in the age to come" (*The Christ of the Covenants* [Philipsburg, NJ: Presbyterian and Reformed Publishing Co., 1980]), 222. Rayburn comments similarly: "As Augustine ('The Spirit and the Letter.' *Augustine's Later Works*, LCC 8, ed. J. Burnaby [London: 1955], 223, 225) saw long ago, this promise of the universal knowledge of God can refer to

nothing less than the universal, spiritual knowledge of God, and as such can refer only to the time of the consummation when all believers enter into the full enjoyment of the covenant's eternal reward, 'which is the most blessed contemplation of God himself.' Certainly with respect to its context in Jeremiah, where it is presented as a contrast to the state of national unbelief and alienation from God, let alone with respect to the obvious meaning of the words themselves, the promise that all shall know can only by the most desperate expedient be made to refer to another period in which apostasy was rife, belief in need of challenge and support, and the church a small society in an evil and hostile world. The correlation of promise and new covenant in Hebrews suggests that the promises of fellowship with God and the universal knowledge of God contained in Jeremiah's oracle are promises, the full realization of which believers can expect only in the world to come." Ibid., 196. Cf. Willard, *The Divine Conspiracy*, 142, commenting on an eschatological fulfillment of the first provision of the New Covenant: "A time will come in human history when human beings will follow the Ten Commandments and so on as regularly as they now fall to the ground when they step off a roof. They will then be more astonished that someone would lie or steal or covet than they now are when someone will not. The law of God will then be written in their hearts, as the prophets foretold (Jer. 31:33; Heb. 10:16). This is an essential part of the future triumph of Christ and the deliverance of humankind in history and beyond."

4. Cf. Isa. 58:4–10; Matt. 5:16; 25:31–46.

5. Cf. 1 Pet. 1:20; Rev. 13:8.

6. Cf. Gen. 15:6–18; 22:8–17; John 8:56; John 1:29; 2 Cor. 5:19; Rom. 4:25; 1 Pet. 1:18–20; 2:24.

7. William H. Shea, *The Abundant Life Amplifier: Daniel 7–12* (Boise, ID: Pacific Press Publishing Association, 1996), 160.

# Chapter 4

# New Covenant DNA in the Old Covenant

The essence of the Sinai covenant, referred to by many as the old covenant, is expressed in the Ten Commandments. Hence Moses's statement to Israel, "He declared to you his covenant, the Ten Commandments" (literally, "the Ten Words"; Hebrew, *aseret haddebarim*, Deut. 4:13). This included God's reminder that He delivered them from slavery and bondage, and then His fatherly instruction regarding "the Ten Principles of covenant relationship"[1] (Exod. 20:1–17; Deut. 5:6–21). The additional laws, judgments, and regulations recorded in Exodus 20:22–23:33 "may be interpreted as elaborations and practical explications of the Decalogue"[2] and were referred to by Moses as "the book of the Covenant" (Exod. 24:7). Regulations regarding the sanctuary ritual, the numerous calls to holiness, coupled with assurances that God would make them holy, qualify the book of Leviticus as a further "exposition of the nature of Israel's covenant relationship with Yahweh."[3] Many scholars also refer to Deuteronomy as the Covenant Book of Israel, as it contains Moses's reiteration of God's covenant with Israel. The structure of Deuteronomy parallels that of Near Eastern treaties of Moses's day.[4]

The old and new covenants have been pitted against one another by some Bible students who describe the new covenant as grace-based, gospel-bearing, faith-inducing and mission-directed in apparent contrast to the Mosaic (Sinai) covenant, which they describe as legalistic in orientation, bondage-producing, and exclusive in intention. While

others avoid such explicit accusations and characterizations, they make statements that seem carefully calculated to lead their readers toward a similar conclusion. Two such statements are examined here.

*"Because of the minutiae of detail contained in the old covenant the* sons of Israel *stumbled as they applied the specifics of these laws to their real-life experiences."*[5] This statement implies that God gave Israel a covenant at Sinai that was so encumbered with minutiae that anyone who attempted to apply it to daily life was destined to stumble.

*"Paul's argument in Romans 8 is that 'the requirement of the law' can be fulfilled* only *within the arrangements of the new covenant."*[6] This statement does not acknowledge the clear distinction between the grace-based, gospel-bearing historical old covenant given by God and the *old covenant experience* testified to in Galatians 4 and elsewhere as a perversion of the pure covenant which God gave (the contrast between old covenant and new covenant experiences will be examined in chapters 6 and 7). Failing to take this distinction into account, the statement that "'the requirement of the law' can be fulfilled *only* within the arrangements of the new covenant" suggests that the unfortunate citizens of the Old Testament period who attempted to live according to the Sinai covenant, under which they served God for 1500 years, were destined to never have the requirement of the law fulfilled in their lives.

The book these quotations were drawn from contains many similar statements. The author never directly accuses God of imposing a legalistic system on His Old Testament people, but the cumulative weight of his statements makes the accusation, despite his occasional statement to the contrary. He establishes a straw old covenant, then sets it on fire, something the New Testament does not do.

In contrast, since we have identified the DNA markers that God imprinted in the new covenant, we can now examine the Sinai covenant to see whether it contains the DNA markers of the new covenant/ everlasting gospel. It should come as no surprise that we will find that all four markers are indeed embedded in the Sinai covenant.

## New Covenant DNA Marker 1—Sanctification

*Evidence in the Sinaitic covenant for Promise/Provision 1 of the new covenant:* "'I will put my law in their minds and write it on their hearts'" (Heb. 8:10)—*Sanctification.* When Peter admonished Christians to the highest level of sanctification, he quoted from the Sinai covenant and appealed to it as his authoritative source: "Just as he who called you is holy, so be holy in all you do; for it is written: 'Be holy, because I am holy'" (1 Pet. 1:15–16; quoting Lev. 11:45; 19:2).

God's call for obedience was premised on His promise to empower people in every way necessary for them to comply. God's appeal in the Sinaitic covenant that Israel "be holy…keep my decrees and follow them" was immediately accompanied with His enabling promise, "I am the LORD, who makes you holy" (Lev. 20:7–8). His biddings were His enablings. God invested the weekly Sabbath with that very meaning. As He "blessed the seventh day and made it holy," so He instructed His covenant people to "observe my Sabbaths" each week as "a sign between me and you for the generations to come, so you may know that I am the LORD who makes you holy"[7] (Gen. 2:3; Exod. 31:12–13). The Sabbath was a symbol and constant reminder

> It should come as no surprise that we will find that all four DNA markers of the new covenant/everlasting gospel are indeed embedded in the Sinai covenant.

to God's people of His promise to sanctify them, to write His laws in their hearts, to restore His image within them—"I am the LORD, who makes you holy."

Lest we be accused of putting words in God's mouth that He would inscribe His laws on the hearts of His covenant people who put their trust in Him, Moses himself proclaimed it in his reiteration of the Sinaitic covenant in Deuteronomy:[8] "The LORD your God will circumcise your hearts and the hearts of your descendants, so that you may love him with all your heart and with all your soul, and live....Now what I am commanding you today is not too difficult for you or beyond your reach.... No, *the word is* very near you; it is in your mouth and *in your heart* so that you may obey it...*to love the* L ORD *your God*, to walk in his ways, and *to keep his commands*, decrees and laws" (Deut. 30:6, 11–16, italics added).

In Romans 10:6–10 the apostle Paul quoted from this passage in Deuteronomy 30 to support his own teaching of righteousness by faith and introduced it with these words: "But the righteousness that is by faith says." Thus we see that Deuteronomy 30 is a classic Sinai covenant statement of "the righteousness that is by faith" through which the gospel was preached to Israel (Rom. 10:5–13). Sadly, Paul had to lament concerning Israel, "but they have not all obeyed the gospel" that was preached to them (Rom. 10:16).

So strong is the argument from Deuteronomy 30:11–14 and Romans 10:5–16 that the Sinai covenant was a grace-based, righteousness-by-faith-encoded, gospel-bearing covenant that dispensationalist Wayne Strickland labors to make this Deuteronomic passage prophetic of a future time beyond the scope of the Sinai covenant. He does this to support his claim that "The righteousness of the law was operable during Moses' life, but that a future time would see righteousness based on faith."[9] But O. Palmer Robertson rightly states, "the setting of Deuteronomy 30 requires that it be understood as reporting nothing other than a renewal of the Mosaic covenant of law" proving that "grace clearly may be found in the Mosaic covenant of law" even as "law clearly may be found in the Abrahamic covenant of promise."[10] McComiskey concurs: "[Christ] may be seen by Paul in the Old Testament word just as vividly as he is in the new Testament. Paul could see Christ in Deuteronomy 30....In that passage [Deut. 30:11–14] Christ became the facilitating principle of obedience."[11]

Thus the psalmist, who lived during the era of the Sinai covenant and had accepted the everlasting gospel message communicated through that covenant, could testify, "I desire to do your will, O my God; your law is within my heart" (Ps. 40:8). And God addressed His trusting children of that historical old covenant era who had a similar experience with God: "Hear me, you who know what is right, you people who have my law in your hearts" (Isa. 51:7).

Clearly, God's call for an obedient, sanctified life, a life of holiness that bore the divine image, was accompanied by God's own promise/provision, embedded within the Sinai covenant itself, that enabled His holy law to be ingrained in the hearts of His people, not just inscribed in granite. Such a sanctified experience is only possible for those who have responded in faith to the everlasting gospel appeal and whose hearts have been converted and transformed by the Holy Spirit (John 3:3–6; Rom. 8:4, 7–9).

## New Covenant DNA Marker 2—Reconciliation

*Evidence in the Sinaitic covenant for Promise/Provision 2 of the new covenant*: "I will be their God and they will be my people" (Heb. 8:10)— *Reconciliation.* Leviticus 26 is a key chapter that outlines protective stipulations as part of "the decrees, the laws and the regulations that the LORD established on Mount Sinai between himself and the Israelites through Moses," specifying rewards for obedience and a series of gradually intensifying punishments for repeated disobedience (Lev. 26:46). Just as a parent will punish children for dangerous behavior to protect them, so every punishment listed in Leviticus 26 was designed to lead habitual sinners back to God.[12] This chapter is one of the many Bible passages that reveal that the various covenants are all part of one unified, developing covenant. Here God puts forth His disciplinary intervention in the lives of the Israelites as evidence that He hasn't forgotten the covenants He made with their fathers. "I will remember my covenant with Jacob and my covenant with Isaac and my covenant with Abraham…For their sake I will remember the covenant with their ancestors whom I brought out of the land of Egypt in the sight of the nations to be their God. I am the LORD" (Lev. 26:42, 45).

God's covenant promise to Abraham and his descendants, including Moses, that He would do everything possible to save their nation and to empower them as His missionary nation to take the gospel to the world, included His disciplinary intervention in their lives. And right in the middle of this revelation in Leviticus

> God's call for an obedient, sanctified life was embedded within the Sinai covenant itself and enabled His holy law to be ingrained in the hearts of His people, not just inscribed in granite.

26 God reiterates the bottom-line goal of His covenant(s) with them: "I will walk among you and be your God, and you will be my people" (Lev. 26:12). God's greatest desire is to be reconciled to His lost children and to draw them back into the kind of close, covenant relationship with Himself that Adam and Eve had in Eden. As the ultimate fulfillment of this desire, He will one day return for them and take them to be with Him forever.[13]

## New Covenant DNA Marker 3—Mission

*Evidence in the Sinaitic covenant for Promise/Provision 3 of the new covenant*: "No longer will a man teach his neighbor or a man his brother, saying, 'Know the LORD,' because they will all know me, from the least of them to the greatest" (Heb. 8:11)—*Mission*. The Sinaitic covenant called the entire nation to become a "kingdom of priests and a holy nation" (Exod. 19:5–6). Since this Israelite "kingdom of priests" had a Levitical priesthood of its own who ministered to their nation, who was the nation of Israel itself, as a kingdom of priests, to minister to? And what was the nature of their mission to those they were called to serve?

It was understood that the nation as a whole was commissioned by God as priestly bearers of the everlasting gospel of salvation to the ends of the earth. This mission statement was divinely encoded into their history as a people. To Jacob, their father, God had said: *"All peoples on earth* will be blessed through you.... Your descendants will be like the dust of the earth, and you will spread out to the west and to the east, to the north and to the south. *All peoples on earth* will be blessed through you and your offspring" (Gen. 12:3; 28:14, italics added).

Devout Israelites prayed, "May God be gracious to us and bless us and make his face shine upon us, that your ways may be known on earth, your salvation among all nations" (Ps. 67:1–2). Israel's failure to fulfill their evangelistic mission led Isaiah to the national confession: "We have not brought salvation to the earth; we have not given birth to people of the world" (Isa. 26:18).

When Peter wanted to assert the missionary purpose of God's new covenant people, he relied on the most authoritative source he knew—God's own word established in Scripture and encoded in His covenant(s) of old: "But you are a chosen people, a royal priesthood, a holy nation, a people belonging to God, that you may declare the praises of him who called you out of darkness into his wonderful light.... Live such good lives among the pagans that, though they accuse you of doing wrong, they may see your good deeds and glorify God on the day he visits us" (1 Pet. 2:9, 12; cf. Exod. 19:5–6).

Their proclamation was not to be limited to declaring the laws of God. They were also to reveal His plan for the salvation of the world as depicted in the sanctuary. And their most important mission was to reveal His loving character in their actions: "'*The nations* will know that I am the LORD,' declares the Sovereign LORD, 'when I show myself holy through you before their eyes'" (Exod. 19:5–6; Ezek. 36:23, italics added).

Through the prophets, themselves members of the Sinai covenant, God appealed for His covenant people to first know Him themselves that they might better make Him known: "For I desire mercy and not sacrifice, and the knowledge of God more than burnt offerings" (Hos. 6:6). Commenting on this divine appeal through Hosea, Geerhardus Vos comments: "All the demands made of the people are summed up in this one thing, that there should be the knowledge of God among them, and that not as a theoretical perception of what is Jehovah's nature, but as a practical acquaintance, the intimacy of love.…This knowledge is intended to make Israel like unto Jehovah, it has a character-forming influence."[14]

Isaiah, who also lived under the covenant of Sinai and was a prophetic voice for that covenant, wrote: "You are my servant, Israel, in whom I will display my splendor [NKJV: in whom I will be glorified].…It is too small a thing for you to be my servant to restore the tribes of Jacob and bring back those of Israel I have kept. I will also make you a light for the Gentiles, that you may bring my salvation to the ends of the earth" (Isa. 49:3, 6). While this divinely mandated mission statement to be a "light for the Gentiles" ultimately had the Messiah in mind, it was first directed to "my servant, Israel." As such, it has been called "the great commission of the Old Testament."[15]

Paul and Barnabas authenticated their own mission to preach the gospel to the Gentiles by quoting from this very passage in Isaiah, showing that they were simply obeying the mission statement of God to His covenant people through the ages (Acts 13:46–47).[16]

God's covenant people at Sinai were His ambassadors through whom He had chosen to spread the knowledge of God and His glory universally, with the ultimate end in mind that one glorious day "they will all know me, from the least of them to the greatest." Through them the world was to hear the passionate appeal of the One who would give His life for their salvation: "Turn to me and be saved, all you ends of the earth" (Isa. 45:22).

## New Covenant DNA Marker 4—Justification

*Evidence in the Sinaitic covenant for Promise/Provision 4 of the new covenant*: "For I will forgive their wickedness and will remember their sins no more" (Heb. 8:12)—*Justification*. Surprisingly, *the first time the Bible refers to God as a forgiver of sins, or even announces that forgiveness is available, is on the occasion of the second giving of the Ten Commandments.*

The LORD said to Moses, "Chisel out two stone tablets like the first ones, and I will write on them the words that were on the first tablets, which you broke....So Moses chiseled out two stone tablets like the first ones and went up to Mount Sinai early in the morning, as the LORD had commanded him; and he carried the two stone tablets in his hands. Then the LORD came down in a cloud and stood there with him and proclaimed his name, the LORD. And he passed in front of Moses, proclaiming, "The LORD, the LORD, the compassionate and gracious God, slow to anger, abounding in love and faithfulness, maintaining love to thousands, and *forgiving wickedness, rebellion and sin.* Yet he does not leave the guilty [unrepentant and unbelieving] unpunished." (Exod. 34:1–7, italics added)

> God's covenant people at Sinai were His ambassadors through whom He had chosen to spread the knowledge of God and His glory universally.

Davidson comments on the terms God used in this passage to identify Himself at the giving of His law on Sinai:

- "Merciful" [compassionate]…from the verb *hanan*, to be "full of mercy, grace, and favor."
- "Slow to anger"—literally "long of nose!" God's anger fuse is very long! Incredible patience.
- "Abounding in *hesed*"—this is the covenant term par excellence; *hesed* is steadfast covenant love, best summarized in the hymn: "O Love That Will Not Let Me Go!" That's God's *hesed*.
- "Abounding in *emet*"—this implies stability, reliability, faithfulness, trustworthiness, sureness, truth.
- "Keeping *hesed* for thousands"—here he returns to the ultimate covenant word, God's lovingkindness, his covenant love, is steadfast unto thousands—and not just thousands, but what is

implied here in the Hebrew is the thousandth generation! God's *hesed* is to the thousandth generation! (NRSV; NJPS[17])

- "Forgiving iniquity, transgression and sin"—all kinds of sin! Even *awon* (perverse iniquity), and *pesha'* (rebellion—there is no sacrifice in the sanctuary service for this kind of sin); but God can forgive even the worst and apparently most hopeless sinner![18]

Once God's compassionate, forgiving, empowering grace had been formally revealed in the Law, the prophets adopted the theme. Dybdahl comments: "[The Exodus 34:6–7] classic description of God is recalled repeatedly in the rest of the Old Testament—more than any other passage. Major repetitions with similar wording include Numbers 14:18; Nehemiah 9:17; Psalm 86:15; 103:8; 145:8; Jeremiah 32:18; Joel 2:13; Jonah 4:2; and Nahum 1:3. In most cases, the passages form either the basis of an appeal for God's forgiveness or an explanation of why God was gracious to His people."[19]

It is important to remember that *God chose the law as the vehicle in which to reveal Himself as a forgiver*. Through the law God revealed that forgiveness would be mediated through animal sacrifice (Leviticus 4–5). Such sacrifices served as the visible type of the yet-to-come atoning sacrifice that was first promised to Adam through the seed of the woman, and later to Abraham through whose seed all nations of the world would be blessed. Through the giving of the law, God depicted more clearly than ever His way of salvation in the types and symbols of the sanctuary (Ps. 77:13). In the sanctuary imagery it was not only the *way* of His gospel that God revealed more clearly, but *Himself*: "I have seen *you* in the sanctuary and beheld *your power* and *your glory*. Because *your love* is better than life, my lips will glorify *you*" (Ps. 63:2–3, italics added). On the basis of God's revelation and promise in the Sinai covenant, historical old covenant believers could experience the reality and assurance that God had forgiven their sins.

On this foundation of God's forgiving grace revealed in the law and reiterated throughout the Old Testament, the New Testament grounded its own gospel message of salvation by grace. When Paul quoted Scripture to authenticate and explain his own preaching on justification by faith, he quoted from Psalm 32, David's testimony on forgiveness. This is highly significant when one bears in mind that, in Rayburn's words, "David's religion was the religion of Moses."[20] "However, to the man who does not work but trusts God who justifies the wicked, his faith is credited as righteousness. David says the same thing when he speaks of the blessedness of the man to whom God credits righteousness apart from works: 'Blessed are they whose transgressions are forgiven, whose sins are covered. Blessed is the man whose sin the Lord will never count against him'" (Rom. 4:5–7, quoting Ps. 32:1–2).

The prophet Isaiah's message was a further step in God's progressive covenantal revelation, more clearly identifying God's Messiah as the suffering servant whose own sacrifice would bear the sins of the world: "The LORD has laid on him the iniquity of us all" and "by his wounds we are healed" (Isa. 53:6, 5).

Throughout the 1500 years between the giving of the law on Sinai and the advent of Christ, God continued through varied imagery to assure His covenant people that their sins were forgiven: "Though your sins are like scarlet, they shall be as white as snow; though they are red as crimson, they shall be like wool" (Isa. 1:18). "Who is a God like you, who pardons sin and forgives the transgression of the remnant of his inheritance? You do not stay angry forever but delight to show mercy. You will again have compassion on us; you

> God chose the law as the vehicle in which to reveal Himself as a forgiver.

will tread our sins underfoot and hurl all our iniquities into the depths of the sea" (Mic. 7:19).

## Sinai Covenant a Covenant of Grace and Pure Gospel

After reviewing numerous evidences that the law God gave His covenant people at Sinai was grace-based, Davidson concludes that the covenant at Sinai bore "all the elements of the valid covenant of grace. It was based upon an experience and statement of prior redemption preceding the Ten Words [Exod. 20:1–2], and upon the blood of the sacrifice which ratified the covenant [Exodus 24], pointing to the atoning work of their Substitute and Surety. The covenant on Mt Sinai, on God's part, was totally a covenant of grace, a phase of the one everlasting covenant presented throughout the Bible."[21]

With the four DNA markers of God's everlasting gospel/new covenant with humankind embedded so deeply and explicitly in the Sinai covenant, it is not surprising to find the author of Hebrews writing, "We [in the New Testament era] also have had the gospel preached to us, just as they [in the Old Testament era, and more specifically during the period immediately following the giving of the law on Sinai, Israel's sojourn in the desert] also did" (Heb. 4:2).[22] In His covenant with them at Sinai, God gave His people a thoroughly grace-based, gospel-bearing, mission-directed covenant.

God's gospel-bearing promise to humanity at Adam's fall (Gen. 3:15) constituted the core component of each succeeding and expanded expression of His covenant for humankind's benefit—given to and through Noah, Abraham, Israel, David, etc.

- "Abram believed the LORD, and he credited it to him as righteousness" (Gen. 15:6).
- "Through the righteousness that comes by faith" "Abraham and his offspring [including his descendants at Sinai] received the promise that he [and they] would be heir of the world" (Rom. 4:13).
- "The law [God's covenant with Israel at Sinai], introduced 430 years later [than God's covenant with Abraham], does not set aside the covenant previously established by God [with humankind

in Genesis 3:15 and later reiterated and expanded to Abraham and his descendants] and thus do away with the promise. For if the inheritance depends on the law [alone—i.e., on obedience divorced from faith], then it no longer depends on a promise [the core component of every expression of God's covenant(s) with humankind, including His covenant at Sinai], but God in his grace gave it to Abraham [and his descendants, including Israel at and subsequent to Sinai] through a promise" (Gal. 3:17–18).

The gospel God embedded in the Sinai covenant—that covenant most often referred to by biblical scholars as the old covenant—was the pure gospel, not "a different gospel" that Paul warned "pervert[s] the gospel of Christ" and leads anyone who promotes it to be "eternally condemned" (Gal. 1:6–9). For "we [in the New Testament era] also have had the gospel preached to us, just as they [the recipients of God's covenant with Israel at Sinai] also did" (Heb. 4:2).[23] Thus Stephen could testify, "On Mount Sinai…[Moses] received *living words* to pass on to us" (Acts 7:38, italics added).

Had Israel, under the supervision of the Holy Spirit, been faithful to this pure gospel covenant, faithfully teaching and modeling its essential message to their children, the Spirit could have used it to instill within their successive generations a saving "trust in God" and a heart inclined to "keep his commands," His "living words": "He decreed statutes for Jacob and established the law in Israel, which he commanded our forefathers to teach their children…and they in turn would tell their children. Then they would put their *trust in God* and would not forget his deeds but would *keep his commands*" (Ps. 78:5–7, italics added). Jesus later identified "faith"[24] as one of the weightier matters of the law (Matt. 23:23, NKJV, NRSV). God's covenant with Israel was fully grace-based, gospel-bearing, and faith-inducing.

## Law Given Through Moses/Grace and Truth Came Through Jesus

Some commentators interpret John 1:17 ("For the law was given through Moses; grace and truth came through Jesus Christ") to mean that God's purportedly "law-based" historical old covenant given through Moses at Sinai was replaced by His grace-based new covenant which came when Jesus came. This interpretation carries the implicit, if not explicit, message that the covenant God gave at Sinai was not based on grace but on something other than grace.

But if God did not ground the Sinai covenant in grace, on what grounds did He give it to His people—works? As we have seen, the biblical record clearly establishes the historical old covenant in its entirety as a grace-based, gospel-bearing, faith-inducing, and mission-directed covenant throughout.

Apparently part of the problem comes in how one verse is translated. The New King James Version translates John 1:17, "For the law was given through Moses, *but* grace and truth came through Jesus Christ." The word "but" isn't in the original Greek text. The New International Version more accurately renders the text, "For the law was given through Moses; grace and truth came through Jesus Christ." Along with most modern translations, the NIV doesn't insert the conjunction that seems to set up a conflict between the old and new covenants.

John never intended that his reference to "the law…through Moses" should be pitted against "grace and truth…through Jesus Christ." In fact, the context reveals that his intention was exactly the opposite. An extended look at this context will make this point clear.

John opens his gospel with the shocking affirmation to the people of his day that Jesus, the one who lived among us in the flesh, was none other than the eternal God, the Creator, the source of all light and truth (John 1:1–3, 14). Then follows the passage in question, John 1:15–18: "John [the Baptist] testifies concerning him. He [John the Baptist] cries out, saying, 'This was he of whom I said, "He who comes after me has surpassed me because he was before me.'" From the fullness of his grace we have all received one blessing after another. For the law was given through Moses; grace and truth came through Jesus Christ. No one has ever seen God, but God the One and Only, who is at the Father's side ["close to the Father's heart," NRSV], has made him known."

Note first that John the Baptist pointed to Jesus's pre-existence and divine identity as evidence of Jesus's superiority to himself and all other prophets (1:15). The prophets were *bearers* of truth, but Jesus was the *source* of truth. The prophets testified to God's grace, but Jesus, being Himself God, was the source of that grace. Jesus was the source of the divine grace first announced in God's grace based, gospel-bearing, faith-inducing, mission-directed covenant promise to fallen Adam (Gen. 3:15). God progressively revealed this same grace more fully to the human race through His successive covenants with Noah, Abraham, and Moses. Thus John could write, "From the fullness of his grace we have all received one blessing after another," or, as the New Revised Standard Version translates it more literally from the Greek, "From his fullness we have all received, grace upon grace"[25] (1:16).

In other words, every revelation of divine grace given through the previous covenants came from Jesus Himself in His pre-existent state, for He was one with God from the very beginning. The divine grace revealed in the covenants was His own grace, representing the disposition and commitment of the heavenly council—Father, Son, and Holy Spirit. The covenants revealed His everlasting love for His entire creation, including all humankind, especially the people He had elected to represent and proclaim to the world the revelation of His grace and salvation. "The law...given through Moses" amplified and expanded on through the prophets, represented the culmination of that revelation that had been given to the world prior to the advent of Christ. It contained "the fullness of his grace" revealed to humankind up to that time.[26]

The message of John 1:17 follows naturally. It further establishes Jesus as the source of both the continuity and continuing progression of the revelation of God's grace given through the ages: "For the law was given through Moses; grace and truth came through Jesus Christ."

The verse begins with the word "for,"[27] showing that John intended for this verse to follow the thought he had developed in the previous verses, namely, that the divine revelations given through the ages, constituting "one blessing after another [literally 'grace upon grace'],'" were in fact progressive revelations of the grace of the pre-existent Christ. In verse 17 John declares the divine revelation through Jesus to be the ultimate revelation of that very grace expressed in all previous divine covenants, and expressed most fully up to that point in the revelation of His grace made in "the law." When Jesus was among us, His teachings expounded on and magnified the grace and truth He had progressively revealed to the prophets through the ages. His life, death, and resurrection on our behalf was a demonstration to the entire universe of the divine grace and truth that is eternal in origin and duration and truly universal in its embrace. He who from the beginning was one with God and always "close to the Father's heart" came to earth to reveal the depth of grace that fills God's heart.

> Every revelation of divine grace given through the previous covenants came from Jesus Himself in His pre-existent state, for He was one with God from the very beginning.

From the fullness of his grace we have all received one blessing [the historical old covenant] after another [the historical new covenant]. For the law [the first administration of grace, "the law" being used here as the chief representative of God's revelation through the entire Old Testament era] was given through Moses [not "*came* through Moses" but "*was given* through Moses," for Moses was only the intermediary informing the people of that grace that was given to him by Jesus, the source of grace]; grace and truth [revealed progressively to humankind from the time of Adam, and reaching its fullest revelation in the historic new covenant with the revelation of Christ in the flesh] came through [not "*was given* through" in this instance, but "*came* through," for the Source and Originator is now in view, not merely an intermediary] Jesus Christ. No one has ever seen God, but God the One and Only, who is at the Father's side ["close to the Father's heart," NRSV], has made him known. (John 1:16–18)

Thus, understood in context, John 1:17 affirms that Jesus's revelation of grace in His life on earth continued His progressive revelation, exponentially so, of the grace He had revealed in the law that came through Moses.

## Summary

The same theological DNA identity markers that characterize the new covenant—sanctification, reconciliation, mission, and justification—were divinely imprinted in the old covenant as well. In His covenants with humans, God progressively revealed His nature as a God of grace, compassion, love, justice, righteousness, truth, and forgiveness. In the process, He increasingly clarified the details of His plan of salvation. His covenant with His people at Sinai constituted a vital link in the chain of revelations running from humanity's fall in Eden to the restoration of all things in the earth made new. The divine grace and truth proclaimed in God's word to His people at Sinai became flesh at the incarnation of Christ and dwelled among us.

The old and new covenants are not opposed to each other, but the new covenant is presented in Scripture as being different from the old. How so? And if both covenants proclaim the same gospel, what should be made of the differences? We'll address these questions in our next chapter.

# Notes

1. Daniel I. Block, "Preaching Old Testament Law to New Testament Christians," *Ministry*, vol. 78, no. 5 (May, 2006), 9.

2. Ibid., 10.

3. Ibid.

4. Richard M. Davidson, *A Love Song for the Sabbath* (Washington, DC: Review and Herald Publishing Association, 1988), 37–38: "Scholars have uncovered ancient treaties, or covenants, from about the time of Moses that Hittite overlords (suzerains) made with their subordinate (or vassal) states. The external form of the Hittite suzerainty treaty went as follows: 1. *Preamble*—the suzerain identifies himself. 2. *Historical prologue*—description of previous relationship between suzerain and vassal, stressing the benevolence and generosity of the suzerain in the past as a basis for the vassal's gratitude and future obedience. 3. *Stipulations*—the basis and detailed obligations laid on the vassal by the suzerain, calling for commitment of loyalty by the vassal to the suzerain and establishing a covenant relationship between the two. 4. *Document clause*—statement about the preservation of the treaty in the vassal's sanctuary and provision for periodic readings of the treaty. 5. *Witnesses*—list of gods (particularly of the suzerain) and inanimate objects—anything beyond change—who are witnesses to the making of the treaty. 6. *Blessings and curses*—the call for faithfulness and loyalty, with promises of blessings for compliance and curses for breach of confidence.... The book of Deuteronomy has many parallels to the formal elements of the Hittite treaty. We may diagram the covenant renewal structure of Deuteronomy as follows: 1. *Preamble*: Deut. 1:1–6a. 2. *Historical Prologue*: Deut. 1:6b–4:49. 3. *Stipulations*: Deut. 5–11. 4. *Document Clause*: (Deposit) Deut. 10:5; 31:9, 24–26, (Reading) Deut. 31:10, 11. 5. *Witnesses*: Deut. 30:19; 31:19; 32:1. 6. *Blessings and Curses*: Deut. 11:26–32; 27–28; 33." For further discussion, Davidson recommends Meredith Kline, *Treaty of the Great King: The Covenant Structure of Deuteronomy* (Grand Rapids, MI: Eerdmans, 1983); Kenneth Kitchen, *Ancient Orient and Old Testament* (Downers Grove, IL: InterVarsity, 1966), 90–102; Peter Craigie, *The New International Commentary of the Old Testament: Deuteronomy* (Grand Rapids, MI: Eerdmans, 1976), 36–45.

5. Ratzlaff, 202.

6. Ibid., 203.

7. Some have suggested that God's statement that He is the one who makes His covenant people holy was not a reference to holiness of character, but rather to being set apart, as sheep who have been separated from the flock are said to be "holy to the Lord." However, when God appealed to His people, "Be holy, because I am holy" (Lev. 11:45; 19:2), He seems quite clearly to have in mind holiness of character, patterned after His own character, not simply set apart like sheep. This is how Peter understood it (1 Pet. 1:15–16).

8. Robertson, 218: "The entire book of Deuteronomy presents itself in covenantal form as a renewal of the bond which God established originally with Israel at Sinai."

9. Wayne G. Strickland, "The Inauguration of the Law of Christ with the Gospel," in Stanley N. Gundry, ed., *Five Views on Law and Gospel* (Grand Rapids, MI: Zondervan Publishing House, 1993), 248–252.

10. Robertson, 218.

11. McComiskey, *The Covenants of Promise*, 228.

12. Ranko Stefanovic, *Revelation of Jesus Christ: Commentary on the Book of Revelation*

(Berrien Springs, MI: Andrews University Press, 2002), 216: "The covenant curses [of Leviticus 26 and Deuteronomy 32, cf. Revelation 6] were, in the initial phase, preliminary judgments from God on his people. They were intended to wake them from their apostate condition, lead them to repentance, and move them toward a positive relationship with God."

13. Robertson, 293–294: "What is the point of the covenant? It is to establish a oneness between God and his people. That oneness which was interrupted by the entrance of sin must be reconstituted through the covenant of redemption. 'I shall be your God and You shall be my people,' functioning as the central unifying theme of the covenant, underscores the role of oneness as the essence of the goal of the covenant."

14. Geerhardus Vos, *Biblical Theology: Old and New Testaments* (Edinburgh: Banner of Truth Trust, 1948), 261.

15. *NIV Study Bible* (1088), note on Isaiah 49:3: "Together with Ge 12:1–3; Ex 19:5–6, this verse is sometimes called the 'great commission of the OT' and is quoted in part by Paul and Barnabas in Ac 13:47."

16. Hans K. LaRondelle, *Our Creator Redeemer: An Introduction to Biblical Covenant Theology* (Berrien Springs, MI: Andrews University Press, 2005), 34: "God's election of Israel was therefore an election to a special responsibility to be a blessing to all as a 'kingdom of priests' and a 'holy nation.' This bestowed on Israel the mission to be *priestly mediators* to all Gentile nations, in continuity with the Abrahamic covenant (see Exod. 19:5–6). For this missionary purpose God made a covenant (*berit*) with Israel—a bond of a redemptive fellowship."

17. NJPS is the abbreviation for *Tanakh—The Holy Scriptures: The New JPS Translation according to the Traditional Hebrew Text* (Philadelphia: Jewish Publication Society, 1988).

18. Richard M. Davidson, "Blazing Grace (The Graciousness of God in the Sinaitic Covenant)," an unpublished manuscript presented at the 2003 spring meeting of the Gospel Study Committee (see footnote on p. x), 17.

19. Dybdahl, *A Strange Place for Grace*, 82. Commenting on Joel's reference to God as "gracious and compassionate, slow to anger and abounding in love" (2:13), the NIV Study Bible scholarly note says, "Recalls the great self-characterization of God in Ex 34:6–7, which runs like a golden thread through the OT."

20. Rayburn, "The Contrast Between the Old and New Covenants in the New Testament," 19.

21. Davidson, "Blazing Grace," 9.

22. This truth was aptly stated by Geerhardus Vos: "There was real gospel under the theocracy. The people of God of those days [Old Testament] did not live and die under an unworkable, unreceptive system of religion, that could not give real access to and spiritual contact with God. Nor was this gospel-element contained exclusively in the revelation that preceded, accompanied, and followed the law; it is found *in the law itself.* That which we call 'the legal system' is shot through with strands of gospel and grace and faith. Especially the ritual system is rich in them. Every sacrifice and every lustration proclaimed the principle of grace." *Biblical Theology*, 129.

23. Refers specifically to "those Moses led out of Egypt" (Heb. 3:16), as well as more generally to the entire Old Testament generation.

24. This term, translated "faithfulness" by the NIV and several other translations in Matthew 23:23 is the Greek term for "faith," *pistin,* and is translated predominantly as "faith" elsewhere in those same translations.

25. The Greek phrase is *karin anti karitos.* William F. Arndt and F. Wilbur Gingrich

describe the use of *anti* in John 1:16 "to indicate that one thing is equivalent to another," and translate the complete phrase "*grace after grace* or *grace upon grace* (i.e., grace pours forth in ever new streams;…)." *A Greek-English Lexicon of the New Testament and Other Early Christian Literature* (Chicago: The University of Chicago Press, 1957), 73. Thus the New Revised Standard Version translation: "grace upon grace."

26. Willard, *The Divine Conspiracy*, 141: "The law that God had truly given to Israel was, until the coming of the Messiah, the most precious possession of human beings on earth. *That* law consisted of fundamental teachings such as the Ten Commandments, the 'Hear, O Israel…' of Deuteronomy 6:4–5, the great passage on neighbor love in Leviticus 19:9–18, and the elaborations and applications of them by the Jewish prophets up to John the Baptist.

"'What great nation is there,' Moses exclaims, 'that has statutes and judgments as righteous as this whole law that I am setting before you today?' (Deut. 4:8). The ancient writers knew well the desperate human problem of knowing how to live, and they recognized the law revealed by Jehovah, Israel's covenant-making God, to be the only real solution to this problem.

"God's true law also possessed an inherent beauty in its own right, as an expression of the beautiful mind of God. It is profound truth and therefore precious in its own right. In Ps 119 and elsewhere we see how the devotee of the law, Jehovah's precious gift, was ravished by its goodness and power, finding it to be the perfect guide into the blessed life in God. It was a constant delight to the mind and the heart.

"We must understand that Jesus, the faithful Son, does not deviate at all from this understanding of the law that is truly God's law. He could easily have written Psalm 119 Himself."

27. Arndt and Ginrich list John 1:17 as one of the verses in which *hoti* is best translated "for." *A Greek-English Lexicon of the NT*, 594.

# Chapter 5

# How the Old and New Covenants Differ

So far we have observed that all the covenants, including the Sinai covenant, were encoded with the same grace-based, gospel-bearing, faith-inducing, mission-directed DNA markers as the new covenant. We've also seen that all proclaimed the same everlasting gospel and were progressively revealed expressions of the covenant-love of the Trinity. So we must ask, why then did God say that the new covenant would "not be like the covenant I made with their forefathers when I took them by the hand to lead them out of Egypt"? (Jer. 31:32; Heb. 8:9). And further, why would Moses say of the covenant God made with Israel at Sinai: "It was not with our fathers that the LORD made this covenant, but with us, with all of us who are alive here today" (Deut. 5:3).

Some authors interpret these texts to mean that the covenant God made with Israel at Sinai was entirely different from both the covenant He made with Abraham and the new covenant.[1] That view can be summarized in the following table:

| Abrahamic Covenant | Sinai Covenant | New Covenant |
|---|---|---|
| Promise/Faith | Law/Obedience | Promise/Faith |
| | | Holy Spirit/Love |
| | Not like the covenant made with their fathers. | Not like the covenant made with those redeemed from Egypt. |
| | Deuteronomy 5:3 | Hebrews 8:8–9 |

These interpreters thus attempt to isolate God's covenant at Sinai, including the Ten Commandments, from its surrounding covenants of grace, and identify it with the "letter that kills" (2 Cor. 3:6), "the ministry that brought death" (2 Cor. 3:7), and "the ministry that condemns men" (2 Cor. 3:9). They further charge that God's covenant at Sinai was written in stone and letter only, not in the heart or by the Spirit, and was not designed so that the majority of covenant members could know God personally. They see the Sinai covenant and law as the target of all the apparent anti-law texts of the New Testament, making that covenant ineffectual and liberating the new covenant believer from its oppressive bondage. This interpretation would seem plausible if Deuteronomy 5:3, Jeremiah 31:32, and Hebrews 8:9 meant what such interpreters claim, namely that the Sinai covenant was different in character from God's previous covenants and the new covenant.

Let's examine these texts and see whether they necessarily contradict the conclusion we came to in chapter 4 that the covenant God made with Israel at Sinai is consistent with, and of the same character as, His other covenants with humanity.

There are at least six ways in which the new covenant is different:

- A different response was anticipated.
- It was like the new commandment to love, which wasn't new.
- It was a new and more powerful revelation than previously given.
- It was to make the older covenant new and more real to us.
- It replaced the older, fulfilled ceremonies with new ones.
- Jesus came in the middle.

None of these differences affects the essential nature of the covenant, which is still a grace-based, gospel-bearing, faith-inducing, mission-directed expression of the covenant love of the Trinity. In this chapter, we will examine these six differences.

## A Different Response Anticipated

The immediate context within the new covenant itself provides the most obvious and probable resolution of Jeremiah 31:31 and Hebrews 8:8. The full statement in Jeremiah's edition reads: "[The new covenant] will not be like the covenant I made with their forefathers when I took them by the hand to lead them out of Egypt, because they broke my covenant [made with them at Sinai], though I was a husband[2] to them." Hebrews 8:8 replaces "though I was a husband to them" with "because they did not remain faithful to my covenant, and I turned away from them."

Clearly, what God intended to be different about the new covenant from the one made with Israel at Sinai was the faithfulness of the recipients of the covenant. It was an appeal for the new covenant believer to be faithful where the recipients of the covenant He made at Sinai had been unfaithful.

The master of the vineyard in Jesus's parable, after having his servants beaten and killed by the tenants of his property, finally "sent his son to them. 'They will respect my son,' he said" (Matt. 21:33–37). So too in the new covenant God is effectively saying, having killed My prophets and rejected their appeals for repentance and offers of a new heart and spirit by My grace, surely My people will not reject My Son whom I have resurrected from the dead for their justification. Surely, He says, this covenant will be new in the positive way My people respond to it. How could they reject My Son?

## Like the New Commandment to Love, which Wasn't New

There is the further possibility that the new covenant differed from the one given at Sinai in the same way that the Old Testament commandments to love and obey God and to love one another (Deut. 6:5; Lev. 19:18) were reiterated in the New Testament as a commandment that wasn't new, but yet it was: "Dear friends, I am not writing you a new command but an old one, which you have had since the beginning. This old command is the message you have heard. Yet I am writing you a new command; its truth is seen in him [Jesus]" (1 John 2:7–8). "I am not writing you a new command but one we have had from the beginning. I ask that we love one another. And this is love: that we walk in obedience to his commands. As you have heard from the beginning, his command is that you walk in love" (2 John 5–6).

The Old Testament commandments to love God and neighbor were expressed with the very same words in the New Testament, but Jesus lived that love in a way that made the law of love shine with new splendor—almost as though it were a new law.[3]

Similarly, each of the four DNA promise/provisions of the covenant of redemption, while already explicitly stated in the Old Testament, could be seen in a gloriously new light after people had seen them lived out in the life of Jesus. These were the same truths but now wondrously illuminated. So much so that even though the promises had been operative from the implementation of the covenant at Adam's fall and progressively expanded upon with each succeeding covenant, once we saw those promises lived out in the life of Jesus, it was as though we hadn't seen them before. They seemed like new promises even though they had been around from the beginning.

## A New and More Powerful Revelation

Closely related to the previous point is one related to the name by which God made Himself known to Moses and to Abraham. God told Moses, "I am the Lord [Hebrew *YHWH* or *Yahweh*]. I appeared to Abraham, to Isaac and to Jacob as God Almighty [Hebrew *El-Shaddai*], but by my name the Lord [*Yahweh*] I did not make myself known to them" (Exod. 6:2–3). And yet, it was precisely as the Lord, *Yahweh*, that God *did* make Himself known to Abraham and entered into a covenant relationship with Him: "Abram believed the Lord [*Yahweh*], and he credited it to him as righteousness. He also said to him, 'I am the Lord [*Yahweh*], who brought you out of Ur of the Chaldeans to give you this land to take possession of it.'…On that day the Lord [*Yahweh*] made a covenant with Abram" (Gen. 15:6–7, 18).

And it was by that very name that Abraham knew and addressed

God: "Abram said, 'O Sovereign LORD [*Yahweh*]...'; Abraham...called upon the name of the LORD [*Yahweh*], the Eternal God" (Gen. 15:2; Gen. 21:33). Furthermore, Isaac and Jacob also knew God by the name Yahweh (Gen. 27:20; 28:13; 32:9). In what possible way then could God have said to Moses that He had not made Himself known to Abraham "by my name the LORD [*Yahweh*]"?

If the context of God's statement to Moses is carefully studied (Exod. 6:1–8), it will be seen that God was about to reveal Himself in a new way to Moses and Israel, a way that Abraham and the patriarchs had not seen. His new revelation would be so much greater than the old that by comparison it would seem as if God had never before revealed Himself as Yahweh. God's statement to Moses that He had not made Himself known to Abraham by His name "the LORD" (*Yahweh*) "reveals that the fullness of God's nature and the total meaning of His name was not yet manifest."[4] He was about to work mighty miracles to deliver His people from their slavery. God had worked miracles previously (e.g., Gen. 12:10–20; 19:24; 21:1–7; 22:12–14), but not to the same extent as they were about to see happen in Egypt and throughout their wanderings in the desert. God was also about to reveal to them His holy law at Sinai, amidst spectacular displays in nature. And as noted in the previous chapter, it was at the giving of the law at Sinai that Scripture first records God declaring Himself to be a loving God, a forgiving God, a gracious God, a merciful God.

In other words, Abraham had known God by His name *Yahweh* on a limited basis, but Moses and Israel were on the verge of knowing Him by that name on an even grander scale, pursuant to the progressive revelation He was about to give in His "new" covenant at Sinai. The events surrounding and including Sinai were going to be a fuller revelation of who Yahweh was and what His will was for His people than even Abraham himself had been given. God's self-revelation to Moses and Israel was not a *different* revelation but a *fuller* revelation, and in that sense a *new* revelation.

Similarly, when God said that the new covenant would not be like the one He made with Israel at Sinai, He was stating that the new covenant, characterized as it was by the real presence of the Son of God among us, would make known the divine nature and will in a revelation far surpassing anything given previously. Thus the revelation *was not new* in the sense of being *different* in kind from the previous revelation, and yet it *was new*, being a much *fuller* revelation than that which had been given previously. This understanding is consistent with the way God has worked throughout the history of salvation—progressive understanding made known in each successive administration of the covenant of redemption—Adam, Abraham, Moses, historical new covenant.

## Making It New and Real to Us

Edward Heppenstall has made this observation about Deuteronomy 5:3:

> The question may be raised that Deuteronomy distinguishes between the Abrahamic and Sinaitic covenants. "The Lord our God made a covenant with us in Horeb. The Lord made not this covenant with our fathers, but with us, even us, who are all of us here alive this day" Deut 5:2, 3. Moses is not emphasizing the difference between covenants. He is saying that each man must renew that covenant for himself. God made a covenant with Abraham; nevertheless both Isaac and Jacob renewed that holy covenant for themselves. And it must be renewed by their descendants. They cannot be excused by saying that God made this covenant only with their fathers, and so it is not binding. No, he made it with them, "with us, even us, who are all of us here alive this day." What avails it to the children of Abraham according to the flesh, since God is able of the stones to raise up children unto Abraham? This is a covenant that needs to be ratified by every individual for himself apart. Similarly, we urge our own children to seek and to gain a Christian experience for themselves, for they do not inherit it from their parents. This is exactly what Moses was asking the Hebrews to do just before he died.[5]

Moshe Weinfeld, author of the *Anchor Bible Commentary on Deuteronomy 1–11*, and Peter C. Craigie, who wrote a commentary titled *The Book of Deuteronomy*, agree with Heppenstall's argument. They note that the point of Moses's appeal to his audience is not to distinguish between the present covenant and earlier ones but rather that Moses's audience might make the covenant given to their fathers their very own, to adopt it and internalize it personally, to assure that it does not remain in granite but rather becomes ingrained within them.[6]

Similarly, we who live in the New Testament era must not consider a study of God's covenant(s) as an esoteric religious exercise unrelated to our daily lives, but should embrace the most mature and purest expression of God's covenant(s) as seen lived out in the life of Jesus Christ. It must not remain in granite but become ingrained. Viewed in that light, God's timeless, universal invitation to salvation takes the form of a new covenant to each new generation.

## New Ceremonies

Another difference between the new and old covenants was their divinely ordained ceremonial systems. The new covenant no longer maintained the elaborate ceremonial system structured around animal sacrifices. The prophet Daniel had prophesied that the coming Messiah would not only "confirm a covenant with many" but would also "put an end to sacrifice and offering" (Dan. 9:27). Hebrews 7–10 confirms that the animal sacrificial system met its fulfillment in Jesus's once-for-all sacrifice for sin and was no longer to be practiced. In the new covenant, baptism and the Lord's Supper replaced the old covenant's circumcision and animal sacrifices (Luke 22:19–20; 1 Cor. 11:23–26; Col. 2:11–12).

Similarly, the Sinai covenant had differed from earlier covenants in the elaborateness of its ceremonial system. Animal sacrifices were certainly part of the system previous to Sinai (e.g., Gen. 4:4; Exod. 3:18). But the instruction to build a sanctuary as a dwelling place of God, as well as to provide a structure for the administration of an expanded sacrificial system and ceremonial ritual, was new (Exodus 25–40; Leviticus).

## Jesus Came in the Middle

Of all the ways that the new covenant differs from the old, the most significant is that in the old "God spoke to our forefathers through the prophets," but in the new "he has spoken to us by his Son, whom he appointed heir of all things, and through whom he made the universe" (Heb. 1:1–2). The prophets were godly men, to be sure. They knew God. In them God was restoring His image. Their messages are as valuable to us today as to their original hearers. But Jesus "is the radiance of God's glory and the exact representation of his being, sustaining all things by his powerful word" (Heb. 1:3).

In a biblically illiterate society, many people do not know the most fundamental difference between the Old Testament and the New. The difference, of course, is that Jesus came in the middle. That's a cataclysmic difference! The whole Old Testament looks forward to His coming. The New Testament looks back at it and now anticipates His return.

Conversion is an experiential form of Jesus's coming in the middle. Many believers have testified that their own personal conversion to Christ, itself an act of grace, changed the way they view the world. My own conversion was no exception. The day after my conversion I well remember looking at trees and grass as though seeing them for the first time and marveling at how they were an expression of God's love for me. People in my life I had hardly noticed before became important to me when I realized the value that God places on them. The personal experience of conversion to Christ transforms one's whole perspective on life. It enables the believer to see old things as new in some beautiful way.

The same happened to history itself when Jesus came in the middle. Now we have BC/AD, Old Testament/New Testament, made so because Jesus came in the middle. His advent is the epicenter of history.

Simply in terms of God's progressive revelation through the

covenants, think of what it means that Jesus who was "from everlasting," Jesus who was "with God in the beginning," Jesus who sat on the most holy Trinitarian council where covenant was born before time was born, Jesus whom John declared "was God" and whom the prophet Isaiah called "Mighty God, Everlasting Father"—think of what it means that this very Jesus actually came into our world

> In a biblically illiterate society, many people do not know the most fundamental difference between the Old Testament and the New. The difference, of course, is that Jesus came in the middle.

and lived with us! (Mic. 5:2; John 1:1–3, 14; Isa. 9:6). After Jesus came, the gospel was focused like a laser beam on the events of His death and resurrection for us (1 Cor. 15:1–3).

## Floodlight on the Law

John could say, "For the law was given through Moses; grace and truth came through Jesus Christ. No one has ever seen God, but God the One and Only, who is at the Father's side, has made him known" (John 1:17–18). "The law given through Moses" was a huge advance in God's progressive revelation of his covenantal relationship with His people. The psalmist declared, "Your law is truth" (Ps. 119:142 NKJV). God's law—His commandments and the symbolic sanctuary depiction of the Messiah's atoning death—revealed the way to life. But Jesus, the Author and Giver of that very law, could say, "*I am* the way and the truth and the life" (John 14:6, italics added). What the law testified to, He was. The law was a transcript of His character.

God revealed a fleeting and wonderful glimpse of Himself to Moses as a merciful, gracious, loving, forgiving God (Exod. 34:6–7). But Jesus was "at the Father's side" from the beginning and could say something that Moses and the prophets could never say: "Anyone who has seen me has seen the Father" (John 14:9). He *was* the gracious one, the one who loved us to the death, the forgiver. Nothing the law said became untrue once Jesus came. Rather, His coming shined a floodlight on the truths revealed in the law. In His most famous address, the Sermon on the Mount, He said: "Do not think that I have come to abolish the Law or the Prophets; I have not come to abolish them but to fulfill them. I tell you the truth, until heaven and earth disappear, not the smallest letter, not the least stroke of a pen, will by any means disappear from the Law until everything is accomplished" (Matt. 5:17–19).

The new that had come in Christ was not to the denigration of the old but in fulfillment of it. Those who watched Him, listened to Him, and lived with Him began to view everything, including God's eternal laws and promises and character, in a new light: "But now a righteousness from God, apart from law, has been made known, to which the Law and the Prophets testify" (Rom. 3:21). As Paulien has noted, "Righteousness is whatever God does."[7] Righteousness is His character. And righteousness is His actions which are always consistent with His character. The law prescribed it. Jesus lived it. His life magnified what the law taught.

## Everlasting Covenant Personified

In Jesus the Old Testament covenant symbols met their reality—the promise met its fulfillment. He was "the Lamb of God who takes away the sin of the world" (John 1:29). He "was without sin," and credits to us His own righteousness so we shall be "saved through His life" (Heb. 4:15; 2 Cor. 5:21; Rom. 5:10). He who voluntarily placed Himself on death row to spare our race from extinction, who had been depicted through the covenants as the hope of the race, had finally come to the execution…and the resurrection! In every conceivable sense, in Jesus the new had come. In Him God's progressive revelation through His covenant(s) reached its pinnacle. So much, so in fact, that in a Messianic prophecy written centuries before the advent, God revealed that in the

Messiah humanity would be in the presence of the very One who is *Himself* the covenant: "I, the LORD, have called you in righteousness; I will take hold of your hand. I will keep you and will make you to be a covenant for the people and a light for the Gentiles, to open eyes that are blind, to free captives from prison and to release from the dungeon those who sit in darkness" (Isa. 42:6–7; cf. Gal. 3:19–20). In Him "the Word [the everlasting covenant itself] became flesh and made his dwelling among us" (John 1:14).

The DNA of the everlasting covenant was His DNA. Promise/Provision 1 (Sanctification): In Him, in His humanity, we saw one whose heart was so dependent on the heavenly Father that God could fully write His eternal law on it. Promise/Provision 2 (Reconciliation): In Him we saw one in whom God could bring to fullest realization His promise, "I will be their God and they will be my people." Promise/Provision 3 (Mission): In Him we saw one who needed no one to teach Him about God, for He knew God, and none was ever so passionate as He to make God known to those who knew Him not (Luke 19:10; John 14:7–9; 17:25–26). Promise/Provision 4 (Justification): In Him symbol met reality, promise met fulfillment (Heb. 9:12–14). In Him the effective sacrifice and atonement for our sin has been finally made and need never be repeated (Heb. 9:25–28). In Him the devil received his ultimate sentence and awaits his final disposition (Heb. 2:14). In Him death itself has lost its sting, and "those who all their lives were held in slavery by their fear of death" are set free (1 Cor. 15:20–22, 55; Heb. 2:15).

## Cosmically New

The New Testament authors viewed the entire revelation and history of the Old Testament through the new lens provided by the life, teachings, death, and resurrection of Jesus. If they had failed to do so, their eyes and hearts would have remained veiled (2 Cor. 3:14). They understood Jesus as the new Adam, the new exodus (the new "way out"), the new Moses, the new Israel, the new temple, the new king, the new Elijah, the new redeemer from exile.[8] Where Adam and Israel failed, Jesus succeeded. The covenant curse that Adam and Israel, and all humanity, merited through disobedience was borne by Jesus.

- "Christ redeemed us from the curse of the law by becoming a curse for us, for it is written: 'Cursed is everyone who is hung on a tree'" (Gal. 3:13, quoting Deut. 21:23).
- "We all, like sheep, have gone astray, each of us has turned to his own way; and the LORD has laid on him the iniquity of us all"; "by his wounds we are healed" (Isa. 53:6, 5).
- "For if, by the trespass of the one man, death reigned through that one man, how much more will those who receive God's abundant provision of grace and of the gift of righteousness reign in life through the one man, Jesus Christ. Consequently, just as the result of one trespass was condemnation for all men, so also the result of one act of righteousness was justification for all men" (Rom. 5:17–18).
- "For as in Adam all die, so in Christ all will be made alive" (1 Cor. 15:22).

Jesus's atoning death on the cross seems to have not only made God's covenant with *humanity* a new covenant, but in ways we don't fully understand it appears to have made His everlasting covenant with the other inhabitants of the universe a new covenant as well. Note this astounding revelation: "For God was pleased to have all his fullness dwell in him, and through him to reconcile to himself all things, whether things on earth or things in heaven, by making peace through his blood, shed on the cross" (Col. 1:20).

Jesus's death on the cross put God's everlasting covenant on display before the universe itself in a way it had never been seen before. God used Jesus's death on the cross to, in some profound way, "reconcile to himself *all things*, whether things on earth or *things in heaven*" (italics added). In what way did Jesus's death "reconcile to himself...things in heaven" that have never been estranged from Him through sin? Before such great mysteries we stand on holy ground with bowed heads and awed hearts. But at least this much can be said: in the Christ event God was revealing something breathtakingly new, even to the universe that lies beyond sin's borders, about His everlasting covenant promise and commitment to His creation.

## The Holy Spirit's New Ministry

One of the most amazing evidences of how the New Testament writers, and Jesus Himself, understood the "newness" of His everlasting covenant in the New Testament historical era was in the way they treated the work of the Holy Spirit. The Holy Spirit had been operative in the Old Testament as a creating (Gen. 1:1–2), convicting (Ps. 51:9–12), converting (1 Sam. 10:6–10), reviving (Ezek. 37:1–14), empowering/sanctifying (Ezek. 36:25–27), indwelling (Exod. 31:1–3), gift-imparting (Exod. 31:1–3), miracle-working (Gal. 4:29), all-pervading presence (Ps. 139:7) who strove for the conversion of all humankind (Gen. 6:3) and who could be longed for (Ps. 51:11), resisted (Ps. 106:33), and grieved (Isa. 63:7–10).

Conversion and sanctification have never been available except through the ministry of the Holy Spirit. All the sanctified qualities of a godly, righteous, holy, divine-image-bearing life are but the fruits of the Spirit (John 3:3–6; Gal. 5:19–23). It has also been revealed that "those controlled by the sinful nature cannot please God," and that only "if the Spirit of God lives in you" (Rom. 8:8–9) can one be redeemed from this spiritually bankrupt condition. This is a timeless and universal truth. Jesus was amazed that Nicodemus, a Jewish leader, did not understand it (John 3:3–6).

One recent writer on the covenants claimed, "In the old covenant only the key leaders were filled with the Holy Spirit and had a personal knowledge of God."[9] This is a serious misunderstanding of the biblical record. While Old Testament believers in general did not know much about the Holy Spirit's unique role and work, just as they did not know much about the identity and role of Jesus, that does not mean that these members of the Trinity were not fully and globally active throughout that period—convicting, converting, and indwelling those who believed to sanctify them and restore the divine image within them.[10]

Even so, the apostle John, who experienced the powerful display of the Holy Spirit's ministry manifested at Pentecost, could look back on the whole of salvation history, including the years that Jesus was on earth, and conclude, "Up to that time the Spirit had not been given, since Jesus had not yet been glorified" (John 7:39). And Jesus Himself said, "Unless I go away, the Counselor will not come to you" (John 16:7). In light of the abundant scriptural testimony regarding the pervasive work of the Holy Spirit throughout the entire period of the Old Testament, in what possible way could it be said that the Holy Spirit had not come or been given until Jesus was glorified?

Robertson shares a valuable insight: "The self-revelation of God throughout the ages may be regarded as the 'raw material' used by the Holy Spirit to apply the benefits of redemption to the life-experience of the believer."[11] The Holy Spirit's work is not different in the New Testament era than it was in the Old. What *is* different is the "raw material" the Holy Spirit has to work with. Previously He used the wonderful stories of creation, the flood, the exodus from Egypt, the manna from heaven and water from a rock, the law given from Sinai, and the animal sacrifices in the sanctuary to impress people of their spiritual need and of God's covenant promise to save them to the uttermost if they do not reject Him.

> The Holy Spirit's work is not different in the New Testament era than it was in the Old. What is different is the "raw material" the Holy Spirit has to work with.

Once Jesus had completed His earthly mission and was glorified, the Holy Spirit had powerful new "raw material" to work with. The new story didn't discount the older ones. It supercharged them. Even a quick read of the book of Acts reveals that the Holy Spirit still used the old stories, but they had become subservient now to the new story—the resurrection of Jesus! The old had been gathered up and made even more effective by the new. But now that the new had come, it must forever after take center stage. "When he, the Spirit of truth, comes, he will guide you into all truth....He will bring glory to me by taking from what is mine and making it known to you" (John 16:13–14).

In every way, God's long-standing covenant with His people had entered a profoundly new phase. Something indescribably new had taken place. Not the final consummation yet, but the guarantee of it.

## Caveat

The underlying assumption of evangelical dispensationalism appears to be that the nature of the Sinai covenant itself contributed in some way to the general unbelief and failure of Israel to live up to their covenant privileges and obligations. In essence this is an accusation against God who gave the covenant. But pointing to the general failure of Israel as proof that God's covenant at Sinai was faulty would be similar to pointing to the dark ages of Christian history as evidence that there was something faulty about the New Testament because it left generations of supposed Christians in such spiritual darkness.

And what about our own generation, with Bibles in practically every home in the Western world and churches dotting our landscape? Is Jesus's plaintive query a warning to our generation, "However, when the Son of Man comes, will he find faith on the earth?" (Luke 18:8). Perhaps we should listen anew and take to heart the appeal Moses made to the covenant people who were poised to enter the Promised Land: "The LORD our God made a covenant with us....It was not with our fathers that the Lᴏʀᴅ made this covenant, but with us, with all of us who are alive here today."

## Summary

In Deuteronomy 5:3 Moses differentiates the covenant God made with the generation of Israelites who were about to enter Canaan under the leadership of Joshua from the one He made with their fathers. Jeremiah 31:31 and Hebrews 8:9 differentiate God's new covenant with Israel from the one He entered into with the generation of Israelites He delivered from Egypt. How are we to understand this differentiation?

God's own answer to this question was that He expected a different response from those in the New Testament period to whom the gospel would be preached than He had received from those in the Old Testament period to whom that same gospel had been preached. Also, the New Testament ceremonies of baptism and the Lord's Supper replaced the Old Testament animal sacrificial services. Furthermore, whenever a new generation receives God's covenant, it comes as a new covenant to them in the sense that they cannot rely on the response of their forbearers to God's invitation to salvation but must make that choice for themselves.

In addition, Jesus's advent in human history made everything new— the age-old commandment to love became a "new" commandment; the grace and truth depicted in the law given to the world through Moses came into our world personified in Jesus Christ as though it were a new revelation; the Holy Spirit, the divine sanctifying agent who had been drawing and sealing men and women to God from the beginning, was introduced by Jesus as though He had not been active previously. The cataclysmic advent of Jesus, the unifying agent in God's covenant(s) with humanity, made everything that came before it "old" and everything that came with and after it "new." God's entire revelation through the prophets came to be regarded as the "Old" Testament, and His subsequent inspired revelation the "New." The "old" revelation was not old in the sense of somehow being less inspired, valid, or applicable than it had been previously, but rather "old" in the sense that it could never again be fully understood without reading it in the light of the everlasting gospel revealed in Jesus. To read it any other way would be to do so with veiled eyes and hardened hearts.

We are now prepared to understand and appreciate the all-important theme of the next two chapters—how Scripture refers to the old and new covenants at some times with a *historical* application in mind, and at other times with an *experiential* application in mind. The significance of recognizing this scriptural demarcation can hardly be overestimated. On the one hand, the failure to recognize these distinct applications has resulted in scriptural interpretations that fracture the unity of the covenant of redemption/everlasting gospel. On the other hand, discriminately applying these distinctions erases apparent conflicts between some passages of Scripture and preserves the scriptural unity and coherence of the everlasting gospel.

## Notes

1. E.g., Ratzlaff, 39–40, 43, 48, 85, 189, 193.

2. Jeremiah elsewhere speaks of God's marriage to Israel and subsequent divorce when Israel became an unfaithful spouse (3:6–14). Ezekiel portrayed God's covenant with Israel as a covenant between a husband and wife (16:8, 32). The spousal relationship between God and His covenant people would be renewed in the new covenant (Hos. 2:14–23).

3. Similarly, at the end of His life on earth Jesus converted the Matthew 7:12 principle— "So in everything, do to others what you would have them do to you"—into the John 13:34 principle—"A new commandment I give you: Love one another. As I have loved you, so you must love one another." Once Jesus's disciples had seen the Golden Rule lived out in His life, Jesus could restate it as He did in a much safer form for us to follow (if we truly know Him), and that in essence made the old commandment to love one another a new commandment— "As I have loved you, so you must love one another" (rather than, "Do unto others as you want them to do to you").

4. Gerhard F. Hasel, *Biblical Interpretation Today* (Washington, DC: Biblical Research Institute, 1985), 22. Cf. LaRondelle, *Our Creator Redeemer*, 32: "The Patriarchs had known Yahweh only as the God of *promises*, but under Moses Israel came to know Yahweh as the *Fulfiller* of His promises. This gave the name *Yahweh* a new character and meaning to Moses that was not known by the patriarchs."

5. Heppenstall, *The Covenants and the Law*, 447.

6. Moshe Weinfeld, *Anchor Bible Commentary on Deuteronomy 1–11* (New York: Doubleday,

1991), 237–238. "According to the traditions in Numbers and Deuteronomy, the Exodus generation, which stood at Sinai, died out during the forty years of wanderings in the desert (cf. Num 14:23, 30; Deut 1:35; 2:14–16). In order to make the Sinaitic covenant binding for the new generation, the author had to make the Israelites declare that the Sinaitic covenant was actually directed to them and not just to their fathers: 'not with our fathers…YHWH made this covenant, but with us, the living, all of here today.' The generation that stands on the plains of Moab is then conceived as standing at Sinai.…A similar explanatory digression is found in Deut 11:2–9. There the author stresses the fact that the signs and miracles done by God at the Exodus were experienced, not by the sons of the listeners (who are the ones actually being spoken to), but by the listeners themselves (11:7; cf. 29:1). The blurring of generations concerning the covenantal commitment is clearly expressed in 19:13–14: 'I make this covenant not with you alone, but with those who are standing here with us this day, and with those who are not with us here this day.…' Israel throughout its generations is thus presented in Deuteronomy as one body, a corporate personality."

Peter C. Craigie, *The Book of Deuteronomy*, The New International Commentary on the Old Testament (Grand Rapids, MI: Eerdmans, 1976), 148: "In a literal sense, the covenant was made with the fathers of most of those standing there on the plains of Moab. The essence of the covenant, however, was its present reality, so that Moses drives home very forcefully the direct identification of the principally new and young generation with those involved in the making of the Horeb covenant. It was made with us, each one of us, these present today, all of us who are living—the syntax of this part of the Hebrew sentence is at first sight rather awkward, but it functions effectively in a hortatory sense to drive home the direct relationship between the people present and the Lord of the covenant."

One point at which these scholars differ with Heppenstall is their interpretation of "our fathers." They hold that Moses's reference to "our fathers" does not refer to Abraham at all, but rather to the real fathers and grandfathers of Moses's own audience who forty years earlier were actually present at Sinai when the law was given. In Deuteronomy, Moses, shortly before his death, addressed their children who had come safely through the 40–year wilderness pilgrimage and were poised to go in and take the land of Canaan. He urged those children, now adults, not to ignore the covenant God made with their fathers as something that was designed for their fathers only, but rather to embrace as their very own that same covenant that God made with their fathers forty years earlier at Sinai.

7. Paulien, *Meet God Again for the First Time*, 94.

8. Ibid., 55–75.

9. Ratzlaff, 191.

10. Cf. 1 Cor. 12:1–11; Gal. 5:22–25; Titus 3:3–8. The Holy Spirit's work during the historical old covenant period was equally as encompassing and ubiquitous, but more quiescent. The law could never accomplish any of the Holy Spirit's salvation ministries on humanity's behalf, but has ever been a tool of the Spirit's. Ratzlaff's statement, "*The role the law filled in the old covenant is filled by the Holy Spirit in the new*" (*The Sabbath in Crisis*, 184), is a great misunderstanding of the roles of the law and the Holy Spirit in both God's old and new covenant historical eras. Apart from the work of the Holy Spirit no human beings in any era have ever been convicted of sin, converted, born into the eternal kingdom of God, had God's law written on their hearts or been empowered for ministry. When God told Elijah, "I have reserved for myself seven thousand who have not bowed the knee to Baal" (1 Kings 19:18;

Rom. 11:4), those were 7,000 who had submitted themselves in faith to the work of the Holy Spirit in their lives. For "the sinful mind is hostile to God. It does not submit to God's law, nor can it do so. Those controlled by the sinful nature cannot please God. You, however, are controlled not by the sinful nature but by the Spirit, if the Spirit of God lives in you" (Rom. 8:7–9). That is an eternal truth not bound by historical ages but only by the limitations of faith and submission to God's will. Though the Holy Spirit doesn't get as much press in the Old Testament as in the New, He is fully active for the salvation of men and women of every era. Nor was He limited by the boundaries of race, nationality, or religion. Throughout the ages even "Gentiles who do not have the law," yet by the moral and loving way they live "show that the requirements of the law are written on their hearts," bear witness in their lives of the Holy Spirit's convicting, converting, cleansing, transforming, saving, indiscriminating work among all people, "(…their [sanctified] consciences also bearing witness, and their thoughts now accusing, now even defending them.)…on the day when God will judge men's secrets through Jesus Christ, as my gospel declares" (Rom. 2:14–16).

11. Robertson, 191.

# Chapter 6

# The Two Covenants in History and Experience

We have seen thus far that God's covenant(s) with humanity emanated from the everlasting, primordial covenant of love that existed within the Trinity and embraces all of God's creation, involving His whole-souled commitment to their ultimate welfare and His expectation of their whole souled commitment and loving loyalty to Him in return. When Adam and Eve sinned against God's covenant with them, God adapted His everlasting covenant into a covenant of redemption, His plan to save humanity and restore the eternal hope He designed for them.

The details of God's covenant of redemption/plan of salvation were revealed progressively through covenants God made with chosen human agents who were elected by God as stewards to proclaim His everlasting gospel to the world. Each covenant bore DNA markers that characterized it as a fully grace-based, gospel bearing, faith-inducing, mission-directed revelation of God's covenant of redemption/plan of salvation. God would write His law on believers' hearts, be their God, forgive their sins, and spread through them the fragrance of the knowledge of Himself until the final restoration of all things when all would know Him. Even when the covenants were differentiated, their essential unity as expressions of the everlasting gospel/everlasting covenant was preserved. God was at work by His Spirit, throughout both Old Testament and New Testament times, to reveal Himself to people,

convict them of sin, forgive the repentant, and write His law on the hearts of those who responded in faith that they might obey Him in love.

But what about the New Testament claims that the old covenant and law are engraved on stone only, not in the heart (2 Cor. 3:7), and that they are not based on faith (Gal. 3:12)? The law is called the power of sin (1 Cor. 15:56); something we must die to in order to be married to Christ and receive salvation (Rom. 7:1–4; Gal. 2:19); that which will prevent those who try to live by it from ever sharing in the inheritance of the saints (Gal. 4:30); something no longer needed as a tutor to bring us to Christ once we've been converted and come to Christ (Gal. 3:24–25); a letter that kills (Rom. 7:10–11; 2 Cor. 3:6) and engenders a curse (Gal. 3:13); death (2 Cor. 3:7); condemnation (2 Cor. 3:9); spiritual imprisonment (Gal. 3:23); and slavery (Gal. 4:24–25, 30–31). One biblical scholar characterized the covenant God made with Israel at Sinai as "sin-provoking," "sin-inducing," and "sin-producing."[1] Is this the character of the law that the God of the everlasting covenant gave to His people during the Old Testament era? Instead of the law and covenant God gave His people on Sinai being grace-based, gospel-bearing, faith-inducing, and mission-directed, was it instead sin-provoking, sin-inducing, and sin-producing? Was God's law and covenant a divine instrument of salvation or something His covenant people had to be rescued from to find salvation?

> Was God's law and covenant a divine instrument of salvation or something His covenant people had to be rescued from in order to find salvation?

The answer lies in part in a crucial distinction between *history* and *experience* that underlies the biblical presentation of the old and new covenants. The old and the new covenants each have dual applications: a *historical* application and an *experiential* application.

## The Historical Old and New Covenants

The plan of salvation by which God saves us is referred to by many theologians as the "covenant of redemption." The covenant of redemption is God's everlasting covenant molded around the needs of fallen humanity for the purpose of reconciling them with God and restoring the eternal inheritance God offered them at creation—that He might be their God and they might be His people.

But the covenant of redemption was itself divided into two historical periods, which may also rightly be called "the two dispensations"[2]—the Old Testament period (the historical old covenant) and the New Testament era (the historical new covenant). "The bond of God with man before Christ may be called 'old covenant' and the bond of God with man after Christ may be called 'new covenant.'"[3] This historical divide was marked by the coming of Jesus. The monumental fact of His presence among us marked the watershed of spiritual history. Before He came, there was no Old Testament or old covenant, historically speaking. But after He came, everything prior to His advent was considered "old" and everything that followed was considered "new." Thus, we live in the historical new covenant/New Testament era.

## The Historical Old Covenant

The historical old covenant was characterized by redeeming acts of God; a system of moral and civil laws based on love and the Ten Commandments; and an elaborate ceremonial system eventually focused in a localized sanctuary, administered by imperfect priests, and centered on animal sacrifices that could never take away sin but served as an anticipatory type and shadow of the atoning ministry of the Messiah who was yet to come. The historical old covenant was ratified by the blood of animals (Gen. 4:4; 8:20; 15:6–18; Exod. 24:4–8; 40:29; Heb. 9:22).

The covenant God made with Israel at Sinai—including moral and civil laws, along with the more elaborated ceremonial system through which the everlasting gospel was preached to Israel—came to represent the historical old or "first" covenant (Hebrews 7–10). But this covenant more accurately encompasses the entire Old Testament (2 Cor. 3:14) and covers the full historical period of God's gracious dealings with human beings from Adam's fall to the incarnation of Christ. The historical old covenant was a grace-based, gospel-bearing, faith-inducing, mission-directed covenant encoded with all four promise provisions residing in the new covenant. God purposed with the historical old covenant to groom a people through whom He could reveal His holiness and extend His salvation appeal to every nation, tribe, tongue, and people: "Turn to me and be saved, all you ends of the earth" (Isa. 45:22; Ezek. 36:23).

## The Historical New Covenant

The historical new covenant era was characterized by several things:

- the once-for-all redemptive act of God in Jesus Christ (the foundational core of the gospel—1 Cor. 15:1–4) for the salvation of the world and the reconciliation to Himself of all things in heaven and on earth (2 Cor. 5:19; Col. 1:19–20);
- an even greater clarification and intensification of moral expectations based on the magnification of love and the Ten Commandments as revealed in the life and teachings of Jesus Christ (Matt. 5:17ff.; 22:35–40);
- a simpler ceremonial system consisting of baptism and the holy communion; a deeper understanding of God based on God's self-revelation in Jesus (John 14:7–9); a new and intensified phase of the Holy Spirit's work based on the superlative, new "raw material" provided Him by the sacrificial death, resurrection, and glorification of Jesus (John 7:39; 17:4); and
- believers' heightened awareness of the availability, role, and work of the Holy Spirit as the convicting, converting, character-producing, ministry-empowering agent of the Trinity (John 3:3–5; 7:37–39; 14:26; 15:26).

The historical new covenant was ratified by the blood of Jesus (Luke 22:20; Heb. 9:22–26). (See table 2 on pages 294–296 in appendix D for a side-by-side comparison of the historical old and new covenants.)

## The Experiential Old and New Covenants

When discussing old covenant/new covenant concepts, New Testament authors, and Paul in particular, often had in mind not the two historical divisions of spiritual history represented by the Old and New Testaments, but rather two vastly different religious experiences.

### The Experiential Old Covenant

The experiential old covenant represented an illegitimate and perverted use of God's law/covenant as a system of merit to earn God's acceptance and establish one's righteousness before God—an application of God's law/covenant He never intended.

An old covenant experience is an externalized religion, engraved on stone (in granite) only, not ingrained in the heart. An old covenant experience is going through the motions of religion with an unconverted heart, "having a form of godliness but denying its power" (2 Tim. 3:5). It's a religion of "the flesh," represented by Paul's pre-conversion experience—"as for legalistic righteousness, faultless" (Phil. 3:4–6). It takes the "holy, righteous and good" law of God and converts it into a legalistic instrument of spiritual bondage and death, into a letter that kills: "I found that the very commandment that was intended to bring life actually brought death. For sin, seizing

> When discussing old covenant/new covenant concepts, Paul often had in mind not the two historical divisions of spiritual history represented by the Old and New Testaments, but rather two vastly different religious experiences.

the opportunity afforded by the commandment, deceived me, and through the commandment put me to death" (Rom. 7:12, 10–11). When viewed from the perspective of "all who rely on observing the law" for their salvation, "the law is not based on faith" (Gal. 3:10, 12).

Though the everlasting gospel was preached to Adam, Abraham, and Israel through the grace-based, gospel-bearing, faith-inducing, mission-directed covenants of the Old Testament historical era, "not all the Israelites accepted the good news" (Rom. 10:16). "Israel, who pursued a law of righteousness, has not attained it. Why not? Because they pursued it not by faith but as if it were by works" (Rom. 9:31–32). An old covenant experience is not of faith. It is something we must die to in order to be married to Christ, and it is something that will prevent those who try to live by it from sharing in the inheritance of the saints. It is indeed "a different gospel—which is really no gospel at all," but one designed "to pervert the gospel of Christ" (Gal. 1:7).

## The Experiential New Covenant

A new covenant experience, on the other hand, is the real thing. Reflecting on his conversion, Paul wrote:

> But whatever [I used to believe] was to my profit [from my old covenant experience of externalized religious formalism] I now consider loss for the sake of Christ. What is more, I consider everything [associated with that former experience] a loss compared to the surpassing greatness of knowing Christ Jesus my Lord, for whose sake I have lost all things. I consider them rubbish, that I may gain Christ and be found in him, not having a righteousness of my own that comes from the law, but that which is through faith in Christ— the righteousness that comes from God and is by faith. (Phil. 3:7–9)

A new covenant experience involves the acceptance by faith of God's gracious gift of salvation based on the redemptive act of Christ, and the obedience that issues naturally from faith and a restored relationship with

God through a dependent reliance on Jesus's indwelling presence through the Holy Spirit. "Do we, then, nullify the law by this faith [new covenant experience]? Not at all! Rather, we uphold the law" (Rom. 3:31).

Viewed from an experiential rather than historical perspective, the new covenant represents an internalized religious experience lived by one who has been "born of the Spirit" (John 3:3–6), "lives by the Spirit" (Rom. 1:8–17), bears the "fruit of the Spirit" (Gal. 5:22–25), and exercises the "gifts of the Spirit" (1 Cor. 12:1–11). The Holy Spirit puts God's law in the mind and writes it on the heart of believers (Deut. 30:10–14; Isa. 51:7; Rom. 2:12–16), establishing it on the basis of their faith (Rom. 3:31) and fulfilling its requirements in their lives (Rom. 8:4). Someone enjoying a new covenant experience delights in and loves God's law (Ps. 1:1–3; 119:47, 97; Rom. 7:22). In the Holy Spirit's hands, God's law is "perfect" (Ps. 19:7). The Holy Spirit uses God's law for "converting the soul" (Ps. 19:7 NKJV), creating true freedom (Ps. 119:44–45; James 2:8–12), revealing sin that we might be drawn ever closer to Christ (Gal. 3:23–24; Rom. 3:20; 7:13), and motivating and empowering "the obedience that comes from faith" (Rom. 1:5).

At creation Adam enjoyed a new covenant experience. Even though he needed no forgiveness at that time (promise/provision 4—justification—of the new covenant), that eventuality had already been provided for in the everlasting covenant: "This grace was given us in Christ Jesus before the beginning of time" (2 Tim. 1:9; cf. 1 Pet. 1:18–20; Rev. 13:8). In every other respect, Adam was like a new covenant believer through faith in his creator. God's law was written in his heart (new covenant promise/provision 1—sanctification); God was his God and he was God's child (promise/provision 2—reconciliation); and Adam needed no one, other than God Himself, to teach him about God, for he knew God personally (promise/provision 3—mission). From this perspective, the new covenant (experientially understood) predated both the experiential old covenant initiated by Adam's fall and God's historical old covenant that was ratified by the blood of animals after

Adam's fall. Viewed from this perspective, the new covenant actually preceded the old.

The new covenant experience, as well as the historical new covenant, was also ratified by "the blood of the eternal covenant," for "without the shedding of blood there is no forgiveness" (Heb. 13:20; 9:22).

While dispensational scholars view the old and new covenants exclusively from a historical perspective (equating the old covenant with the Old Testament era, especially from Sinai on, and the new covenant with the New Testament era), other scholars view the covenants strictly from an experiential perspective. Rayburn's views are representative here: "The distinction between the new covenant and the old covenant has nothing to do with the distinction between the situation before Christ came and the situation after or between the religion and revelation before Christ and that after. It is rather the distinction between flesh and Spirit, between the old man and the new man, between death and life, between condemnation and righteousness, and between guilt and the forgiveness of sin....In a proper sense, all salvation is the new covenant."[4]

Both of these groups of interpreters recognize an essential dimension of the scriptural revelation of the old and new covenant themes. But both also err in denying either the historical or the experiential dimensions. While not specifically employing the nomenclature, "*historical* old and new covenants" and "*experiential* old and new covenants," other scholars nonetheless recognize the need to make this distinction when the context requires it for a proper understanding of the New Testament's attitude toward God's law and the way of salvation in the Old Testament era, and more particularly at Sinai.[5] Sheer logical consistency requires that such a distinction be made. (See table 3 on pages 297–300 in appendix D for a side-by-side comparison of the experiential old and new covenants.)

Only after both the historical and experiential dimensions of the old and new covenant themes in Scripture are acknowledged and applied can it be seen that the very same beautiful, unified, coherent plan of salvation has been proclaimed throughout Scripture and all of God's covenants—the plan of salvation by grace through faith alone, resulting in obedient discipleship and involvement in the divine mission. Only with the acknowledgement of the historical and experiential dimensions of the old and new covenants can the consistent appeal and warning of Scripture from beginning to end be discerned. It is an appeal to turn to the Lord and be saved through the regenerating work of His Spirit, who alone can ingrain the divine law in the heart of faith. The appeal is coupled with the warning against a humanistic, externalized religion "written in stone" only, consisting of a self-righteous, judgmental attitude that results in an oppressive, dutiful morality of dead works.

## Gospel-Bearing Historical Old Covenant, but Legalistic Old Covenant Experience, at Sinai

In His Sinai covenant with the nation of Israel, God renewed the covenant of redemption promises He had given to their forefathers. Israel's overall response throughout their history, however, was summed up in these words of Paul: "Since they did not know the righteousness that comes from God and sought to establish their own, they did not submit to God's righteousness" (Rom. 10:3). This old covenant experience of legalism throughout Israel's history will be examined in much more detail in the next chapter. However, early seeds or nuances of their later more matured old covenant experience may perhaps already be detected in their initial response to God's covenant renewal: "Tell us everything the LORD our God tells you. We will listen and obey" (Deut. 5:27). Was this a faith-based, new covenant response, or a legalistically self-dependant one?

Note God's own evaluation of their response as communicated through Moses: "The LORD heard you when you spoke to me and the LORD said to me, 'I have heard what this people said to you. Everything they said was good'" (Deut. 5:28). By God's own evaluation, they spoke the right words.

But there was more to the story. For the very next verse contains these plaintive words of God: "Oh, that their hearts would be inclined to fear me and keep all my commands always, so that it might go well with them and their children forever!" (Deut. 5:29). Davidson comments:

> On God's part, this covenant was a valid covenant of grace—part of the everlasting covenant of God's promised redemption, agreed to by the Father and Son even before the creation of the world, announced to Adam and Eve in the Protoevangelium [first proclamation of the gospel] of Gen. 3:15, promised to Abram in Gen. 12 and codified in the Abrahamic covenant of Gen. 15 and 17. God accepted the people on the basis of the blood of the Lamb of God, "slain from the foundation of the world." On the human side, the people's response contained appropriate wording, but the wrong motivation, and the wrong understanding of the basis of their salvation and ability to stay in covenant relation with God, rooted in their own efforts. On God's part, it was a valid "new covenant" based on the divine promise and the blood of Christ, but on the people's part it was an "old covenant" experience of salvation by works.[6]

Three times the Israelites promised, "We will do everything the LORD has said; we will obey" (Exod. 24:3, 7; cf. 9:8; Deut. 5:27). Yet within weeks they flagrantly broke their covenant promise by building a golden calf, likely to worship "the Egyptian bull-god Apis"[7] (Exodus 32; Deuteronomy 9). That experience, coupled with Israel's subsequent overall history of unbelief, lends support to the conclusion that Israel's response to God's covenant at Sinai essentially represented an old covenant experience.

At the same time, that very same verbal response—"We will do everything the LORD has said; we will obey"—could also be an experientially new covenant response for those who speak those words in faith and dependence on God as the One who can sanctify them.

This has implications far beyond Sinai. On the one hand, it warns of the possibility of living in a gospel-bearing new covenant age while at the same time suffering a heart deficiency that results in an old covenant experience. On the other hand, it also invites us to depend wholly on God as the One who alone can bring the inner transformation and conversion of heart and mind that will enable us to obey Him freely from a heart of love—"the obedience that comes from faith" (Rom. 1:5). The prayers of the psalmist are always appropriate prayers for the believer: "Create in me a pure heart, O God, and renew a steadfast spirit within me....Grant me a willing spirit to sustain me" (Ps. 51:10, 12). "Teach me your way, O Lord, and I will walk in your truth; give me an undivided heart, that I may fear your name" (Ps. 86:11). Similarly applicable is Solomon's prayer at the dedication of the temple: "May the Lord our God be with us as He was with our fathers; may he never leave us nor forsake us. May he turn our hearts to him, to walk in all his ways and to keep the commands, decrees and regulations he gave our fathers" (1 Kings 8:57–58).

## Summary

The old and new covenants are sometimes viewed in Scripture as historical eras and sometimes as contrasting spiritual experiences—contrasting ways of relating to God and His law. The old covenant historical era covers spiritual history before the advent of Christ, while an old covenant experience represents either rebellion against God's law or a legalistic reliance on it as a means of achieving salvation through obedience. The new covenant historical era covers the period of spiritual history that commenced with the advent of Christ, while a new covenant experience represents acceptance of God's salvation by grace through faith and reliance on the Holy Spirit to write God's law on one's heart for the empowerment of loving obedience and faithful witness. The covenant God made with Israel at Sinai was a grace-based, gospel-bearing, faith-inducing, mission-directed historical old covenant that bore all the DNA markers, promises/provisions of God's description of the new covenant in Jeremiah 31:31–33 and Hebrews 8:8–12. On the whole, Israel's response throughout its history to the gospel proclaimed and offered in that covenant was an old covenant experience of overt disregard and disobedience on the one hand and legalistic reliance on law-keeping for salvation on the other. It is just as possible to live in the new covenant historical era, in which we live, and experience an old covenant experience through flagrant, unrepentant disobedience to God's law or reliance on obedience as one's qualification for salvation. Conversely, Scripture affirms that true believers living in the old covenant historical period possessed a new covenant experience (Hebrews 11).

> The old covenant historical era covers spiritual history before the advent of Christ, while an old covenant experience represents rebellion against God's law or a legalistic reliance on it as a means of salvation.

We are now prepared to see the momentous implications this insight provides for interpreting apparently conflicting scriptural views of God's law.

## Notes

1. Moo, "The Law of Christ as the Fulfillment of the Law of Moses," 333, 336.

2. E. G. White, "The Two Dispensations," *Advent Review and Sabbath Herald*, vol. 63, no. 9 (March 2, 1886), 23.

3. Robertson, 57.

4. Rayburn, "The Contrast Between the Old and New Covenants," 166. Cf. J. O. Buswell, *A Systematic Theology of the Christian Religion*, vol. 1 (Grand Rapids, MI: Zondervan, 1962), 307: "The Scriptures themselves used the term 'old testament' [ read 'old covenant' as the Greek term, *diatheke* is the same for both translations] to refer, not to the thirty-nine books which preceded the earthly life of Christ, nor to the revealed system of worship which the thirty-nine books contained, but to refer to a legalistic, self-righteous attitude in the contemplation of those books and their provisions. Similarly the words 'new testament' [read 'new covenant'] in Scripture refer not to the twenty-seven books given since the time of Christ on earth, but to that renewed relationship into which God's elect, in every age since the fall of man, have entered by faith."

Cf. also Paul Penno, following Waggoner (Paul E. Penno, Jr., "Calvary At Sinai: The Law and the Covenants in Seventh-day Adventist History" (master's thesis, Andrews University, 2001, 238): "The new covenant was all about the promise of God to be received by faith alone. This was God's plan for saving mankind ever since Adam fell into sin. God renewed the same covenant with Abraham, Isaac, and Jacob. All of the patriarchs believed God's promise and He accounted them righteous by faith. In effect, the plan of salvation in the new covenant was the same for sinners in any age whether before the cross or after. The new covenant between God and Abraham was all about how the conditions of God's law might be met. Believing in Christ, Abraham fulfilled the only condition for salvation. Christ was his righteousness. Such genuine faith, founded upon the love of God for sinners, always manifested itself in genuine obedience. Christ in the life was the living law in the heart."

5. E.g., Vos, *Biblical Theology*, acknowledges this hermeneutical principle in the following observation: "In Gal 3:23, 25 he [Paul] speaks of the 'coming' of faith, as though there had never been any faith before. And yet the same Paul in Rom. 4:16ff., speaks at length of the role played by faith in the life of Abraham, and how it virtually dominated the entire Old Testament system" (128). Cf. Robertson, 57–58, 180–182.

6. Davidson, *Blazing Grace*, 11.

7. *NIV Study Bible* (133), comment on Exodus 32:4.

# Chapter 7

# Historical and Experiential Applications

Once the distinction between the historical and experiential dimensions of the old and new covenants is understood, much of the apparent tension between biblical statements regarding God's law can be resolved.

This chapter will provide numerous examples as it explores New Testament passages in which the historical/experiential distinction is critical for a proper interpretation.

## The First Covenant is Obsolete

After giving its version of the new covenant first cited in Jeremiah, Hebrews 8:13 says, "By calling this covenant 'new,' he has made the first one [referring to the Sinaitic covenant] obsolete; and what is obsolete and aging will soon disappear." This text has been cited as evidence that the Ten Commandments, and more specifically the Sabbath of the fourth commandment, are now obsolete. But a closer examination yields a different conclusion.

Hebrews is the New Testament's most comprehensive book on the covenants. While both historical and experiential dimensions of the old and new covenants are in view at different places throughout the book, chapters 7–10 focus primarily on the historical dimension. More specifically, the emphasis of these chapters is on the priesthood and sacrificial systems established by the Sinaitic covenant, both of which were imperfect and could not take away sin. The imperfect old covenant

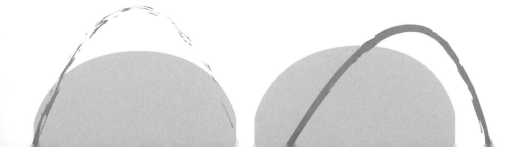

priesthood has been replaced by Christ, "a high priest [who] meets our need—one who is holy, blameless, pure, set apart from sinners, exalted above the heavens" (Heb. 7:26). The animal (typical/symbolic) sacrifices of the old covenant sanctuary services which could not take away sin have been replaced by their corresponding and eternal Type, Jesus Christ, who "appeared once for all at the end of the ages to do away with sin by the sacrifice of himself" (Heb. 9:26). (See appendix A on pages 251–266 for an expanded comparison of the historical old and new covenants in Hebrews 7–10.)

What Hebrews 8:13 declares as "obsolete and aging…soon [to] disappear" is clearly the ceremonial system of the historical old covenant, its priesthood and animal sacrifices which were types of the priesthood and sacrifice of Christ. This fulfillment of the old covenant ceremonial system types in the priesthood and sacrifice of Jesus, replacing the old covenant ceremonies, was definitely a historical transition. This ceremonial transition from the historical old covenant to the historical new covenant had been prophesied in the Old Testament ("the Anointed One…will put an end to sacrifice and offering" [Dan. 9:25, 27]) and was noted in the gospel record itself (at the very moment Jesus died, "the curtain of the temple [where the priests performed the sacrifices] was torn [by God] in two from top to bottom" [Matt. 27:50–51]). Clearly, what Hebrews declares as obsolete is the symbolic and typical priesthood and animal sacrifices of the Old Testament now that Christ, their anticipated Type, has come. The key to understanding Hebrews 8:13 is firmly rooted in the historical perspective of the covenants.

The same is not the case in some other New Testament epistles. When Paul writes about the law and the covenant(s) in Galatians, for example, his emphasis is just as clearly experiential.[1]

## Personal and National Examples of Old Covenant / New Covenant Experiences

Note this highly-instructive treatment of the covenants in Galatians 4:

Tell me, you who want to be under the law, are you not aware of what the law says? For it is written that Abraham had two sons, one by the slave woman and the other by the free woman. His son by the slave woman was born in the ordinary way [Greek, *kata sarka*, "according to the flesh"]; but his son by the free woman was born as the result of a promise.

These things may be taken figuratively, for the women represent two covenants. One covenant is from Mount Sinai and bears children who are to be slaves: This is Hagar. Now Hagar stands for Mount Sinai in Arabia and corresponds to the present city of Jerusalem, because she is in slavery with her children. But the Jerusalem that is above is free, and she is our mother.... 

Now you, brothers, like Isaac, are children of promise. At that time the son born in the ordinary way [Greek, *kata sarka*, "according to the flesh"] persecuted the son born by the power of the Spirit. It is the same now. But what does the Scripture say? "Get rid of the slave woman and her son, for the slave woman's son will never share in the inheritance with the free woman's son" [quoted from Gen. 21:10]. Therefore, brothers, we are not children of the slave woman, but of the free woman.

It is for freedom that Christ has set us free. Stand firm, then, and do not let yourselves be burdened again by a yoke of slavery. (Gal. 4:21–5:1)

Understood historically, this passage would accuse God of making a covenant with Israel at Sinai that would result in spiritual slavery, and of structuring it such that those who remained faithful to it would live "according to the flesh" and "never share in the inheritance" of the saints. But such a covenant would be very different from every other covenant He has ever made. How uncharacteristic of God to make a covenant that would doom those who entered into it to unconverted lives and eternal loss. Such a repugnant idea has been fully discounted by our discovery that the four DNA markers of the new covenant were embedded in God's covenant with His people at Sinai. We've established that the Sinai covenant was grace-based, gospel-bearing, faith-inducing, and mission-directed—the most complete revelation God had given of His grace, forgiveness, and holiness.

A close examination of Paul's list of the characteristics of "the two covenants" in Galatians 4 reveals that the old covenant he speaks of cannot possibly be the grace-based, gospel-bearing, faith-inducing, mission-directed covenant God invited His people into at Sinai. It rather describes Israel's horrible distortion and wrongful application of that covenant and the consequences of their perversion of, and deficient response to, the gospel.

Note the following table that lists the distinctive characteristics of the old and new covenants as described in Galatians 4.

| The First or Old Covenant | The Second or New Covenant |
| --- | --- |
| Abraham's experience with Hagar, the slave woman (4:22) | Abraham's experience with Sarah, the free woman (4:22) |
| Mount Sinai corresponds to the "present" city of Jerusalem (4:24–25) | Corresponds to Jerusalem above which is "free" (4:26) |
| "Born in the ordinary way," literally, "according to the flesh" (4:23, 29) | "Born as a result of a promise," "born by the power of the Spirit" (4:23, 29) |
| The persecutor (4:29) | The persecuted (4:29) |
| Cannot "share in the inheritance" (4:30) | Receives "the inheritance" (4:30) |
| "Burdened by a yoke of slavery" (5:1) | Free in Christ (5:1) |

These two lists do not describe two different covenants initiated by God in sequential *historical* eras, the first spanning the 1500–year period from Sinai to the incarnation, and the second encompassing the generations following. They describe two different human *experiences* based on opposite human responses to the timeless everlasting-gospel invitation God has embedded in every covenant He has ever made with humanity. This becomes unmistakably clear when the following lists of New Testament contrasts between "the flesh" and "the Spirit" are considered:[2]

| The Flesh | The Spirit |
|---|---|
| "That which is born of flesh is flesh" (John 3:6). | "That which is born of the Spirit is spirit" (John 3:6). |
| "The righteous requirement of the law might be fulfilled in us who do not walk according to the flesh" (Rom. 8:4). | "The righteous requirement of the law might be fulfilled in us who...walk... according to the Spirit" (Rom. 8:4). |
| "Those who live according to the flesh set their minds on the things of the flesh" (Rom. 8:5). | "Those who live according to the Spirit, [set their minds on] the things of the Spirit" (Rom. 8:5). |
| "To be carnally [literally, 'fleshly'] minded is death" (Rom. 8:6). | "To be spiritually minded is life and peace" (Rom. 8:6). |
| "The carnal [literally, 'fleshly'] mind is enmity against God: for it is not subject to the law of God, nor indeed can be" (Rom. 8:7). | "If anyone does not have the Spirit of Christ, he is not His" (Rom. 8:9). |
| "Those who are in the flesh cannot please God" (Rom. 8:8). | "You are not in the flesh but in the Spirit, if indeed the Spirit of God dwells in you" (Rom. 8:9). |
| "If you live according to the flesh, you will die" (Rom. 8:13). | "If by the Spirit you put to death the deeds of the body, you will live" (Rom. 8:13). |
| "The flesh [wars] against the Spirit" (Gal. 5:17). | "The Spirit [wars] against the flesh" (Gal. 5:17). |
| "The works of the flesh are...adultery, fornication, uncleanness, lewdness, idolatry....Those who practice such things will not inherit the kingdom of God" (Gal. 5:19–21). | "The fruit of the Spirit is love, joy, peace, longsuffering....Those who are Christ's have crucified the flesh with its passions and desires" (Gal. 5:22–24). |
| "If anyone thinks he may have confidence in the flesh, I more so:... concerning the righteousness which is in the law, blameless" (Phil. 3:4–6). | "What things were gain to me, these I have counted loss for Christ...not having my own righteousness, which is from the law, but that which is through faith in Christ, the righteousness which is from God by faith" (Phil. 3:7–9). |

According to Paul in Galatians 4, those who live according to the first or old covenant are "born in the ordinary way" [literally, "according to the flesh," cf. NKJV ] (4:23, 29), while those who live according to the second or new covenant are "born by the power of the Spirit" (4:29). Jesus said, "Flesh gives birth to flesh [a left column, old covenant experience], but the Spirit gives birth to spirit [a right column, new covenant experience]....You must be born again [i.e., converted from a left column experience to a right column experience]." "I tell you the truth, no one can see the kingdom of God unless he is born again" (John 3:6–7, 3). This is a timeless truth applicable to people in every age. The "old covenant" characteristics of the Galatians 4 list above do not represent the experience of saved people who lived during the era of God's historical old covenant. They represent the old covenant experience into which every human being is born. Everyone must be converted from this experience to enter the kingdom of God.

God did not design the covenant He initiated for His people at Sinai to engender a life "according to the flesh" that would burden them with "a yoke of slavery" and foreordain them to "never share in the [eternal] inheritance" of the saints. But the way many of the people *responded* to the saving gospel of His covenant did engender just such a result.

Note how Galatians 4 refers to "two covenants" (the only place in Scripture where that exact phrase is used) and then illustrates these covenants with contrasting *experiences* from the life of the man who is considered the paragon of the everlasting covenant—Abraham (4:24). God had promised Abraham a son through his aged wife, Sarah. When the promised child was delayed in coming, Abraham grew impatient and took matters into his own hands. He produced a child through Hagar, his wife Sarah's "maidservant" (literally, "maidslave").

Abraham's relationship with the slave woman Hagar represents those who confine themselves to spiritual slavery by attempting to produce through the flesh, their own efforts, what they are incapable of producing, but what God has promised to produce—eternal salvation, obedience, and a godly life that can influence others toward salvation. Abraham's subsequent trust in God and His promise to produce a child through Sarah represents the spiritual freedom of faith and submission to the control of the Spirit who has the power to produce what we cannot produce.

"These women represent two covenants." Abraham's independent efforts with Hagar exemplified an old covenant experience; his dependence on God in his relationship with Sarah exemplified a new covenant experience. When Paul presented his case regarding the two covenants, he presented as his "Exhibit A" these experiences of Abraham, the revered man of God who received the everlasting covenant and became "the father of all who believe" (Rom. 4:11). No greater evidence could be presented that the old and new covenants are rooted in experience and predate both Sinai and the advent of Jesus.

Abraham's personal old covenant experience with Hagar was nationalized through the experience of Israel subsequent to God's covenant with them at Sinai. "The women represent two covenants. One covenant is from Mount Sinai and bears children who are to be slaves: This is Hagar. Now Hagar stands for Mount Sinai in Arabia and corresponds to the present city of Jerusalem, because she is in slavery with her children. But the Jerusalem that is above is free, and she is our mother" (Gal. 4:24–26).

If Paul submitted Abraham's unbelieving actions as "Exhibit A" of an old covenant experience, he presented Israel's experience at Sinai as "Exhibit B." Unfortunately, examples of a national new covenant experience were harder to come by. There were some: "By faith the people passed through the Red Sea....By faith the walls of Jericho fell"

> The "old covenant" characteristics of Galatians 4 represent the old covenant experience into which every human being is born. Everyone must be converted from this experience to enter the kingdom of God.

(Heb. 11:29–30; cf. Exod. 4:31; 14:31; Ps. 106:12–13). But on the whole, "Israel, who pursued a law of righteousness, has not attained it. Why not? Because they pursued it not by faith but as if it were by works" (Rom. 9:31–32). This is the meaning of Paul's statement in Galatians 4:24, "One covenant is from Mount Sinai and bears children who are to be slaves: This is Hagar." The legalistic way Israel tended over the years to respond to God's Sinai covenant exemplified an old covenant experience of legalism and spiritual slavery that leads to spiritual death.

While "the two covenants" in Galatians 4 are exemplified by historical figures—Abraham and Israel at Sinai and beyond—they do not represent historical eras but rather religious experiences, as Rayburn asserts:

> The "covenants" here [Gal. 4:21–31] have *nothing* to do with our division between the Old Testament and the New Testament. There is and always has been only one salvation and only one true relationship with God.... That salvation and that relationship is one of these two covenants in [Galatians] 4:21ff. The other is the religious situation which arises when that true relationship is spurned in unbelief and when legalism instead of grace is embraced as the true principle of righteousness. This point is, in our view, very clear in Galatians. The issues discussed here: legalism versus grace, unbelief versus faith, slavery versus sonship, and the two "covenants," have nothing to do with our division between the time before Christ and the time after his coming. These issues are timeless.[3]

It is difficult to overestimate the significance of this crucial insight. In Galatians 4:21–5:1 Paul reveals what he has in mind when he refers to "the two covenants." They are not historical eras but *experiences*. One covenant represents a life "according to the flesh." Both Jesus and Paul describe such a life as one that is controlled by the sinful nature that is at war with the Spirit and destined for destruction unless converted (John 3:3–6; Rom. 8:5–14; Gal. 5:16–25). At conversion a person moves from the left column to the right in the Galatians 4 list above—moves from an old covenant experience of life in the flesh to a new covenant experience of life in the Spirit.

In Galatians 5:16–25 Paul describes the war between the flesh and the Spirit in the human heart and declares that those who choose to live according to the flesh "will not inherit the kingdom of God." This is a timeless and universal truth. The two covenants of Galatians 4 cannot represent different God-initiated historical eras—one controlled by the flesh or sinful nature and the other lived in submission to the Spirit—because no one living in the first historical era in accordance with the old covenant of the flesh could inherit the kingdom of God. Rather, the two covenants represent two contrasting *responses* to God's grace. Both are human experiences that have existed side by side from the time of Cain and Abel to this very day. Unless this is understood, the Bible's teaching on God's holy law might appear to be a quagmire of contradictions.

Equipped with the understanding that Paul used old and new covenant terminology in an experiential rather than historical sense, we will now examine in detail a number of significant New Testament texts on the covenants and the law.

## Not Under the Law's (Schoolmaster's) Supervision

In a passage related to his discussion of the two covenants in Galatians 4, Paul writes: "But the Scripture declares that the whole world is a prisoner of sin, so that what was promised, being given through faith in Jesus Christ, might be given to those who believe. Before this faith came, we were held prisoners by the law, locked up until faith should be revealed. So the law was put in charge to lead us to Christ that we might be justified by faith. Now that faith has come, we are no longer under the supervision of the law" (Gal. 3:22–25).

Understood from a strictly historical perspective, one would have to conclude from this passage that the generations that lived from the time God gave the law on Sinai until Christ came some 1500 years later were all kept locked in the prison of sin until faith came in with the advent of Christ. And only after faith came with Christ could people finally be released from the prison of sin and be saved by faith. This would mean that no one living in the Old Testament era could have been justified by faith, because saving faith would not have come until Christ came in the flesh. There is virtually no way out of this interpretation if these verses are viewed from a strictly historical perspective. "If it is the temporary character of the law and Christ's bringing it to an end that is contemplated in Gal 3:23ff.,…it follows by a rigorous necessity that there could have been no justification by faith in the Old Testament age (3:24).…In our view this is an unavoidable conclusion."[4]

However, when Galatians 3:22–25 is viewed *experientially*, then the experience of salvation by faith comes back into view. People of every era are held prisoner by sin until faith comes. The phrase "Before this faith came" cannot be read historically, as though such faith came only with the advent of Christ. It must be read experientially. Before faith comes into the life, a person is still kept under lock and key by sin.

But, one might ask, does the text not say, "Before faith came, we were held prisoners *by the law*, locked up until faith should be revealed" (italics added)? Yes. But does this mean that the law itself, and not sin, kept people locked up and under guard up until faith came? No. For God "was a husband to them" when He gave His law as a manifestation of His covenant love for His people (Jer. 31:32). He did not give it to enslave them or keep them spiritually imprisoned. The law in and of itself has no power to do anything. It cannot make "the trespass… increase" (Rom. 5:20), in the sense of causing us to sin even more. Only our own sinful nature leads us to sin more (Rom. 7:21–23; 8:2).

Except by the Holy Spirit's supervision, the law has no power whatsoever to spiritually awaken us to the point that "sin might become utterly sinful" in our eyes, convicting us of our sin and need for God (Rom. 7:13). The law has no power to enable us to obey it except by the power of the Holy Spirit (Rom. 8:2–4). It cannot even lead us to Christ except by the Spirit's tutelage. If it's true that *we* can do nothing without Christ (John 15:5), it must be equally true, if not more so, of the law—the law can do nothing without Christ's Spirit enabling it to do so in the life of an individual.[5] This has always been the case.

Even the best construction that can be placed on Galatians 3:22–25 when it's interpreted historically—that the law acted as a temporary supervisor, tutor, or schoolmaster to get people by until faith would finally come with the advent of Christ—is inadequate. A strict historical interpretation of this passage means that regardless of how benevolent the law's ministry to people in the Old Testament might have been, saving faith did not come in history until Christ came in history.

But that cannot be what Paul meant because in the same letter he writes that Abraham "believed God and it was credited to him as righteousness" (Gal. 3:6, quoting Gen. 15:6), and quotes the Old Testament prophet Habakkuk's teaching that "the righteous will live by faith" (Gal. 3:11, quoting Hab. 2:4).

Those who apply a strictly historical interpretation to this passage often use it to teach that the law God gave on Sinai was only valid until Christ came. But a consistent historical interpretation must conclude that saving faith was not available to humans before Christ's advent.

> The phrase "Before this faith came" cannot be read historically, as though such faith came only with the advent of Christ. It must be read experientially. Before faith comes into the life, a person is still kept under lock and key by sin.

When Galatians 3:22–25 is interpreted from an experiential perspective, it can be understood something like this:

But the Scripture declares that the whole world is [and always has been, experientially] a prisoner of sin ["for God has bound all men over to disobedience so that he may have mercy on them all" (Rom. 11:32)], so that what was promised [that is, salvation through the everlasting gospel taught consistently in all God's covenants], being given through faith in Jesus Christ [at a person's conversion during any historical era], might be given to those who believe. Before this faith came [i.e., while we were still unconverted], we were held prisoners by the law [the Spirit's first use of the law to constrain wickedness until conversion might occur], locked up until faith should be revealed [through the converting influence of the Holy Spirit on the heart]. So the law was put in charge [or, "was a schoolmaster," KJV; "was our tutor," NKJV; the second use of the law as a convicting influence as the Holy Spirit applies it to the conscience of the sinner in every historical era] to lead us to Christ that we might be justified by faith [at conversion]. Now that faith has come [conversion and a new covenant experience through the Holy Spirit's justifying and sanctifying ministry], we are no longer under the supervision of the law [or, "under a schoolmaster," KJV; "under a tutor," NKJV; the Spirit's use of the law as an instrument to initially awaken us to our lost condition and our need for Christ and conversion[6]].

Concerning this experiential interpretation, two models of the law may be instructive. The first is Calvin's three uses or functions of the law, as summarized by Louis Berkhof:

- [First use—Civil] The law serves the purpose of restraining sin and promoting righteousness,…it serves the purpose of God's common grace in the world at large [i.e., the law serves society as a whole as a guide to social order].
- [Second use—Tutorial] In this capacity the law serves the purpose of bringing man under conviction of sin, and of making him conscious of his inability to meet the demands of the law. In that way, the law becomes his tutor to lead him unto Christ, and thus becomes subservient to God's gracious purpose of redemption.

- [Third use—Normative] This is the so-called *tertius usus legis*, the third use of the law. The law is a rule of life for believers, reminding them of their duties and leading them in the way of salvation.[7]

Paul's reference in Galatians 3:23 to being "held prisoners by the law" could correspond to the first use of the law as a divinely appointed restraining influence in society, with application to the non-believer as well as the believer. Paul's reference in Galatians 3:24–25 to the law as a supervisor, tutor, or schoolmaster could correspond to Calvin's second use of the law. Indeed, it was in his discussion of his "second use" that Calvin acknowledged that "the law was a schoolmaster to bring them to Christ": "For all who have lived for a considerable time in ignorance of God will confess it to have been their experience, that they were constrained by the law to a certain kind of fear and reverence of God, till, being regenerated by his Spirit, they began to love him from their hearts."[8] It is this second use of the law—its specific, Spirit-supervised role as a tutor or schoolmaster to initially bring sinners to Christ and conversion—from which the believer is released "now that faith [conversion] has come" (Gal. 3:25).

But if believers are released from the first and second uses of the law at their conversion, it is done so that they might graduate to its third use as a guide for holy living, "giving joy to the heart" and "light to the eyes," serving as "a lamp to my feet and a light for my path" (Ps. 19:8; 119:105). In his commentary on Galatians 3:25 and its reference to the believer's no longer being under the law as a schoolmaster once "faith is come," Calvin wrote: "Is the law so abolished that we have nothing to do with it? I answer, the law, so far as it is a rule of life, a bridle to keep us in the fear of the LORD, a spur to correct the sluggishness of our flesh, —so far, in short, as it is 'profitable for doctrine, for reproof, for correction, for instruction in righteousness, that believers may be instructed in every good work,' (2 Tim. iii. 16, 17)—is as much in force as ever, and remains untouched."[9]

Indeed, Calvin taught that this "third use of the law...is the *principal* one...[which] relates to the faithful, in whose hearts the Spirit of God already lives and reigns"[10] (italics added). "Wherefore, when David represents the life of a righteous man as spent in continual meditations on the law (Ps 1:2), we must not refer it to one period of time only, because it is very suitable for all ages, even to the end of the world.... This truth remains for ever unshaken, that the law has sustained no diminution of its authority, but ought always to receive from us the same veneration and obedience."[11]

A second, complimentary model of the law, "embedded in the very grammatical structure of the Decalogue," also supports an experiential understanding of Galatians 3:22–25. Davidson points out that the grammatical form of the original Hebrew construction of the Ten Commandments allows for them to be understood either in their traditional portrayal as commands ("emphatic imperative"[12]) or as promises ("emphatic promise"[13]). Thus, "while it is possible to interpret the commandments as prohibitions, we can also interpret them as divine promises. For those redeemed by the blood of the Lamb, it is no longer the command 'You may not have any other gods before Me,' but instead, the promise 'You will not have any other gods before Me.' You will not make any graven images, you will not take My name in vain. I promise you! You will no longer want to do those things that interrupt our intimate personal relationship."[14]

We may view the *prohibitive* nature of the Ten Commandments as representative of its role as supervisor, tutor, and schoolmaster. Only converted believers, in whom the Spirit of God dwells, can appreciate and experience the *promissory* role of God's law to which they graduate upon conversion.

To one who is used to reading Galatians 3:22–25 from a historical perspective, this experiential interpretation may seem strained at first. But in light of what we have learned about the unity of the covenants, the experiential interpretation proves to be the most natural and consistent one.

Here is what Galatians 3:22–25 might look like when rendered interpretively from a strictly historical perspective:

> But the Scripture declares that the whole world is a prisoner of sin, so that what was promised [salvation by faith as exemplified in God's covenant with Abraham], being given through faith in Jesus Christ [at such a time when such faith would become available], might be given to those who believe. Before this faith came [i.e., before Christ came in history], we were held prisoners by the law [as God gave it at Sinai], locked up [by God Himself through His covenant, without faith] until faith should be revealed [at the advent of Christ]. So the law was put in charge [at the time God gave it to Israel on Sinai] to lead us to Christ [at the point He would come in history, some 1500 years after God gave the law on Sinai] that we might be justified by faith [at the advent of Christ when faith would come]. Now that faith has come [with the advent of Christ], we are no longer under the supervision of the law [i.e., now that Christ has come, and faith with Christ, whatever role the law played in the lives of His people before He came is no longer needed, because Christ, and more specifically, faith, saving faith, is finally available at long last].

No reputable scholar holds to this strictly historical interpretation, for that would mean that justifying faith was not available until Christ came. But such an interpretation is demanded if this passage, and others like it, is meant to be interpreted from a historical perspective. Yet many commentators assign the historical perspective to the phrase, "we are no longer under the supervision of the law," in an attempt to render the law of God of no effect for those who live in the new covenant historical era. They use such texts in Galatians in an attempt to pit the Abrahamic covenant against the Mosaic covenant, and in so doing miss the vital point of the passage. Robertson holds that Galatians "clearly indicates that the ultimate contrast in Paul's mind is not between the Abrahamic and the Mosaic covenants, but between the way of justification advocated by the Judaizers and the way of justification provided by Christ."[15]

It is indeed true, as Hebrews 7–10 attests and as was prophesied in the Old Testament, that the ceremonial priestly and sacrificial system was fulfilled and abrogated with the atoning sacrifice and priestly enthronement of Jesus (Dan. 9:27). But the same cannot be true of God's moral law, which is as "holy, righteous and good" (Rom. 7:12) as "spiritual" (Rom. 7:14), and as necessary for the hearts of God's people (Ps. 40:8; Isa. 51:7; Jer. 31:33; Heb. 8:10) in the historical new covenant era as when it was written into the very nature of Adam and later codified and issued by God to His covenant people.[16]

There are segments of Galatians 3–5 that must be understood from a historical perspective. But Paul uses these historical references primarily to drive home the experiential point he makes. When Paul writes, "The law, introduced 430 years later, does not set aside the covenant previously established by God and thus do away with the promise" (Gal. 3:17), he certainly has historical developments in mind. He spotlighted God's covenant with Israel at Sinai and His covenant with Abraham 430 years earlier to establish that the law God gave on Sinai did not contain a different gospel from that communicated to Abraham in which God first explicitly stated His promise of righteousness by faith. Hebrews 11:4–7 makes it clear that this promise was first made available immediately after the entrance of sin. The timeless, universal gospel promise of righteousness by faith contradicted the Pharisaical interpretation of Paul's day that the law offered righteousness to those only who "rely on observing the law" and "pursued it not by faith but as if it were by works" (Gal. 3:21; Rom. 9:32). That was the point Paul drove home in Galatians 3:17 by his statement that God's covenant with Israel at Sinai did not change the gospel promise of righteousness by faith in any way.

Faithfulness to the wider scriptural teaching on the continuity and unity of the covenants and the plan of salvation requires that Galatians 3:23–25 be understood from an experiential perspective.

## Not Under Law but Under Grace

Paul's statement, "You are no longer under law, but under grace" (Rom. 6:14) is also an experiential statement. There is a historical element to it because before conversion we are all under "the law of sin," the control of the sinful nature (Rom. 7:25). Sin has its way with us as "the law of sin," the sinful nature, bends some of us toward immorality and others toward legalism, both of which are expressions of sin and antithetical to grace (Gal. 5:19–21; Phil. 3:4–6). But after conversion we are bent by the Spirit toward grace and "the obedience that comes from faith" (Rom. 1:5). Not that life "under grace" is free from intense struggles with sin, as Scripture and any Spirit-led believer can testify. Indeed, Paul characterizes Christian experience as spiritual warfare (Eph. 6:10ff). The difference is that before conversion we are "hostile to God" (Rom. 8:7), but at the moment of conversion we switch sides and begin fighting as citizens of heaven against "the spiritual forces of evil in the heavenly realms" (Eph. 6:12ff.).

The context of Romans 6:14 demands an experiential interpretation, for the full text says: "For sin shall not be your master, because you are not under law, but under grace." C. E. B. Cranfield concludes similarly: "[Romans 6:14] may then be interpreted as a promise that sin will no more be their lord, because another lord has taken possession of them, namely, Christ."[17]

The mistaken interpretation that the phrase "under law" in this text addresses the historical period from Sinai to Calvary, and that since Calvary we no longer need to live by the moral commands of Sinai, conveys a skewed view of salvation history. It suggests that when God gave the law He made sin the master over His covenant people, and that He intended that this tyranny would last until Christ's atoning sacrifice was made—that the promise that "sin shall not be your master, because you are not under law, but under grace" has been in effect only since Jesus established the new covenant.

Some have used Romans 11:6—"if by grace, then it is no longer by works"—to further promote the idea that the old covenant promoted a system of works while the new covenant is entirely grace-oriented. But God did not institute a system of works righteousness as a method for His people's salvation at Sinai. Salvation has always been by grace through faith. Understood experientially, this text teaches that until sinners are converted they seek to placate God with good works. But following conversion, God's redeemed children understand that their salvation "is no longer [nor ever was] by works" but "by grace." Salvation "by works" can legitimately be spoken of only if it is the perfect works of Christ that are meant—works that have been vicariously performed and graciously imputed to sinners to be applied by faith. (See appendix B on pages 267–284 for a more complete discussion of the "under law" versus "under grace" texts.)

## Died to the Law

Another text often used to pit the new covenant against the Ten Commandments is Galatians 2:19: "Through the law I died to the law so that I might live for God." But reading this text experientially leads to understanding it as grace-based: "Through the law [the true gospel insights gained through the grace-based, gospel-bearing, faith-inducing, mission-directed historical old covenant God gave His people at Sinai], I died to the law [an old covenant experience of unbelief and legalistic self-righteousness] so that I might live for God [the goal-directed intent of every covenant God has ever made with humankind, enabling people to live for God]."

A related passage (Rom. 7:1–6) speaks to the same point:

> Do you not know, brothers—for I am speaking to men who know the law—that the law has authority over a man only as long as he lives? For example, by law a married woman is bound to her husband as long as he is alive, but if her husband dies, she is released from the law of marriage. So then, if she marries another man while her

husband is still alive, she is called an adulteress. But if her husband dies, she is released from that law and is not an adulteress, even though she marries another man.

So, my brothers, you also died to the law through the body of Christ, that you might belong to another, to him who was raised from the dead, in order that we might bear fruit to God. For when we were controlled by the sinful nature, the sinful passions aroused by the law were at work in our bodies, so that we bore fruit for death. But now, by dying to what once bound us, we have been released from the law so that we serve in the new way of the Spirit, not in the old way of the written code.

The Galatians 2:19 formula, "Through the law I died to the law so that I might live for God," becomes in Romans 7:4, "You also died to the law through the body of Christ, that you might belong to another." The two expressions carry the same meaning. An internalized relationship with God by means of the new birth, born of the Spirit, puts to death a legalistic marriage to the law. A few verses later (Rom. 8:2) Paul reiterates this same timeless truth: "Through Christ Jesus the law of the Spirit of life [a new covenant experience through the converting, justifying, sanctifying influence of the Holy Spirit] set me free from the law of sin and death [an old covenant experience of being married to law rather than to God, and relying on obedience to the law rather than on the righteousness of God as the basis of salvation]."

The "law of the Spirit of life" (Rom. 8:2) is the holy law of God applied by the Holy Spirit to sinners as a converting influence and to believers as a sanctifying influence as the Spirit writes it on their hearts (Ps. 19:7; Rom. 8:4; Jer. 31:33; Heb. 8:10). The "law of sin and death" (Rom. 8:2) is that same holy law of God at work under the power of the evil one and the sinful nature, perverting it into an illegitimate system of works righteousness—"sin, seizing the opportunity afforded by the commandment, deceived me, and through the commandment put me to death" (Rom. 7:11). Indeed, "the law of the Spirit of life" is none other than God's law ingrained in the heart by the Spirit of God—a new covenant experience enjoyed by every believer in every age. On the other hand, "the law of sin and death" is God's law externalized in granite and relied on as a basis for salvation—an old covenant experience.

Thus Paul could say, "By dying to what once bound us [that is, the sinful nature], we have been released from the law [that is, the illegitimate use of and reliance on the law], so that we serve in the new way of the Spirit [a new covenant experience, the law ingrained in the heart], and not in the old way of the written code [an old covenant experience, externalized obedience, the law in granite only]" (7:6). Paul's contrast of "the new way ['newness,' NKJV] of the Spirit" with "the old way of the written code ['oldness of the letter,' NKJV]" clearly contrasts the proper and improper use of the law.

As Cranfield observes: "[Paul] does not use 'letter' as a simple equivalent of 'the law.' 'Letter' is rather what the legalist is left with as a result of his misunderstanding and misuse of the law. It is the letter of the law in separation from the Spirit. But, since 'the law is spiritual' (v. 14), the letter of the law in isolation from the Spirit is not the law in its true character, but the law as it were denatured. It is this which is opposed to the Spirit whose presence is the true establishment of the law."[18]

The story is told about Melissa. As a young girl she was married to a mean, abusive husband named Edgar who wrote out a long "to do" list for her every day before he went to work. If she hadn't finished everything to his satisfaction by the time he returned, he would beat her. She lived in fear and misery, and, needless to say, when Edgar died she hardly missed him. A few years later she fell deeply in love with a man named Allen. His loving concern for her made her life totally different. Rather than ordering her to do things, he discussed with her what needed to be done, and they divided their duties around the house.

A few years later Melissa came upon one of Edgar's old lists up in the attic. She felt the rush of adrenaline and a crawling sensation on her skin as she began to read the list. But then suddenly she realized that everything on that list was something she was still doing regularly. But now she loved doing it because she loved the man she was doing it for!

What a great illustration of Romans 7:1–6! The law hasn't changed. But love can transform begrudging subservience into joyful cooperation. Is that not what conversion and covenant is all about?

## Law Not Based on Faith

In Galatians 3:12 Paul states, "The law is not based on faith; on the contrary, 'The man who does these things will live by them'" (quoting Lev. 18:5). Since Paul is quoting from the Sinaitic law, does this text teach that the Sinai covenant was not a grace-based, gospel-bearing, faith-inducing covenant? Is Paul saying that God made a covenant with Israel that was designed to keep them from saving faith?

Our study thus far has already demonstrated that this is not what Paul meant. Trust/faith was central to the covenant relationship God invited His people into at Sinai. When Moses struck the rock in disobedience to God's command that he simply speak to it, God indicted Moses for his lack of faith, using the same Hebrew word, *aman*, translated "believed" in Genesis 15:6: "Abraham *believed* the LORD, and he credited it to him as righteousness"—"you did not trust [Hebrew, *aman*] in me enough to honor me as holy" (Num. 20:2–12). In the covenant book, Deuteronomy, Moses similarly indicted the people for failing to respond to God in faith—"You did not trust in the LORD your God" (Deut. 1:32; cf. 9:23). Thus Barton Payne concludes, "The fundamental requirement of the law was faith, belief in God (Deut. 1:32; 9:23)."[19] Jesus Himself identified "the weightier matters of the law [as] justice and mercy and *faith*" (Matt. 23:23 KJV, NKJV, NRSV, ASV). The law *taught* faith! Remember that when God gave His law to Israel, it was the most complete revelation of God's character of love, grace, mercy, and forgiveness given to humankind, and it pointed forward to Christ's atoning sacrifice. God's Sinai covenant was a grace-based, gospel-bearing, faith-inducing, mission-directed covenant.[20]

In context, Leviticus 18:5 addresses life in the land that God had promised to them and their descendants: "The man who does these things [obeys God's laws—civil and health laws as well as moral and ceremonial] will live by them [will reap the practical and positive benefits—good health, rewarding relationships with family and neighbors, etc.]." Over the years, however, this principle had become misapplied into a salvation principle—obey God's commandments in order to gain a right standing before God and to merit eternal life. It is this misunderstanding of God's law that Paul seeks to remedy in Galatians 3. Leviticus 18:5, isolated from the gospel elements of the law, cannot bring sinners into a right relationship with God. Paul wants his readers to understand that God proclaimed the gospel throughout His Sinaitic covenant law and embedded Leviticus 18:5 within that gospel context.

This being true, how could Paul say that "the law [which teaches faith, induces faith] is not based on faith"? Again, the juxtaposition of the historical and experiential dimensions helps us understand. The historical old covenant was a grace-based, gospel-bearing, faith-inducing, mission-directed law. But that same law can be perverted into an old covenant experience of unbelief and legalism.

That this is certainly what Paul meant is clear from the immediate context. Here is the text again, including the verses just preceding it, with interpretative comments in brackets:

> All who rely on observing the law [an old covenant experience of pursuing righteousness "not by faith but as it were by works"—Rom. 9:32] are under a curse, for it is written: "Cursed is everyone who does not continue to do everything written in the Book of the Law" [i.e., someone who relies on the law, rather than on God and His righteousness, must live a perfect life, for perfection is demanded by the law]. Clearly no one is justified before God by the law [because no one has lived a perfect life, except Jesus], because "The righteous will live by faith" [quoting Hab. 2:4]. The law [an old covenant experience

of relying on the law] is not based on faith; on the contrary, "The man who does these things will live by them" [quoting Lev. 18:5—i.e., those who rely on their law keeping as the basis for their acceptance with God or even as the basis for their ongoing sanctification will have to live without fault, for

> The historical old covenant was a grace-based, gospel-bearing, faith-inducing, mission-directed law. But that same law can be perverted into an old covenant experience of unbelief and legalism.

they will have no other righteousness to rely on but their own]."

## The End of the Law

Paul writes in Romans 10:4, "Christ is the end of the law so that there may be righteousness for everyone who believes." Is he saying that the law God gave to Moses at Sinai, and God's expectations of obedience, were terminated by Christ? In *Christ the End of the Law: Romans 10:4 in Pauline Perspective*, Robert Badenas argues that in Romans 10:4 Paul uses the term "law" in reference to the Torah (the entire Old Testament Scripture), and the term "end" to mean "purpose, goal or ultimate meaning," not "termination."[21] This is the position that most interpreters from the early church through the Reformation held. Badenas further points out that the gospel was deeply embedded in the Torah. "Since for Paul there is only one gospel (Gal. 1:6–9) and Christ is both the *telos* (sum, apex, climax, etc.) of the Torah and the center of the gospel, the gospel was heard wherever the Torah was heard, and therefore, it should have been known all through Israel's history....For Paul the eternal gospel of God is the true meaning of every passage of the Torah....From such a perspective, Paul saw that the law always required a response of faith."[22]

A similar view is represented by the scholarly note on Romans 10:4 in the *NIV Study Bible:*

> *Christ is the end of the law.* Although the Greek word for "end" (*telos*) can mean either (1) "termination," "cessation," or (2) "goal," "culmination," "fulfillment," it seems best here to understand it in the latter sense. Christ is the fulfillment of the law (see Mt 5:17) in the sense that he brought it to completion by obeying perfectly its demands and by fulfilling its types and prophecies. The Christian is no longer "under the law" ([Rom.] 6:15), since Christ has freed him from its condemnation, but the law still plays a role in his life. He is liberated by the Holy Spirit to fulfill its moral demands (see 8:4).[23]

If we take "Christ is the end of the law so that there may be righteousness for everyone who believes" to mean that Christ is the *termination* of the law God gave to Moses, or the *termination* of God's expectations of obedience to that law as a standard of righteousness, then we must ask, does that mean that before Christ came into the world the only way to achieve righteousness was by obeying the law? Isn't that the very idea Paul argues so vehemently against throughout Romans (e.g., 4:1–24; 9:30–32)?

If "Christ is the *end* of the law" has any nuance of *termination* intended, it must be because Paul uses "the law" in this passage to mean a *mistaken use* of the law to establish one's own righteousness. The immediate context supports this reading, for the previous verse says, "Since they did not know the righteousness that comes from God and sought to establish their own, they did not submit to God's righteousness" (10:3). And just a few verses earlier Paul pointed out that "Israel, who pursued a law of righteousness, has not attained it. Why not? Because they pursued it not by faith but as if it were by works" (9:31–32). In this light Paul could be understood to have legalistic works, an old covenant experience, in view in Romans 10:4, resulting in the following interpretation: "Christ [His perfect righteousness imputed to the sinner] is the end [termination] of the law [legalistic efforts to establish our own righteousness and merits before God based on our own works—an old covenant experience] so that there may be righteousness [the only true saving righteousness] for everyone who believes

> If "Christ is the end of the law" has any nuance of termination intended, it must be because Paul uses "the law" in this passage to mean a mistaken use of the law to establish one's own righteousness.

[a new covenant experience]." The truth expressed in this passage is timeless and eternal.

## The Power of Sin is the Law

In his chapter on the resurrection of the righteous dead at the second coming of Jesus, Paul wrote, "The sting of *death* is *sin*, and the power of *sin* is the *law*. But thanks be to God! He gives us the victory through our Lord Jesus Christ" (1 Cor. 15:56–57, italics added).

A casual reading of this text might lead someone to conclude that just as death results from sin, so sin results from the law, and that if God had never given humankind any laws, there would have been no sin. But of course He did, and yet we know that neither He nor His holy law is the instigator of sin.

But, some will say, the law Paul is referring to here is not just law in general but specifically the law God gave to Moses for Israel at Sinai. And yet Paul himself wrote, "Before the law was given [at Sinai], sin was in the world" (Rom. 5:13). The degenerative conditions that developed in the antediluvian world certainly illustrate that truth. So, sin certainly had power over people before Sinai. Does anyone think that Israel would have been better off, less sinful, more holy, and better equipped to be God's representatives to the nations if only God had not come down to them at Sinai and invited them into the expanded covenant He designed for them?

Moses asked, "What great nation is there that has statutes and judgments as righteous as this whole law that I am setting before you today?" (Deut. 4:8). The most truly righteous people in Israel delighted in God's law and meditated on it day and night (Ps. 1:1–2). They loved God's law, which they cherished as a revelation of the One who loved and cared for them (Ps. 119). "Jesus, the faithful Son, does not deviate at all from this understanding of the law that is truly God's law. He could easily have written Psalm 119 Himself."[24] What then might Paul have had in mind by referring to the law as "the power of sin"?

The triad "*death…sin…law*" Paul uses in 1 Corinthians 15:56 occurs several times in Romans 7:7–8:2. Indeed, the entire thought of 1 Corinthians 15:56–57 is included in Romans 8:1–2: "Therefore, there is now no condemnation for those who are in Christ Jesus, because through Christ Jesus the *law* of the Spirit of life set me free from the *law* of *sin* and *death*" (italics added). In the extended passage Paul testified that "in my inner being I delight in God's law" which is "holy, just, good,…spiritual," and "intended to bring life" (Rom. 7:22, 12, 14, 10). But at the same time Paul found "the *law* of *sin* [i.e., his sinful nature] at work within my members," a powerful law which "seizing the opportunity afforded by the commandment, deceived me, and through the commandment put me to *death*" (Rom. 7:23, 11, italics added). Paul did not find fault with God's law, but with his sinful nature that maliciously commandeered God's holy law and converted it into a law of sin and death. Thus his phrase, "the power of sin is the law," as used in 1 Corinthians 15:56, addressed an experiential salvation issue.[25]

The law, any law from God, is "the power of sin" because the sinful nature will war against it by urging us to break it, or to observe it legalistically. The law is "the power of sin" in that under the influence of the Holy Spirit its holy and righteous precepts alert us to the spiritual reality that all is not well with us and we need help—"through the law we become conscious of sin" (Rom. 3:20). The law is "the power of sin" because the eternal consequences of sin remain embedded in it—"the wages of sin is death" (Rom. 6:23; cf. Deut. 30:19).

But "thanks be to God! He gives us the victory through our Lord Jesus Christ" (1 Cor. 15:57). Jesus was stung with the sting of the second death, exhausting it of its poison for all who put their wholehearted trust in Him. Thus the grace of God makes possible "the gift of God [which] is eternal life in Christ Jesus our Lord" (Rom. 6:23). "Therefore, there is now no condemnation for those who are in Christ Jesus" (Rom. 8:1).

## The Ministry of Death Versus the Ministry of the Spirit

Paul's discussion in 2 Corinthians 2:14–4:6 about two ministries that represented two covenants focuses on how those ministries were *received* rather than on the gospel-sufficient *content*, or lack thereof, of those ministries. The complete passage involved follows:

*2 Corinthians 2:14–17*
But thanks be to God, who always leads us in triumphal procession in Christ and through us spreads everywhere the fragrance of the knowledge of him. For we are to God the aroma of Christ among those who are being saved and those who are perishing. To the one we are the smell of death; to the other, the fragrance of life. And who is equal to such a task? Unlike so many, we do not peddle the word of God for profit. On the contrary, in Christ we speak before God with sincerity, like men sent from God.

*2 Corinthians 3:1–18*
Are we beginning to commend ourselves again? Or do we need, like some people, letters of recommendation to you or from you? You yourselves are our letter, written on our hearts, known and read by everybody. You show that you are a letter from Christ, the result of our ministry, written not with ink but with the Spirit of the living God, not on tablets of stone but on tablets of human hearts.

Such confidence as this is ours through Christ before God. Not that we are competent in ourselves to claim anything for ourselves, but our competence comes from God. He has made us competent as ministers of a new covenant—not of the letter but of the Spirit; for the letter kills, but the Spirit gives life.

Now if the ministry that brought death, which was engraved in letters on stone, came with glory, so that the Israelites could not look steadily at the face of Moses because of its glory, fading though it was, will not the ministry of the Spirit be even more glorious? If the ministry that condemns men is glorious, how much more glorious is the ministry that brings righteousness! For what was glorious has no glory now in comparison with the surpassing glory. And if what was fading away came with glory, how much greater is the glory of that which lasts! Therefore, since we have such a hope, we are very bold. We are not like Moses, who would put a veil over his face to keep the Israelites from gazing at it while the radiance was fading away. But their minds were made dull, for to this day the same veil remains when the old covenant is read. It has not been removed, because only in Christ is it taken away. Even to this day when Moses is read, a veil covers their hearts. But whenever anyone turns to the Lord, the veil is taken away. Now the Lord is the Spirit, and where the Spirit of the Lord is, there is freedom. And we, who with unveiled faces all reflect [alternate reading: "contemplate"] the Lord's glory, are being transformed into his likeness with ever-increasing glory, which comes from the Lord, who is the Spirit.

*2 Corinthians 4:1–6*

Therefore, since through God's mercy we have this ministry, we do not lose heart. Rather, we have renounced secret and shameful ways; we do not use deception, nor do we distort the word of God. On the contrary, by setting forth the truth plainly we commend ourselves to every man's conscience in the sight of God. And even if our gospel is veiled, it is veiled to those who are perishing. The god of this age has blinded the minds of unbelievers, so that they cannot see the light of the gospel of the glory of Christ, who is the image of God. For we do not preach ourselves, but Jesus Christ as Lord, and ourselves as your servants for Jesus' sake. For God, who said, "Let light shine out of darkness," made his light shine in our hearts to give us the light of the knowledge of the glory of God in the face of Christ.

While Paul does not specifically use the term "the two covenants" as he did in Galatians 4, his reference to Moses's ministry and his own, with Paul's ministry representative of "a new covenant," seems to have the two covenants in mind. Note some of the major characteristics of these two covenants.

| The Covenant Represented by Moses's Ministry | The New Covenant Represented by Paul's Ministry |
| --- | --- |
| "Written with ink" (3:3) | "Written…with the Spirit of the living God" (4:22) |
| "On tablets of stone," "in letters on stone" (3:3, 7) | "On tablets of human hearts" (3:3) |
| "The letter [that] kills" (3:6) | "The Spirit [that] gives life" (3:6, 17) |
| "The ministry that brought death [and] condemns men" (3:7, 9) | "The ministry that brings righteousness" (3:9) |
| A "glory" that "was fading away" (3:11) | "Ever-increasing glory" "which lasts" (3:18, 10) |
| "A veil that covers their hearts" (3:15) | "The veil is taken away" (3:17) |
| | "Freedom" (3:17) |

Many interpreters view this passage from a dispensational, historical perspective, understanding the characteristics in the left column as representative of the teaching of the Old Testament, and more specifically of God's covenant with Israel at Sinai. These same interpreters understand the characteristics in the right column to refer to the full gospel teaching of the New Testament which was lacking in the Old. But such a strictly historical interpretation would leave all Old Testament people without hope of salvation.

In reality, the left-column characteristics describe a lost condition, not a partially enlightened salvation. They describe stone cold hearts that resist the appeal of God's covenant. And the right-column characteristics describe the results of the Holy Spirit's work in the life of "anyone [who] turns to the Lord" (3:16) and is "being transformed into his likeness" (3:18)—a saving condition fully experienced by all believers in both Old and New Testament eras. In other words, Paul employed these terms primarily to describe experiential, not historical, conditions which apply to all believers (right column) and unbelievers (left column) of all time. Thus the characteristics in these two columns represent experientially-based, timeless, and eternal truths describing *responses* to the gospel by believers and unbelievers, rather than different gospels (or even differing levels of understanding of the one true gospel) ordained by God for separate historical eras.

This is not to deny that 2 Corinthians 2:14–4:6 contains some historical elements, particularly events associated with Sinai on the one hand and the church at Corinth on the other. However, the historical elements serve as the canvas on which Paul paints a primarily experiential theme, namely, the contrasting *responses* to the gospel "among those who are being saved and those who are perishing" (2:15). Implicit in his presentation is the appeal made explicitly just a few verses later: "We implore you on Christ's behalf: Be reconciled to God" (5:18).

Paul bracketed this passage with statements that focus on the *results* of gospel preaching to different populations—namely, to those who received the gospel by faith on the one hand, and to those who resisted through unbelief on the other. "For we are the aroma of Christ among those who are being saved and those who are perishing. To the one we are the smell of death; to the other the fragrance of life" (2:15–16). "If our gospel is veiled, it is veiled to those who are perishing" (4:3).

In these passages, the references to "those who are being saved and those who are perishing" apply timelessly and universally to all people to whom the gospel has ever been preached throughout the history of the covenant of redemption, from its first announcement at the fall of Adam to the second coming of Christ.

It is within the context of this truth, universally applied, that Paul's contrast of "the ministry that condemns men" and "the ministry that brings righteousness" (3:9) must be understood. These terms describe the contrasting *responses* of specific populations to Moses's ministry at Sinai and Paul's ministry at Corinth.

Moses's ministry of the gospel to the covenant nation of Israel met largely with unbelief and/or a self-reliant spirit, responses that would result in eternal death. According to Paul, God's law and gospel proclaimed at Sinai got no further for these unbelieving, self-reliant Israelites than the "tablets of stone" they were written on or the "ink" they were written with (3:3).

By making such statements Paul was not suggesting that the historical "old covenant" (3:14) God gave to Israel through Moses was not grace-based, gospel-bearing, or faith-inducing, or that its gospel message was not received by many in Israel by faith, resulting in their salvation and sanctification—a new covenant experience. Rather, he focused in this particular instance on the majority of Israel who hardened their hearts in unbelief and perverted the gospel into a system of works righteousness (Rom. 9:31–32), holding them up as examples of those in every age who "are perishing." Even though "on Mount Sinai…[Moses] received living words to pass on to us" (Acts 7:38), the persistent unbelief and disobedience of the majority of Israel had perverted the law and its gospel into "the smell of death" (2 Cor. 2:16) and "the letter that kills" (3:6). Through their own willful and stubborn unbelief, Moses's potentially life-saving ministry to them became a "ministry that brought death" (3:7) and a "ministry that condemns men" (3:9). In that it offered them the hope of salvation, his ministry still "was glorious" (3:10), but in that it was rejected and/or perverted, its glory "was fading away" (3:10).[26]

Here we should remind ourselves how God introduced the new covenant: "The time is coming, declares the Lord, when I will make a new covenant with the house of Israel and with the house of Judah. It will not be like the covenant I made with their forefathers when I took them by the hand to lead them out of Egypt, *because they did not remain faithful to my covenant*, and I turned away from them, declares the Lord" (Heb. 8:8–9, italics added).

In this passage God clearly distinguished the old covenant from the new in terms of the experiential response of His people.

> To be a minister of the new covenant is to be a minister who, having preached the gospel, finds that the Spirit has written the message on the heart of the hearer and given him faith and life. To be a minister of the old covenant is to preach the same message but find that the words have fallen on hearts of stone which will not believe....Paul is a minister of the new covenant because he, by God's grace, has ministered salvation to the Corinthians. Moses is a minister of the old covenant, and according to the argument of 2 Cor. 3 this can only be because he ministered the gospel to a stiffnecked people—to "old" men who took the covenant offered to them by God and broke it, perverting it into something old, dead, and ineffectual. The message is the same, but the results are different.[27]

While Paul's ministry in Corinth did not convert the entire city to Christ, he focused in 2 Corinthians 2:14–4:6 on those who received his gospel by faith and thus "are being saved" (3:15). These he held up as contemporary examples of new covenant believers who take their place in line with the true believers of all ages (Hebrews 11). In this context Paul described himself and those who labored with him as "ministers of a new covenant...of the Spirit [who] gives life" (3:6).

Because Paul views his ministry from the perspective of those who received the gospel by faith and "are being saved," he describes it as "the ministry of the Spirit" (3:8), "the ministry that brings righteousness" (3:9), and "the glory of that which lasts" (3:11). No one reading Corinthians can harbor the illusion that the believers there had achieved high levels of spiritual understanding and maturity by modern Christian standards, but their lives nevertheless had been transformed into "a new creation; the old has gone, the new has come!" (2 Cor. 5:17; cf. 1 Cor. 6:9–11). And Paul was confident that the work the Spirit had begun in their lives would continue "with ever-increasing glory" (3:18) as they continued to respond in faith to the ongoing sanctifying work of the Spirit and to gospel teaching.

Paul's reference to Moses putting "a veil over his face to keep the Israelites from gazing at it while the radiance was fading away" has been interpreted by many to mean that God's covenant at Sinai, as glorious as it was, was only temporary and was always meant to fade away once the greater glory of the new covenant would come in the earthly ministry of Christ. And while on the one hand that understanding has been misapplied by some who want to deny that the Sinai covenant applies to New Testament Christians, it does on the other hand affirm an important truth, namely, that the coming of Jesus made every previous revelation "old" by comparison. Not "old" in the sense of abolished (cf. Matt. 5:17–19) except in the case of the Old Testament ceremonial/ sacrificial system (cf. Dan. 9:27; Heb. 7–10), but "old" in the sense that once Christ came as the "surpassing glory," all previous revelation could be seen in a glorious new light.

However, Paul's reference to the veil Moses put over his face also seems to represent the guilt, fear, unbelief, and self-reliant spirit with which the Israelites responded to the gospel given to them at Sinai. Note the description of this historical incident recorded in Exodus 34:29–35:

> When Moses came down from Mount Sinai with the two tablets
> of the Testimony in his hands, he was not aware that his face was
> radiant because he had spoken with the LORD. When Aaron and all
> the Israelites saw Moses, his face was radiant, and they were afraid
> to come near him. But Moses called to them; so Aaron and all the
> leaders of the community came back to him, and he spoke to them.
> Afterward all the Israelites came near him, and he gave them all the
> commands the LORD had given him on Mount Sinai. When Moses
> finished speaking to them, he put a veil over his face. But whenever he

entered the Lord's presence to speak with him, he removed the veil until he came out. And when he came out and told the Israelites what he had been commanded, they saw that his face was radiant. Then Moses would put the veil back over his face until he went in to speak with the Lord.

It is important to carefully follow the sequence of events in this incident. As he communed with God on the mount, Moses received the second giving of the Ten Commandments, the renewal of God's covenant with Israel, and a new revelation of God's glory. As a result Moses's face was radiant, physically reflecting in a dimmed but miraculous way the glory of God (34:29).

The Israelites, who recently had crafted and worshiped the golden calf as their deliverer from Egypt, and had experienced the severe discipline of God in their camp, were filled with guilt and fear at the sight of Moses's radiant face, feeling they were still under God's displeasure. As such, "they were afraid to come near him" (34:30). Nevertheless, at Moses's invitation and Aaron's urging, they did come near to Moses, and Moses in an unveiled state told them all God had commanded (34:31–32).

After "Moses finished speaking to them, he put a veil over his face." In other words, after Moses finished speaking to the people, then in deference to the people's fearful *response* to him he compassionately veiled his face (34:33). When Moses went into the tent where he would meet directly with God, "he removed the veil" (34:34). Then when Moses came out from God's presence, he would again in an unveiled state tell the people what God had commanded him (34:34). Once again, after seeing their *response*, no doubt of continuing fear and perhaps their unbelief and/or self-reliant spirit, "Moses would put the veil back over his face" (34:35). This cycle—appearing before God unveiled, speaking to the people unveiled, then veiling himself again as a result of their *response* to him and his message—appears to have continued for some time (34:35).

What is quite clear from this sequence is that Moses's act of veiling his face to protect the people from seeing the glory on his face was a direct result of their response to him and to the messages he was giving them from God. For in each instance he did not veil his face until he "finished speaking to them" (34:35). By veiling his face, Moses symbolically portrayed the guilt, fear, unbelief, and/or self-reliant spirit he saw in their faces and read in their hearts. The veil represented the divine wish, "Oh, that their hearts would be inclined to fear me and keep all my commands always" (Deut. 5:29).

The veil represented not the grace-based, gospel-bearing, faith-inducing, mission-directed historical covenant of God, but rather the fear, unbelief, and even self-reliant spirit of the people. Thus Paul could say, "And even if our gospel is veiled, it is veiled to those who are perishing" (4:3), "but whenever anyone turns to the Lord, the veil is taken away" (3:16)—spiritual realities as true in Moses's day as in Paul's.

The emphasis throughout 2 Corinthians 2:14–4:6 appears to be on the *responses* of the people to the ministries of Moses and Paul, and thus on the results of their ministries more than on the *contents* of their ministries. Because of the general unbelief with which Moses's ministry was received, his ministry can be viewed as a ministry of condemnation and death. Because the church at Corinth believed, Paul's ministry among them proved to be a ministry of righteousness, a ministry of the Spirit who gives life. The universal appeal of this passage is for the conversion of unbelievers—"whenever anyone turns to the Lord, the veil is taken away" (3:16)—and for the sanctification of believers—"we all, with unveiled face, beholding as in a mirror the glory

> The veil represented not the grace-based, gospel-bearing, faith-inducing, mission-directed historical covenant of God, but rather the fear, unbelief, and even self-reliant spirit of the people.

of the Lord, are being transformed into the same image from glory to glory, just as by the Spirit of the Lord" (3:18 NKJV).[28]

A careful exegesis of 2 Corinthians 3 will not allow for an interpretation that nullifies the continuing validity of the role that God intends for His law to play in the life of a believer following conversion. Calvin expresses a similar understanding of 2 Corinthians 3:6–7:

> The passage is deserving of particular notice, as teaching us, in what way we are to reconcile those encomiums which David pronounces upon the law—(Psalm xix. 7, 8)—"the law of the Lord *converteth souls, enlighteneth the eyes, imparteth wisdom to babes,*" and passages of a like nature, with those statements of Paul, which at first view are at variance with them—that it is the *ministry of sin and death*—the *letter* that does nothing but *kill* (2 Cor. iii. 6, 7). For when it is animated by Christ, those things that David makes mention of are justly applicable to it. If Christ is taken away, it is altogether such as Paul describes. Hence, Christ is the life of the law[29] [emphasis in the original].

## Law for Sinners Only

I once received a paper intent on discrediting God's law of Ten Commandments and persuading me to abandon my defense of them. The author referred to many of the texts cited in this chapter but focused especially on Paul's statement in 1 Timothy 1:8–9: "We know that the law is good if one uses it properly. We also know that law is made not for the righteous but for lawbreakers and rebels, the ungodly and sinners, the unholy and irreligious." Paul then lists the kinds of horrible sinners he has in mind—those who murder their parents, slave traders, perverts, etc.—but then also extends the list to include "whatever else is contrary to the sound doctrine that conforms to the glorious gospel of the blessed God, which he entrusted to me" (1 Tim. 1:10–12).

The author of the paper kept asking me whether I considered myself a righteous person saved by grace or a sinner who needed the law. It was a rhetorical question. The way he posed the question strongly implied that to admit that I was a sinner would be tantamount to denying my faith in the efficacy of Christ's atoning sacrifice on my behalf and saving righteousness granted to me as a divine gift. His question disturbed me for several days.

As I prayerfully studied this, I was struck first by Paul's own characterization of himself only three verses later than the ones cited by my questioner: "Jesus came into the world to save sinners—of whom I am [Greek, *eimi*, present tense] the worst" (1 Tim. 1:15). Most scholars believe First Timothy to be one of Paul's last letters. Yet here he is still identifying himself in present tense not only as a sinner but as "the worst." The closer he was drawn to Jesus, and the more sanctified and righteous he became by God's grace, the more he saw himself as a sinner in need of continuing grace. The one time Paul characterized himself otherwise was in Philippians 3:6 where he described himself "as for legalistic righteousness, faultless." And in the same breath Paul repudiated this legalistic righteousness and considered it "rubbish, that I may gain Christ and be found in him, not having a righteousness of my own that comes from the law, but that which is through faith in Christ—the righteousness that comes from God and is by faith" (Phil. 3:8–9). In this confession he again showed his solidarity with the Old Testament/covenant gospel.[30]

Some would suggest that when Paul wrote that "law is made not for the righteous," he had the imputed righteousness of Christ in mind. However, the immediate context in which he characterizes himself as the worst of sinners suggests otherwise. When Jesus was criticized for associating with sinners, He responded, "It is not the healthy who need a doctor, but the sick. I have not come to call the righteous, but sinners" (Mark 2:17). Paul seems never to have outgrown his sense of need for the Physician. The ability to recognize oneself as a sinner in continual need of grace is a healthy component of the experience of sanctification.

Paul's statement—"law is made not for the righteous but for lawbreakers and rebels, the ungodly and sinners"—expresses a timeless, universal truth. And just as the holy law of God was applicable to the daily life of the Old Testament believer who was deemed righteous by faith, it remains applicable for the New Testament believer who is declared righteous by that same faith.

When studied from an *experiential* old and new covenant perspective, other puzzling passages we may not have commented on can also be understood to harmonize with the consistent proclamation of the everlasting gospel throughout the ages and in all of God's covenants (see chart 2—"Graphic Summary of the Covenant[s]"—on page 305 in appendix D).

> Paul seems never to have outgrown his sense of need for the Physician. The ability to recognize oneself as a sinner in continual need of grace is a healthy component of the experience of sanctification.

One cannot interpret the passages we have been discussing and others like them from a strictly historical perspective without making God the author of legalism. Understanding them experientially reveals the unity of Scripture and the divine covenant(s) in harmony with the character of our loving God who changes not.

## Perfection Demanded by the Covenant(s) Supplied in New Covenant Experience

Believers should never lose sight of the timeless truth that not just the law but salvation and the everlasting covenant itself demand perfection. It wasn't just demanded in the historical old covenant but in the new as well: "Be perfect, therefore, as your heavenly Father is perfect" (Matt. 5:48). Doing a word study of Jesus's statement doesn't help us lower the bar the tiniest fraction, for the perfection that Jesus commands and demands is "as your heavenly Father is perfect"! The fact is, it's a perfection beyond our ability to comprehend. It's not a perfection that is somehow less than it first sounds, but greater! That truth must never be compromised. To do so would make a mockery of the perfect life Jesus lived on our behalf: "God made him who had no sin to be sin for us, so that in him we might become the righteousness of God" (2 Cor. 5:21). In the loom of heaven that one perfect life was woven into a robe of perfect righteousness that is draped by grace over every believer so that we might approach God's throne with confidence and receive grace to help us in time of need (Zech. 3:1–7; Isa. 61:10; Gal. 3:27; Rev. 7:13–14; Heb. 4:14–16). It is also true that "he himself bore our sins in his body on the tree, so that we might die to sins and live for righteousness; by his wounds you have been healed" (1 Pet. 2:24).

Note the following classic statement that holds together the major issues and components of God's eternal covenant with humankind and is as clear a statement as any on the nature of the gospel and a new covenant experience:

> It was possible for Adam, before the fall, to form a righteous character by obedience to God's law. But he failed to do this, and because of his sin our natures are fallen and we cannot make ourselves righteous. Since we are sinful, unholy, we cannot perfectly obey the holy law. We have no righteousness of our own with which to meet the claims of the law of God. But Christ has made a way of escape for us. He lived on earth amid the trials and temptations such as we have to meet. He lived a sinless life. He died for us, and now He offers to take our sins and give us His righteousness. If you give yourself to Him, and accept Him as your Saviour, then, sinful as your life may have been, for His sake you are accounted righteous. Christ's character stands in place of your character, and you are accepted before God just as if you had not sinned.
>
> More than this, Christ changes the heart. He abides in your heart by faith. You are to maintain this connection with Christ by faith and the continual surrender of your will to Him; and so long as you do this, he will work in you to will and to do according to His good pleasure. So you may say, "The life which I now live in the flesh I

live by the faith of the Son of God, who loved me, and gave Himself for me." Galatians 2:20. So Jesus said to His disciples, "It is not ye that speak, but the Spirit of your Father which speaketh in you." Matthew 10:20. Then with Christ working in you, you will manifest the same spirit and do the same good works—works of righteousness, obedience.

So we have nothing in ourselves of which to boast. We have no ground for self-exaltation. Our only ground of hope is in the righteousness of Christ imputed to us, and in that wrought by His Spirit working in and through us.[31]

## New Covenant Experience in Old Covenant History

In Hebrews 11, the chapter following his extended treatment of the transition from the priesthood and sacrifices of the old covenant to the priesthood and sacrifice of Jesus, the author of Hebrews did something remarkable. He provided a representative list of believers who lived during the period of God's historical old covenant yet manifested a new covenant experience. Long before the new covenant was articulated by Jeremiah and ratified by Jesus's "blood of the everlasting covenant" (Heb. 13:20), the Holy Spirit was converting sinful hearts and living in them and through them in a new covenant experience—beginning with Abel, son of Adam, who "by faith…was commended as a righteous man" (Heb. 11:4). That sort of deep intimacy with God is possible only through a new covenant experience: "By faith Enoch was taken from this life, so that he did not experience death;…For before He was taken, he was commended as one who pleased God" (Heb. 11:5).

Hebrews 11 extends the list through the major representatives of God's covenants—Noah, Abraham, Moses, and David. But the list doesn't stop there. The author also mentions Isaac, Jacob, Joseph, Rahab, Gideon, Barak, Samson, Jephthah, Samuel, and the prophets. The list includes some rough characters, to be sure. But whoever the Spirit draws to faith and salvation surrenders also to the operation of the Spirit, whether it be Samson in the Old Testament or the thief on the cross in the New, both of whom appear to have come up far short of a high level of spiritual maturity, and yet seem to have been included in God's list of saved new covenant believers (Heb. 11:32, 39–40; Luke 23:40–43).[32]

But still the list in Hebrews 11 goes on, including large bodies of people. "By faith the people passed through the Red Sea" (Heb. 11:29). Aren't these the ones who only a few weeks later were making a golden calf? Yes, for the most part. Faith doesn't always equate with spiritual maturity. And "not all the Israelites accepted the good news" (Rom. 10:16), but some did. And God honored their faith. "By faith the walls of Jericho fell" (Heb. 11:30).

The list further includes many unnamed believers who were persecuted, tortured, even martyred: "all commended for their faith" (Heb. 11:35–39). "Before this faith came" through the Holy Spirit's converting influence, every one of them was "a prisoner of sin" (Gal. 3:22–23). Yet because of their submission to the work of the Spirit, "all these people were still living by faith when they died. They did not receive the things promised; they only saw them and welcomed them from a distance. And they admitted that they were aliens and strangers on earth.…Therefore God is not ashamed to be called their God, for he has prepared a city for them" (Heb. 11:13, 16).

These representative believers of God's historical old covenant era, even though most of them lived historically *after* Sinai, did not live "according to the flesh," but "by the power of the Spirit" (Gal. 4:23, 29). They were not the persecutors of the saints but were themselves the persecuted (Gal. 4:29; Heb. 11:25, 35–38). Many will find it hard to imagine that the Old Testament believer who testified, "I delight in your commands because I love them" (Ps. 119:47), "your statutes…are the joy of my heart" (Ps. 119:47), and obedience to Your law is for me to "walk about in freedom" (Ps. 119:44–45), would have described this experience in covenant relation with God as being "burdened by a yoke of slavery" (Gal. 5:1). An Old Testament believer who sang from his or her heart, "The law of the LORD is perfect, reviving the soul" (Ps. 19:7), and "I will never forget your precepts, for by them you have preserved my life" (Ps. 119:93), surely would have been shocked to hear others describe God's gracious covenant with them as "the letter that kills" and a "ministry that brought death [and] condemned [them]," a covenant which they understood only through a dull mind and veiled eyes since they had never "turned to the Lord" (2 Cor. 3:6–9, 14–16). It is only reasonable to envision them as people who embraced His covenant and law as that which is "perfect, reviving the soul," "holy, righteous and good," "spiritual," "of the Spirit [that] gives life" and "brings

> The author of Hebrews provided a representative list of believers who lived during the period of God's historical old covenant yet manifested a new covenant experience.

righteousness" with "ever increasing glory," one that lasts and "gives freedom" (Deut. 4:7–8; 10:13; Ps. 119:39, 119; Rom. 7:12, 14; 2 Cor. 3:6–9, 17–18; James 2:10–12). Far from being a people who related externally to God's covenant as something written on stone only, they were people on whose hearts His law was being written by "the Spirit of the living God" (2 Cor. 3:3; cf. Deut. 30:6, 11–14; Ps. 40:8; Isa. 51:7).

These heroes of faith were not a hopeless people who "will never share in the inheritance with the [saints]" but rather a people who "admitted that they were aliens and strangers on earth," "looking forward to the city with foundations, whose architect and builder is God" (Gal. 4:30; Heb. 11:10, 13). "Therefore God is not ashamed to be called their God, for he has prepared a city for them" (Heb. 11:16). By virtue of their experience with God—an experience initiated and sustained by grace and responded to through faith—they bore the divine credentials of new covenant believers.

God was writing His law on the hearts of each of those in this list— promise/provision 1 (sanctification) of the new covenant. God's law was more perfectly written in Enoch's heart than Samson's, just as it was more perfectly written in the apostle John's than in the heart of the thief on the cross. It is always a work in process short of Christ's return, but a new covenant work nonetheless. Of all those on the list it could be said that God was their God and they were His people—promise/provision 2 (reconciliation). All of them were ambassadors of the knowledge of the true God to the darkened minds of their generation until that Day when no one will need to teach neighbors about God, for all will know Him—promise/provision 3 (mission). Each was no less forgiven "through the blood of the everlasting covenant" (Heb. 13:20) than was any of us in the new covenant era, though each looked forward to the promise of Christ's atoning act by means of lamb sacrifices while we look back on it in remembrance by means of the holy communion—promise/provision 4 (justification).

Each believer in the Hebrews 11 list lived in God's old covenant historical era; each manifested a new covenant experience. Christ was the Author and Finisher of their faith (Heb. 12:2). Hebrews 12:23 classifies them as part of "the church of the firstborn, whose names are written in heaven,…the spirits of righteous men made perfect." The *NIV Study Bible* note on Hebrews 12:23 says: "For the most part, these were pre-Christian believers such as Abel (11:4) and Noah (11:7). They are referred to as…righteous because God credited their faith to them as righteousness, as he did to Abraham (see Ro 4:3). Actual justification was not accomplished, however, until Christ made it complete by his death on the cross (see 11:40; Ro 3:24–25; 4:23–25)."[33]

## Old Covenant Experience in New Covenant History

There was another group of people living in God's new covenant historical era who were "turning to a different gospel—which is really no gospel at all" (Gal. 1:6, 7): the Galatians. Having tasted a new covenant experience, they were in danger of regressing into an old covenant experience: "You foolish Galatians!…Did you receive the Spirit by observing the law, or by believing what you heard [the gospel]? Are you so foolish? After beginning with the Spirit [of grace and faith—a new covenant experience], are you now trying to attain your goal [of salvation and sanctification] by human effort [reliance on observing the law—an old covenant experience]?" (Gal. 3:1–3, 10; 4:21).

Paul countered the Galatians' regression into an old covenant experience with this theme: "We who are Jews by birth and not 'Gentile sinners' know that a man is not justified by observing the law, but by faith in Jesus Christ. So we, too, have put our faith in Christ Jesus that we may be justified by faith in Christ and not by observing the law, because by observing the law no one will be justified" (Gal. 2:16). The author of the *NIV Study Bible* commentary note considers Galatians 2:16 "a key verse" in which Paul "is arguing against an *illegitimate use of the OT law* that made the observance of that law the grounds of acceptance with God" [italics added][34]—*which is precisely the old covenant experience.*

The very fact that by the Spirit's inspiration this warning letter to the Galatians was adopted into the canon of Scripture is evidence of the possibility of living an old covenant experience within the new covenant historical era. The serious tone of Galatians warns every sincere seeker of the truth about the lethal effect that such an experience can have on one's spiritual life, converting it into a burdensome yoke of slavery, transforming the holy covenant into "the letter that kills" and a ministry that brings death and condemnation, whose end "will never share in the inheritance with the [saints]" (Gal. 4:30; 5:1; 2 Cor. 3:6–9).

This may be the meaning of Jesus's teaching about the need for new wine to be poured into new wineskins: "No one pours new wine into old wineskins. If he does, the new wine will burst the skins, the wine will run out and the wineskins will be ruined. No, new wine must be poured into new wineskins" (Luke 5:37–38; cf. Matt. 9:17; Mark 2:22). Jesus did not mean that the gospel God taught through His historical old covenant era, a gospel which was able to make them "wise for salvation" (2 Tim. 3:15; Heb. 4:2), was incompatible with the gospel He was proclaiming in the new covenant historical era. Jesus was responding to those who questioned why the disciples of John the Baptist and the Pharisees fasted but Jesus's disciples did not. [35] Jesus's answer pointed away from judging ourselves or others based on external observances. The temptation to rely on one's religious practices to earn merit with God will always be present as long as the sinful nature maintains any influence in the matter. Luke adds Jesus's statement to this incident: "And not one after drinking old wine wants the new, for he says, 'The old is better'" (5:39). By this He acknowledges the powerful pull of the sinful nature to keep people of every historical era steeped in legalistic attitudes and practices, and resistant to the gospel, a condition that Paul himself experienced for much of his life as his testimony in Philippians 3:4–6 reveals.

A converted person who backslides into legalism has reverted to "a different gospel—which is really no gospel at all," and unless reconverted stands in jeopardy of being "eternally condemned" (Gal. 1:6–9). This concern forms the basis for Paul's admonition to the Colossians, "Just as you received Christ Jesus as Lord [by grace through faith], continue to live in him [by grace through faith]" (Col. 2:6). With this same concern that had loomed into a present threat he confronted the Galatian church more directly: "Did you receive the Spirit by observing the law, or by believing what you heard? Are you so foolish? After beginning with the Spirit, are you now trying to attain your goal by human effort?" (Gal. 3:2–3). Living in the historical new covenant era, even learning about and teaching the new covenant, does not insulate any of us from the age-old temptation to attempt to attain to righteousness by our own works. Even the New Testament, when read through the veil of a legalistic understanding, and apart from prayer and reliance on the Holy Spirit, can be converted into a "letter that kills" and a "law of sin" that produces an old covenant experience (1 Cor. 2:10–14). "But whenever one turns to the Lord, the veil is taken away"—a profound spiritual truth and promise that is timeless and universal, offering hope and salvation to every nation, kindred, tongue, and people (2 Cor. 3:16; Rev. 14:6).

## Covenant Love in Focus

Paul concluded his intense letter to the Galatians warning against an old covenant experience and appealing for a life of faith: "But God forbid that I should boast except in the cross of our Lord Jesus Christ, by whom the world has been crucified to me, and I to the world" (Gal. 6:14). For new covenant Christians, the cross of Christ becomes the cross on which the world is crucified to them, and they are crucified to the world. In context, "the world" in this text represents both the evil "acts of the sinful nature" and reliance "on observing the law" as a means of righteousness and salvation (Gal. 5:19–21; 3:10). Both are crucified on the cross of Christ from which grace streams and hope is born. Just as a magnifying glass can focus the rays of the sun to a pinpoint that can start a fire, so the cross of Christ gathers the rays of God's covenant love and focuses them to a pinpoint that can ignite faith and inscribe His law in the heart.

> Living in the historical new covenant era, even learning about and teaching the new covenant, does not insulate any of us from the age-old temptation to attempt to attain to righteousness by our own works.

## Summary

The interpretative key to understanding the New Testament's position on God's covenant(s) and law is found in a prayerful discernment and application of the historical and experiential dimensions of the covenants to the texts in question. In general, Hebrews 7–10 focuses on the *historical* old and new covenants (the historical periods before and after the coming of Jesus), while the other epistles usually focus on the *experiential* old and new covenants (disobedience and legalism produced by the sinful nature versus faith and loving obedience that proceed from faith as produced by the Holy Spirit). Hebrews emphasizes Christ's fulfillment of the Old Testament sacrificial and priesthood system, making the former ceremonial system obsolete. In the other epistles, Paul's contention with "the law" seeks to rescue it from the misunderstanding and misapplication of it experienced by the majority in Israel, and to restore it to its original grace-based, gospel-bearing, faith-inducing, mission-directed purpose. This understanding results from a careful examination of the immediate and wider scriptural context of the texts involved, and reveals the symmetry and unity of God's plan of salvation throughout the covenant of redemption which spans from paradise lost to paradise restored.

## Notes

1. Robertson (57–58, 180–182) shows respect for this distinction when he discusses the historical perspective on the covenants dominant in Hebrews while recognizing the experiential treatment of the covenants in Galatians:

"The incarnation of Christ represents the most basic differentiation-point in this history. The bond of God with man before Christ may be called 'old covenant' and the bond of God with man after Christ may be called 'new covenant'…

"The entire structure of the letter to the Hebrews builds on this basic distinction. Essential to the total presentation of the Christian gospel in that Epistle is the concept of promise in the old covenant achieving fulfillment in the new.

"In his letter to the Galatians, the apostle Paul sets several dynamic concepts over against one another. Central among contrasting covenantal perspectives is his development of the distinction between the old covenant and the new.

"Paul's ultimate purpose in the entire discussion is to contrast the legalism of current Judaizers with the graciousness of the new covenant (Gal. 2:14–16; 3:1; 4:31–5:2)."

2. The NKJV is used throughout these columns as the NIV sometimes translates *sarx*, the Greek term for "flesh," as "sinful nature" and at other times as "flesh," while the NKJV and a number of other translations translate *sarx* more consistently as "flesh," though they do translate it as "carnal" on occasion. "Sinful nature" is a good translation of *sarx* in many instances, but the inconsistency in translation, sometimes as "sinful nature" and sometimes as "flesh," makes it more difficult to appreciate the strong contrast the New Testament builds between the two, a distinction it is essential to grasp in order to gain an accurate understanding of the nature of the two covenants in Galatians 4.

3. Rayburn, "The Contrast Between the Old and New Covenants," 127; cf. Robertson, 180–182, 60–61: "In Galatians 4:21, Paul addresses himself to those who want to be 'under law.'

He speaks to those who would attempt to achieve righteousness before God by personal law-keeping....

"It is the legalistic misapprehension of the Sinaitic law-covenant that is in the mind of the apostle. Slavery inevitably will result from resorting to natural human resources as a means of pleasing God. Ishmael, the current Judaizers, and unbelieving Israel conjointly find themselves to be slaves.

"...the understanding of Mosaic law with which Paul is contending cannot be viewed as the divinely intended purpose of the giving of the law at Sinai. Even though the middle member of this first triad (Hagar-Sinai-Present Jerusalem) is identified as 'Mount Sinai' (v. 25), it does not represent the true purpose of Sinaitic law-giving.

"Ultimately in Galatians 4, Paul specifically traces the antithesis which he has in mind to the contrast between the 'present Jerusalem' and the 'Jerusalem above' (Gal. 4:25f.). By his reference to the 'present Jerusalem,' Paul alludes to the understanding of the Mosaic law-covenant maintained by the contemporary Judaizers. The new covenant obviously stands in starkest contrast with the legalism of the Judaism current in Paul's day. But this misappropriation of the Mosaic law-covenant certainly cannot be equated with God's original intention in the giving of the law. The Judaizers of Paul's day were not correct in their understanding of Mosaic law. The full force of the apostle's polemic is directed against their misunderstanding."

4. Rayburn, "The Contrast Between the Old and New Covenants," 120–121. The full statement is even stronger: "If it is the temporary character of the law and Christ's bringing it to an end that is contemplated in Gal 3:23ff., reflecting the idea of 3:19, it follows by a rigorous necessity that there could have been no justification by faith in the Old Testament age (3:24). The issue in 3:23ff. is not a relative freedom from an obligation to an external code that the coming of Christ has secured. There is no suggestion that the coming of Christ has transformed the relationship of God's people to the law in the senses often imagined. For example, these verses say nothing about a transformation of one's service to law from an externalism characteristic of the Old Testament to a heart response of the New. Nor do these verses suggest that Christ has released the Christian from bondage by trimming the Pentateuch to a few simple exhortations summarized in the call to love. Explicitly at issue is slavery as opposed to sonship. If Christ's coming and his ending of the law are the middle term in this argument, then it will be with great difficulty that one preserves justification by faith in the Old Testament or consistency in Paul's argument as a whole. In our view this is an unavoidable conclusion. The slavery to law contemplated here is prior to and leads to justification by faith. So an insistence on a religio-historical interpretation of 3:23ff. requires the elimination of the central pillar of Paul's argument—justification by faith is the message and reality of the Old Testament."

5. There is a "law of sin and death" (Rom. 8:2) that misappropriates God's law, enticing us to disobey it (Rom. 7:8, 21–23) or to rely on obedience to it as the basis of our salvation (Rom. 7:11), either way producing death in us (Rom. 7:11). And there is a "law of the Spirit of life" (Rom. 8:2) that convicts us that we have broken the law, draws us to repentance, engenders faith in Christ, and writes His law on our hearts "in order that the righteous requirements of the law might be fully met in us, who do not live according to the sinful nature but according to the Spirit" (Rom. 8:4) through a life of "obedience that comes from faith" (Rom. 1:5). These two contrasting laws—"the law of sin and death" and "the law of the Spirit of life"—are the same holy law of God in the hands of two great, contrasting spiritual powers: Satan and the

sinful nature on the one hand, and the Holy Spirit on the other. Under the influence of Satan and the sinful nature, the law of God becomes a law of sin and death, stirring up rebellion against God on the one hand and enticing us to assign to it meritorious powers on the other. Under the influence of the Spirit of God, the law of God becomes a convicting, converting, and sanctifying instrument—holy, just, good, and spiritual—just as God intended originally (Deut. 10:12–13; Psalm 19; Rom. 7:12, 14, 22). God's holy law has always had a legitimate role in the plan of salvation, but that role has always been perverted when His law has been commandeered by the sinful nature and divorced from the ministry of the Holy Spirit and faith. It operates perfectly, however, when it is kept constantly under the influence of the Spirit and within the context of saving faith in God. This is a timeless, universal truth.

6. Regarding Paul's statement that we are held in prison until faith comes and that once "faith has come, we are no longer under the law" (Gal. 3:23–25), Rayburn clarifies: "In Pauline thought generally this imprisoning work of the law takes place in the life of the individual prior to his justification, indeed serves to lead to that justification, and this work of the law is finished when it has realized its goal, namely, the man's casting himself on Christ in faith for his salvation." Rayburn, "The Contrast Between the Old and New Covenants," 109.

7. John Calvin, *Institutes of the Christian Religion*, Bk II, Chap VII, Sects VI–XV. As listed in Louis Berkhof, *Systematic Theology* (Grand Rapids, MI: Eerdmans, 1941), 614–615.

8. John Calvin, *Institutes of the Christian Religion*, trans. John Allen (Grand Rapids, MI: Eerdmans, 1949), 388.

9. John Calvin, *Calvin's Commentaries: Romans-Galatians* (Wilmington, DE: Associated Publishers and Authors, n.d.), 1898.

10. Calvin, *Institutes of the Christian Religion*, p. 388. Cf., John R. W. Stott, *The Message of Romans* (Downers Grove, IL: InterVarsity Press, 1994), 191: "The moral law remains a revelation of God's will which he still expects his people to 'fulfil' by living lives of righteousness and love ([Rom.] 8:4; 13:8, 10). This is what the Reformers called 'the third use of the law.'"

11. Ibid., 390, 392.

12. E. Kautzsch, ed., *Gesenius' Hebrew Grammar* (Oxford: Claredon, 1910), par. 113bb.

13. Ibid., par. 113cc.

14. Richard M. Davidson, *A Love Song for the Sabbath* (Hagerstown, MD: Review and Herald Publishing Association, 1988), 36.

15. Robertson, 60.

16. This view corresponds to the Westminster Confession of Faith, chap. XIX, sect. 5: "The moral law doth for ever bind all, as well justified persons as others, to the obedience thereof; (Rom. xiii. 8–10. Eph. vi:6; 1 John ii: 3, 4, 7, 8) and that not only in regard of the matter contained in it, but also in respect of the authority of God, the Creator, who gave it. (James ii. 10, 11) Neither doth Christ in the gospel any way dissolve, but much strengthen this obligation. (Matt. v. 17–19. James ii. 8. Rom. iii. 31.)."

17. C. E. B. Cranfield, *A Critical and Exegetical Commentary on the Epistle to the Romans* (Edinburgh: T&T Clark, 2001), 1:139.

18. C. E. B. Cranfield, *Romans*, vol. 1 (New York: T&T Clark, 1998 ed.), 339–340. Cf. Rayburn, "The Contrast Between the Old and New Covenants," 144–145: "The 'oldness of the letter' refers to that situation in the flesh, that time before conversion while one is yet in opposition to God and to his law ([Rom.] 8:7). The 'newness of the Spirit' refers to the

situation created by the Holy Spirit and the imputation of the righteousness of Christ. The context suggests that Rom. 7:1–6 has nothing to do with any religio-historical [i.e., Old Testament era vs. New Testament era] distinction but only with the distinction between the situation of man prior to conversion and the situation of man after conversion....

"*Gramma* ['letter,' NKJV and 'written code,' NIV] refers to the law as it is viewed by the unbeliever and the legalist, who views it as a means of self-assertion, but to whom it will always remain the cold, dead letter because he does not and cannot obey it from within, from a heart transformed by the Spirit. *Gramma* is thus the law apart from Christ and apart from the Holy Spirit."

19. J. Barton Payne, *The Theology of the Older Testament* (Grand Rapids, MI: Zondervan, 1981), 309.

20. The NIV, and similarly the KJV and NKJV, translates Galatians 2:15–16 thus: "We who are Jews by birth and not 'Gentile sinners' know that a man is not justified by observing the law, but by faith in Jesus Christ." If this translation reflects Paul's intended meaning the message is quite amazing. Paul was speaking specifically to Peter but was also addressing other Jews. All of them grew up being taught from the historical old covenant God gave His people at Sinai, including the wider writings of Moses and the prophets. And Paul says, we Jews, educated in the law from birth, "know that a man is not justified by observing the law, but by faith in Jesus Christ."

21. Robert Badenas, *Christ the End of the Law: Romans 10:4 in Pauline Perspective*, Journal for the Study of the New Testament Supplement Series 10 (Sheffield, England: JSOT Press, 1985).

22. Ibid., 136, 150.

23. *NIV Study Bible*, 1721. Cf., note the *NIV Study Bible* scholarly comment on Matthew 5:17–20 where Jesus said He came not to abolish the law or the Prophets, but to fulfill them, and admonished His disciples to exceed the righteousness of the Pharisees: "*fulfill.* Jesus fulfilled the Law in the sense that he gave it its full meaning. He emphasized its deep, underlying principles and total commitment to it rather than mere external acknowledgment and obedience.

"Jesus is not speaking against observing all the requirements of the Law, but against hypocritical, Pharisaical legalism. Such legalism was not the keeping of all details of the Law but the hollow sham of keeping laws externally, to gain merit before God, while breaking them inwardly. It was following the letter of the Law while ignoring its spirit. Jesus repudiates the Pharisees' interpretation of the Law and their view of righteousness by works," 1449.

24. Willard, *The Divine Conspiracy*, 141.

25. Many commentators agree that Paul is here addressing timeless experiential issues. For the most expansive and glorious exposition of 1 Corinthians 15:55–57 I have found, see Robert S. Candlish, *Studies in First Corinthians 15: Life in a Risen Savior* (Grand Rapids, MI: Kregel Publications, 1989 [first published in 1863]), 308–336. Cf. William Barclay, *The Letters to the Corinthians* (Philadelphia: The Westminster Press, 1975), 160; Eugen Walter, *The First Epistle to the Corinthians* (New York: Herder and Herder, 1968), 181–182; R. C. H. Lenski, *The Interpretation of St. Paul's First and Second Epistles to the Corinthians* (Minneapolis, MN: Augsburg Publishing House, 1937), 749; J. J. Lias, *The First Epistle to the Corinthians* (London: Cambridge University Press, 1878), 162; Charles J. Ellicott, *St Paul's First Epistle to the Corinthians: With a Critical and Grammatical Commentary* (London: Longmans, Green, and Co., 1887), 328.

26. This understanding is analogous to the *NIV Study Bible's* interpretive comments on John 20:23 ("If you forgive anyone his sins, they are forgiven; if you do not forgive them, they are not forgiven"): "God does not forgive people's sins because we do so, nor does he withhold forgiveness because we do. Rather, those who proclaim the gospel are in effect forgiving or not forgiving sins, depending on whether the hearers accept or reject Jesus Christ." Similarly, God's covenant/gospel mediated through Moses at Sinai was not in and of itself a ministry of condemnation and death, nor was Paul's gospel in and of itself a ministry of the Spirit and life, but both were viewed so "depending on whether the hearers accept or reject Jesus Christ."

27. Rayburn, "The Contrast Between the Old and New Covenants," 163, 165.

28. Commenting on 1 Corinthians 3:6, Cranfield observes: "The contrast Paul has in mind is not a contrast between a life lived under the obligation to try to obey the law and a life in which that obligation has been replaced by the guidance of the Spirit, but rather a contrast between the life of those, who, though possessing the law, have not yet been enabled by the Holy Spirit rightly to understand it in the light of Christ, and the life of those whom the Holy Spirit has both enabled to understand the law aright in the light of Jesus Christ and also set free to make a beginning of trying to obey it with humble joy....We may conclude that he continued to find the will of God in [the law], but did so now in a new and distinctively Christian way. It is of the utmost importance that we do not underestimate the newness of the Christian's understanding of, and relation to, the law. He understands it in the light of Christ, in the light of his perfect obedience to it and of his clarification of its intention by his life and work and teaching. He has been freed from the illusion that he is able so well to fulfill it as to put God in his debt. He knows that, while it shows him the depth of his sinfulness, it no longer pronounces God's condemnation of him, since Christ has borne that condemnation for him. He no longer feels its commands simply as an obligation imposed on him from without, but is being set free by the Holy Spirit to desire wholeheartedly to try to obey and thereby to express his gratitude to God for his mercy and generosity. So he receives the law's commands as God's fatherly guidance for his children—not as a burden or an infringement of his liberty, but as the pointing out of the way to true freedom." C. E. B. Cranfield, *On Romans: and Other New Testament Essays* (Edinburgh: T&T Clark, 1998), 122–123.

29. Calvin, *Calvin's Commentaries. Romans-Galatians*, p. 1772. Cf. Rayburn, "The Contrast Between the Old and New Covenants," 146, in his comments on 2 Corinthians 3:6, "the letter kills, but the Spirit gives life," lists sources that show wide support for this interpretation: "Chrysostom writes on 3:6: 'Yet these things he saith not absolutely; but in allusion to those who prided themselves upon the things of Judaism.' *The Homilies of S. John Chrysostom on the Second Epistle of St. Paul the Apostle to the Corinthians*, ET: Oxford, 1848, 82. According to Augustine, 'The truth is that the teaching which gives us the commandment of self-control and uprightness of life, remains, without the presence of the life-giving Spirit, a letter that killeth.' 'The Spirit and the Letter,' *Augustine's Later Works* (LCC), ed. J. Burnaby, ET London, 1955, 209ff. In commenting on Psalm 71 he says more simply that the letter is 'the Law without Grace.' Cited in Luther, *Lectures on Galatians, 1519—Chapters 1–6* (LWks), ed. J. Pelikan, ET: St Louis, 1964, 312. Luther himself goes on to add: '...only then is it a "letter" when the grace to fulfill it is not there. In that case it is a "letter" for me, not for itself, especially if it is understood in the sense that grace is not necessary....For this reason the "letter" kills (2 Cor. 3:6), because it is never rightly understood so long as it is understood without grace, just as it is never rightly kept so long as it is kept without grace. In both cases it is death and wrath.' (313)

Cf. K. Barth, *Church Dogmatics*, I, ii, eds. G.W. Bromiley and T.F. Torrance, ET: Edinburgh, 1956, 514ff.; Barrett, *Second Corinthians*, 112ff.; Cranfield, 'St. Paul and the Law,' 53, 57;... Bultmann, *2 Korintherbrief*, 80ff.; Wallis, *PCOC*, 6ff. Conzelmann concludes that 'Paul defines the nature of the old and new covenants by the timeless conceptuality of letter and spirit. The letter is the law, in so far as it is grasped and can be a means in man's hand.' *An Outline of the Theology of the New Testament*, ET: London, 170." This is only a partial list of the sources he identifies in support of this interpretation of "the letter" in the writings of Paul.

30. E.g., Deut. 30:11–14 (with Rom. 10:5–13); Isa. 61:10; Jer. 23:6; 33:16; Zech. 3:1–7; and the entire OT sacrificial system which represented a substitutionary atonement.

31. Ellen G. White, *Steps to Christ* (Mountain View, CA: Pacific Press Publishing Assoc., 1956), 62–63.

32. This is not to imply that those included in the Hebrews 11 list of Old Testament representatives of faith were by any means perfect, or that they never disobeyed God, or that everything they did was directed by the Spirit of God. "Inspiration faithfully records the faults of good men, those who were distinguished by the favor of God; indeed, their faults are more fully presented than their virtues....Men whom God favored, and to whom He entrusted great responsibilities, were sometimes overcome by temptation and committed sin, even as we at the present day strive, waver, and frequently fall into error. Their lives, with all their faults and follies, are open before us, both for our encouragement and warning. If they had been represented as without fault, we, with our sinful nature, might despair at our own mistakes and failures. But seeing where others struggled through discouragements like our own, where they fell under temptation as we have done, and yet took heart again and conquered through the grace of God, we are encouraged in our striving after righteousness. As they, though sometimes beaten back, recovered their ground, and were blessed of God, so we too may be overcomers in the strength of Jesus. The life of Christ's disciples is to be like His, a series of uninterrupted victories, not seen to be such here, but recognized as such in the great hereafter." Ellen G. White, *God's Amazing Grace* (Hagerstown, MD: Review and Herald Publishing Association, 1973), 255.

33. *NIV Study Bible*, 1875.

34. *NIV Study Bible*, 1783, commentary on Galatians 2:16.

35. The *NIV Study Bible* offers these scholarly comments on Mark 2:18 relative to "fasting": "In the Mosaic law only the fast of the Day of Atonement was required [Lev. 16:29, 31; 23:27–32; Num. 29:7]. After the Babylonian exile four other yearly fasts were observed by the Jews [Zech. 7:5; 8:19]. In Jesus' time the Pharisees fasted twice a week" [see Luke 18:12]. The four additional post-exilic fasts referred to in Zechariach 8:19 were not scripturally-required fasts, as also the Pharisaic practice of fasting twice a week most certainly was not.

# Chapter 8

# Love and Law
# in the Covenant(s)

One of the contentions of some who pit the Sinaitic covenant against the new covenant is that the former places much emphasis on law and little on love, while the latter does just the opposite.[1] It has been stated, "This commandment to love is repeated a number of times in the New Testament, just as the Ten Commandments were repeated a number of times in the old."[2] This is misleading and represents a serious misunderstanding of both Old Testament and New Testament laws. It ignores not only the Old Testament emphasis on love but also the New Testament's direct references to the Ten Commandments (e.g., Matt. 19:16–19; Rom. 13:9–10; Eph. 6:1–3; James 2:11) as well as many indirect references. This chapter explores the relationship of law and love in the covenant(s).

## The Nature of Biblical Law

Let us first consider some thoughts about law in general. In May, 2004, the American news media released photographs of shocking abuse of inmates by American soldiers at the Abu Ghraib prison in Iraq. President George W. Bush expressed outrage at such abuse and went on Iraqi television to apologize to the Iraqi people. The president and members of the U.S. Congress repeatedly assured not only the Iraqi people but the entire world community that the United States of America was "a nation of law," and the abusers who violated the

law would be identified and justly punished. The leaders of the most powerful nation on earth wanted the world to know that the United States of America is "a nation of law." Why? Because good laws ensure order and protection for those governed by them.[3] Communities without any laws would be unpleasant, even frightening, places to live. We probably wouldn't want to live under those conditions for long.

Some authors point out, somewhat accusingly, that the covenant God gave His people at Sinai contained 613 commandments or laws. They feel sorry for the "poor" Israelites who labored under the weight of such a multitude of laws, in contrast to the glorious freedom of new covenant people who have been set free and are called simply to love God and their neighbor as themselves.

However, we must remember that the commandments God gave His people at Sinai covered all areas of life—moral, ceremonial, civil, and health—for a very large nation. Most small towns probably have more than 613 laws on their books today, so God was actually remarkably reserved in giving laws to govern His chosen nation.

Rayburn comments on the nature of law, Hebrew *torah*, in the Old Testament: "It would be a great mistake to view the law as mere regulation; it is divine communication and guidance. The greatest privilege was to be the friend of God and in being his friend there was great reward. In the law was revealed the way to live as God's friend."[4]

Dentan illuminates how *torah* calls up an image

> of an understanding friend or wise parent or, perhaps, a learned priest at a shrine, graciously imparting wisdom, rather than that of a despotic monarch laying down arbitrary rules.... Torah is a relationship word; it calls to mind the image of a particular torahgiver—a teacher—and implies a personal tie between the instructor and the instructed. Whereas disobedience to "law" results in punishment, disregard of torah breaks a relationship. Israel's obedience to the torah was a sacramental sign of her continuing fidelity to a relationship that Yahweh had freely offered and she had freely accepted. Obedience

was not so much an attempt to assure the goodwill of an inflexible and possibly testy ruler as an expression of loyalty to a trustworthy lord, a demonstration of gratitude to a wise and powerful savior who had generously made known the rules by which his people could live in health and peace before him.[5]

## The Covenant Book—Love As the Basis of Law

As pointed out earlier, many scholars generally agree that Deuteronomy was recognized in Israel as the Covenant Book, and that it summarizes the Sinaitic covenant, referred to by many as the old covenant. A master copy of Deuteronomy was kept in the sanctuary. When a new king was enthroned in Israel, he was to make a copy of the Covenant Book for himself, study it regularly, and obey its instruction (Deut. 17:18–20). He was also to convene public gatherings to read the Covenant Book to the people, and to instruct them regarding it through "special agents."[6] Thus, it is highly significant that in Deuteronomy, the Covenant Book, the word "love," referring to God's love for His people or their need to love Him and others, occurs more times than in any other Bible book except Psalms, Hosea, John, and 1 John. This revelation comes as a surprise to many people because of the way the Sinai covenant has been caricatured.

Note how Deuteronomy establishes God's love for His people as the foundation for all genuine religious experience:

> In Deuteronomy, the Covenant Book, the word "love," referring to God's love for His people or their need to love Him and others, occurs more times than in any other Bible book except Psalms, Hosea, John, and 1 John.

- "I, the Lord your God, am a jealous God,…showing love to a thousand generations of those who love me and keep my commandments" (5:10; cf. Exod. 20:6). (The Ten Commandments contain the first explicit biblical reference that God loves people, and more specifically His covenant people.[7])

- "But it was because *the LORD loved you* and kept the oath he swore to your forefathers that he brought you out with a mighty hand and redeemed you from the land of slavery, from the power of Pharaoh king of Egypt. Know therefore that the LORD your God is God; he is the faithful God, keeping *his covenant of love* [NKJV: covenant and mercy] to a thousand generations of those who love him and keep his commands" (7:8–9, italics added).

- "Yet the LORD set his affection on your forefathers and loved them" (10:15, italics added).

- "[God] defends the cause of the fatherless and the widow, and *loves the alien*, giving him food and clothing" (10:18, italics added).

- "However, the LORD your God would not listen to Balaam but turned the curse into a blessing for you, because *the LORD your God loves you*" (23:5, italics added).

- "This is the blessing that Moses the man of God pronounced on the Israelites before his death. He said: 'The LORD came from Sinai and dawned over them from Seir; he shone forth from Mount Paran. He came with myriads of holy ones from the south, from his mountain slopes. Surely *it is you who love the people*; all the holy ones are in your hand. At your feet they all bow down, and from you receive instruction, the law that Moses gave us, the possession of the assembly of Jacob'" (33:1–4, italics added).

## Obedience—the Service and Allegiance of Love

Just as God's love for humanity was not explicitly stated in Scripture until the giving of the law at Sinai, so God's two great commandments to love Him and one another, and the moral commands He specified in the Ten Commandments, were not specifically given until the giving of the law at Sinai (Lev. 19:18; Deut. 6:5; Matt. 25:35–40). This doesn't mean they didn't exist before then, or that believers were unaware of them or failed to practice them before that time, only that they were not formalized in Scripture before the law was given.[8] Thus John could say, "Dear friends, I am not writing you a new command but an old one, which you have had since the beginning. This old command is the message you have heard.…I am not writing you a new command but one we have had from the beginning. I ask that we love one another. And this is love: that we walk in obedience to his commands. As you have heard from the beginning, his command is that you walk in love" (1 John 2:7–8; 2 John 5–6).

The command to love God and one another had been rooted in God's covenants with humanity "from the beginning," including and especially in the law given on Sinai. God's love overwhelmed the Old Testament believer even as it does the New Testament believer. For example, twenty-six times Psalm 36 repeats this frame—"His love [Hebrew, *hesed*; "mercy" NKJV] endures forever"—a phenomenon not found anywhere in the New Testament. God's love motivated the Old Testament believer's obedient response to Him (e.g., 1 Kings 3:3; Ps. 116). "The love of God for his people (Deut. 7:7ff.; Ps. 47:1ff.)…was personal and spiritual love, the love of a husband for a wife (Hos. 1:1ff.) and of a father for a son (Ex. 4:22). The obedience to individual commandments is thus understood not as some dreary duty to be done but as the response of love and loyalty to the God whose love made the covenant possible."[9] While some portray the Old Testament believer's motivation for obedience as "an obligation to numerous specific laws" in contrast to the New Testament motivation "from a *response to the living Christ*,"[10] the Bible does not portray it that way at all.

God's commandments were established on the foundation of God's love for man. Love for God as the basis for keeping His commandments was structured into the Ten Commandments: "showing love [*hesed*, 'mercy,' NKJV] to a thousand generations of those who love me and keep my commandments" (Deut. 5:10; Exod. 20:6). After love for God and obedience to His commandments had been inseparably linked within the Ten Commandments, then ever afterward when God called for people to obey Him and keep His commandments, the meaning always included "love me and keep my commandments." This is not to deny that some of these same passages may not contain more threatening sounding statements either embedded in them or associated with them. But such statements are to be understood as a loving parent warning a child away from at-risk behaviors rather than as a cruel master threatening to punish his slaves for any slight infraction of his whimsical and irrational commands.

Note the following references in Deuteronomy where this principle is not merely implied but made explicit to reinforce love as the underlying, prevailing principle and command of the law:

- "Hear, O Israel: The Lord our God, the Lord is one. *Love the Lord your God with all your heart and with all your soul and with all your strength.* These commandments that I give you today are to be upon your hearts. Impress them on your children. Talk about them when you sit at home and when you walk along the road, when you lie down and when you get up. Tie them as symbols on your hands and bind them on your foreheads. Write them on the doorframes of your houses and on your gates" (6:4–9, italics added). This passage, which the Jews called the *Shema* (the Hebrew word for the first word in the passage—"hear"), were the first words spoken by the devout Jew over a newborn child, and the last to be spoken before death—the first to be spoken every morning and the last to be spoken every night. They were to be ever present in the consciousness and conversation of the faithful throughout the day—"when you sit at home and when you walk along the road, when you lie down and when you get up." Obedience to God's commandments was always to be understood as the natural outgrowth and expression of wholehearted love for

God. When the teacher of the law in Jesus's day commented, "To love [God] with all your heart and with all your strength, and to love your neighbor as yourself is more important than all burnt offerings and sacrifices," Jesus noted "that he had answered wisely." He "got it!" (Mark 12:32–33).

- "Know therefore that the LORD your God is God; he is the faithful God, keeping his covenant of love to a thousand generations of *those who love him and keep his commands*" (7:9, italics added). Note Jesus's equivalent statement to New Testament believers: "Whoever has my commands and obeys them, he is the one who loves me. He who loves me will be loved by my Father, and I too will love him and show myself to him" (John 14:21).

> When God called for people to obey Him and keep His commandments, the meaning always included "love me and keep my commandments."

- "And now, O Israel, what does the LORD your God ask of you but to fear the LORD your God, to walk in all his ways, *to love him, to serve the LORD your God with all your heart and with all your soul, and to observe the LORD's commands and decrees* that I am giving you today for your own good? To the LORD your God belong the heavens, even the highest heavens, the earth and everything in it. Yet the LORD set his affection on your forefathers and loved them, and he chose you, their descendants, above all the nations, as it is today. Circumcise your hearts, therefore, and do not be stiff-necked any longer. For the LORD your God is God of gods and Lord of lords, the great God, mighty and awesome, who shows no partiality and accepts no bribes. He defends the cause of the fatherless and the widow, and loves the alien, giving him food and clothing. And you are to love those who are aliens, for you yourselves were aliens in Egypt" (10:12–22, italics added). This command that calls God's covenant people to love the less fortunate and aliens even as God had loved them is the Old Testament equivalent of Jesus's New Testament command, "As I have loved you, so you must love one another" (John 13:34).

- "*Love the* LORD *your God and keep his requirements, his laws and his commands* always....So if you faithfully obey the commands I am giving you today to *love the* LORD *your God and to serve him with all your heart and with all your soul*—then I will send rain on your land in its season....If you carefully observe all these commands I am giving you to follow—to *love the* LORD *your God, to walk in his ways and to hold fast to him*—then the LORD will drive out all these nations before you, and you will dispossess nations larger and stronger than you" (11:1, 13–14, 22–24, italics added). The blessings God promised, conditional upon the love and obedience of His covenant people, were no more to be understood and applied legalistically by recipients of God's Sinai covenant than was Jesus's equivalent statement to New Testament believers in John 14:21 (quoted above).

- "The LORD your God is testing you to find out whether you *love him with all your heart and with all your soul*. It is the LORD your God you must follow, and him you must revere. Keep his commands and obey him; serve him and hold fast to him" (13:3–4, italics added).

- "If the LORD your God enlarges your territory, as he promised on oath to your forefathers, and gives you the whole land he promised them, because you *carefully follow all these laws I command you today—to love the* LORD *your God and to walk always in his ways*— then you are to set aside three more cities" (19:8–9, italics added).

- "*The* LORD *your God will circumcise your hearts* and the hearts of your descendants, *so that you may love him with all your heart and with all your soul, and live*" (30:6, italics added). This empowering promise for obedience is one of several historical old covenant promises[11] equivalent to historical new covenant promises, such as, "for it is God who works in you to will and to act according to his good purpose" (Phil. 2:13).

- "For I command you today to *love the LORD your God, to walk in his ways, and to keep his commands, decrees and laws*" (30:16, italics added).
- "This day I call heaven and earth as witnesses against you that I have set before you life and death, blessings and curses. Now choose life, so that you and your children may live and that you may *love the LORD your God, listen to his voice, and hold fast to him*. For the LORD is your life" (30:19–20, italics added).

Clearly any effort to portray the old covenant as weak on love or to portray the New Testament emphasis on love as something unique to the new covenant fails to accurately depict the great emphasis God placed on love in the covenant He made with His people at Sinai. Indeed, when Paul wrote to the believers at Rome, "The commandments, 'do not commit adultery,' 'do not murder,' 'do not steal,' 'do not covet,' and whatever other commandment there may be, are summed up in this one rule: 'Love your neighbor as yourself'" (Rom. 13:9), he was as surely expressing the sentiment of the Sinai law as he was the sentiment of the new covenant. The whole Bible, including if not especially God's Sinai covenant, acknowledges implicitly and explicitly that "love is the fulfillment of the law" (Rom. 13:10).

> The prophets appeal to the Sinai Covenant with emotional overtones drawn from human experiences to explain the relationship between God and His people. Israel is the flock, and the Lord is the shepherd. Israel is the vine, and the Lord the vinedresser. Israel is the son, and the Lord is the Father. Israel is the spouse, and the Lord is the bridegroom. These images, as Pierre Grelot and Jean Giblet[12] bring out, "make the Sinaitic covenant appear as an encounter of love (cf. Ez

16:6–14): the attentive and gratuitous love of God, calling in return for a love which will translate itself in obedience."[13]

The obedience of the Old Testament believer was inspired by love, motivated by love, rendered in love. Such is the nature of new covenant experience.

## New Testament Commands

Some suggest that the many commandments of the law (most of which were ceremonial stipulations relative to the priests' duties) was "a yoke of slavery" for those to whom God gave them, and that the sheer number of commandments itself engendered bondage for those under the Sinaitic covenant. Attempts have been made to characterize the new covenant as different from the old in that allegedly "the new covenant has general principles rather than detailed laws," "general principles rather than specific details," and "a different emphasis (grace [done] rather than law [do])"[14] (parentheses and brackets used by the original author). To this can be added the additional claim that "*the role the law filled in the old covenant is filled by the Holy Spirit in the new*" (author's own emphasis).[15] But these characterizations are both misinformed and misleading. The same is true for attempts to characterize the historical old covenant as a time when "sinners [are] punished" in contrast to the historical new covenant when "Christ suffered on our behalf."[16]

What is not taken into account by such statements is the sheer quantity and force of New Testament commands. New Testament commands are divine laws in the same tradition and with the same weight as those given on Sinai.[17] A reading of the New Testament looking for the commandments it contains will find over nine hundred direct commands and three hundred indirect commands.[18] Three points became clear to me from such a study. First, the long list of New Testament commandments makes unmistakably clear that no one in a position of spiritual authority in the New Testament—not Jesus, not

Paul, not Peter, not James, nor any New Testament author—trusted "love" as a safe single command, or trusted the Holy Spirit's internal guidance as a safe replacement for all law and very specific divine commandments. The New Testament authors recognized that, on its own, the command to love is not adequate for sinful people, even for those who are being sanctified and in whom the Holy Spirit dwells. The second relevant point is that it is not the mere number of commands that inclines people toward legalism but an attitude toward those commands. Even one command, including the great commandment itself (Matt. 22:37–38) or the new commandment to love others as Jesus loved us (John 13:34) or even the commandment to believe in Jesus (1 John 3:23), is enough to engender both disobedience and legalism in a heart inclined in that direction by the unconverted sinful nature. The third observation is that to new covenant believers, regardless of the historical age in which they might live, the numerous commands of God represent a treasure chest of divine promises to be claimed by faith. For God's commandments are His promises to His covenant people of what He will accomplish in their lives as they rely on Him in faith (Deut. 30:6, 11–14; Ezek. 36:26–27; Phil. 2:13; 1 John 5:14 15).

Far from simply being general principles or advice, most of the New Testament commands are direct and very specific, and those who gave them fully intended that they be kept. There would be serious consequences if they were not. For example, Paul commanded the Ephesians: "But among you there must not be even a hint of sexual immorality, or of any kind of impurity, or of greed, because these are improper for God's holy people. Nor should there be obscenity, foolish talk or coarse joking, which are out of place, but rather thanksgiving. For of this you can be sure: No immoral, impure or greedy person—such a man is an idolater—has any inheritance in the kingdom of Christ and of God" (Eph. 5:3–5).

In this text Paul says that people should not consider themselves finally saved (in the sense of having "any inheritance in the kingdom of

Christ and of God") as long as they continue unrepentantly in "even a hint of sexual immorality" (which Jesus extended even to lusting after someone—Matt. 5:28). Paul even includes "foolish talk or coarse joking" in this list of actions that will exclude someone from "any inheritance in the kingdom of Christ and of God."[19] Such an expression is without parallel in the Old Testament.

An example of an indirect command would be Jesus's statements in the Sermon on the Mount: "I tell you that anyone who is angry with his brother will be subject to judgment," and, "if you do not forgive men their sins, your Father will not forgive your sins" (Matt. 5:22; 6:15). These are not direct commandments against being angry or unforgiving, but the intent is clearly to warn us away from anger and an unforgiving attitude. The consequences of failing to heed this counsel are incredibly serious.

> The New Testament authors recognized that, on its own, the command to love is not adequate for sinful people, even for those who are being sanctified and in whom the Holy Spirit dwells.

Regarding the many New Testament commandments, McComiskey concludes, "The importance of obedience must be recognized. The teaching of Jesus is filled with commandments that he expected his followers to obey."[20] McComiskey goes on to warn against treating the NT commands lightly or failing to understand "the believer's obligation to obey them."[21]

To be sure, there is considerable duplication in the 1,200 direct and indirect New Testament commands. Paul often reiterated commands of Jesus and often repeated his own commands when he wrote to the various churches. In Scripture God had no way of raising His voice, or of using bold or italicized fonts, to emphasize a point. For emphasis God employed the tool of repetition. The four gospels which tell Jesus's story four times, with considerable repetition, were God's way of saying, Listen up, this story is **THE** story on which everything else in this book is dependent and around which all other stories orbit. Similarly, under the Holy Spirit's inspiration and direction, the frequent repetition of commandments in the New Testament was God's way of underscoring their importance.

Table 4 on pages 301–303 in appendix D lists New Testament commands which cover vast areas of Christian living and experience. There are so many laws given in the New Testament that at one point Paul came close to apologizing, in a humorous sort of way, that he had given so many commands. After giving a list of sixteen "acts of the sinful nature" that, if habitually committed, will not allow people to "inherit the kingdom of God," he gave a beautiful list of positive qualities that are the "fruit of the Spirit" (love, joy, peace, etc.), and then added, tongue in cheek no doubt, that, by the way, with respect to these positive qualities, "against such things there is no law" (Gal. 5:19–23).

## Meant to Be Taken Seriously

Lest anyone conclude that God did not intend for His commands to be obeyed, He says, "Do not merely listen to the word and deceive yourselves. Do what it says" (James 1:22). "Anyone, then, who knows the good he ought to do and doesn't do it, sins" (James 4:17). "For whoever keeps the whole law and yet stumbles at just one point is guilty of breaking all of it. For he who said, 'Do not commit adultery,' also said, 'Do not murder.' If you do not commit adultery but do commit murder, you have become a lawbreaker" (James 2:10–11; quoting specifically from the Ten Commandments—Exod. 20:13–14; Deut. 5:18).

Though an attempt has been made to portray the old covenant as a time when God "punished sinners" in contrast to the new covenant when "Christ suffered on our behalf,"[22] note some of the consequences described in the New Testament for those who unrepentantly continue to disobey God's commandments:

- "Anyone who breaks one of the least of these commandments and teaches others to do the same will be called least in the kingdom of heaven" (Matt. 5:19).
- "Anyone who does wrong will be repaid for his wrong, and there is no favoritism" (Col. 3:25).
- "There will be trouble and distress for every human being who does evil" (Rom. 2:9).
- "Do you not know that the wicked will not inherit the kingdom of God?" (1 Cor. 6:9).
- "But among you there must not be even a hint of sexual immorality, or of any kind of impurity, or of greed…for of this you can be sure: No immoral, impure or greedy person—such a man is an idolater—has any inheritance in the kingdom of Christ and of God….God's wrath comes on those who are disobedient" (Eph. 5:3, 5–6). This admonition was/is specifically directed to those whom Paul assured had been saved by grace, raised up with Christ and seated with Him in the heavenly realms! (Eph. 2:4–9).
- "The face of the Lord is against those who do evil" (1 Pet. 3:10–12; Ps. 34:12–16).
- By failing to repent, "you are storing up wrath for yourself for the day of God's wrath, when his righteous judgment will be revealed" (Rom. 2:5).
- "Or you will be condemned" (James 5:12).
- "Unless you repent, you too will all perish!" (Luke 13:5).
- "It would be better for him to have a large millstone hung around his neck and to be drowned in the depths of the sea" (Matt. 18:6).
- "Repent therefore! Otherwise, I will soon come to you and will fight against them with the sword of my mouth" (Rev. 2:16).
- "So I will cast her on a bed of suffering, and I will make those who commit adultery with her suffer intensely, unless they repent of their ways. I will strike her children dead. Then all the churches will know that I am he who searches hearts and minds, and I will

repay each of you according to your deeds" (Rev. 2:22–23).

- "I watched as the Lamb opened the first of the seven seals. Then I heard one of the four living creatures say in a voice like thunder, 'Come!' I looked and there before me was a white horse! Its rider held a bow, and he was given a crown, and he rode out as a conqueror bent on conquest. When the Lamb opened the second seal, I heard the second living creature say, 'Come!' Then another horse came out, a fiery red one. Its rider was given power to take peace from the earth and to make men slay each other. To him was given a large sword. When the Lamb opened the third seal, I heard the third living creature say, 'Come!' I looked, and there before me was a black horse! Its rider was holding a pair of scales in his hand. Then I heard what sounded like a voice among the four living creatures, saying, 'A quart of wheat for a day's wages, and three quarts of barley for a day's wages, and do not damage the oil and the wine!' When the Lamb opened the fourth seal, I heard the voice of the fourth living creature say, 'Come!' I looked, and there before me was a pale horse! Its rider was named Death, and Hades was following close behind him. They were given power over a fourth of the earth to kill by sword, famine and plague, and by the wild beasts of the earth" (Rev. 6:1–8). Jon Paulien and Ranko Stefanovic observe that "the language of Revelation 6:1–8 parallels 'the covenant curses in the Pentateuch and their execution in the context of Bablylonian exile.'"[23] In other words, the same redemptive curses that were designed to lead Israel to repentance for breaking the Sinai covenant are applicable to the church of the New Testament era. God's plan and way of working with His covenant people is essentially the same in every historical era.
- "If we deliberately keep on sinning, after we have received the knowledge of the truth, no sacrifice for sins is left, but only a fearful expectation of judgment and of raging fire that will consume the enemies of God. Anyone who rejected the law of

Moses died without mercy on the testimony of two or three witnesses. How much more severely do you think a man deserves to be punished who has trampled the Son of God under foot, who has treated as an unholy thing the blood of the covenant that sanctified him, and who has insulted the Spirit of grace? For we know him who said, 'It is mine to avenge; I will repay,' and again, 'The Lord will judge his people.' It is a dreadful thing to fall into the hands of the living God" (Heb. 10:26–31).

- "Throw them into the fiery furnace where there will be weeping and gnashing of teeth" (Matt. 13:50).
- "This is the second death" (Rev. 21:9).
- "For our 'God is a consuming fire'" (Heb. 10:29; quoting Deut. 4:24).

Rayburn makes a sobering observation often overlooked in studies on the covenants: "The threats and warnings regarding the punishment of apostates are just as harsh now as in the Old Testament days.... Hebrews 2:2, 3; 10:28ff., 12:25 all emphasize the impossibility of escaping punishment for apostates, now as then. Apostasy in Old and New Testaments receives the same penalty—exclusion from the rest of God,...No less now than then, 'It is a terrifying thing to fall into the hands of the living God' (Heb. 10:31)."[24]

It should also be reiterated, however, that the covenant warnings of punishment in the New Testament bear the same saving intent as did the Old Testament covenant curses. "The covenant curses were, in the initial phase, preliminary judgments from God on his people. They were intended to

> The covenant warnings of punishment in the New Testament bear the same saving intent as did the Old Testament covenant curses.

wake them from their apostate condition, lead them to repentance, and move them toward a positive relationship with God."[25]

## Moral Bar Raised to the Heavens

God's covenants in general have progressively called His covenant people to ever deeper experiences of holiness. Each successive covenant incorporates the moral/ethical/spiritual commands of the previous covenant(s) and raises them to a higher level, always with love as the underlying principle. In the New Testament God actually raised the moral/spiritual bar so high that His people would immediately realize that it would be impossible to stand before Him faultless.

If one of God's purposes in giving the Old Testament law was "so that the trespass might increase" (Rom. 5:20) in the sense "that sin might be recognized as sin" (Rom. 7:13) and "we [might] become conscious of sin" (Rom. 3:20) in order "to lead us to Christ that we might be justified by faith" (Gal. 3:24), how much more should the New Testament commandments serve that same purpose. They were to be used by the Spirit to awaken us to the magnitude of our sin and to lead us to look to Jesus alone for our righteousness. When we come to Christ, the Spirit writes these laws in our hearts and minds.

I have heard people claim that they no longer need any such commandments framed as "Do this…Don't do that," for Jesus Himself is their commandment. That sounds very spiritual. But Jesus instructed His new covenant believers "to obey everything I have commanded you" (Matt. 28:20). He warned, "Not everyone who says to me, 'Lord, Lord,' will enter the kingdom of heaven, but only he who does the will of my Father who is in heaven," and "that servant who knows his master's will and does not get ready or does not do what his master wants will be beaten with many blows" (Matt. 7:21; Luke 12:47).

When people say, "I don't need any other commandment than Jesus," they need to be sure they are not simply seeking a Christian ethic which they can bend this way or that, depending on how they feel at the moment. There is no biblical justification for ignoring the teachings of Jesus and the rest of the New Testament and replacing them with the slogan, "Jesus is my commandment." Moreover, anyone who says "Jesus is my commandment" ought to seriously consider the implications. For He "was without sin" (Heb. 4:15). The moral/spiritual standard set in Jesus embodied all the righteousness commanded in both Old and New Testaments. Jesus's example ought to bring us to our knees in humility and repentance for how far we have fallen from the glory of God.

## A Righteousness Revealed Apart from Law

There is, of course, one sense in which it can be said that Jesus is our commandment, our law. Paul testified, "But now a righteousness apart from law, has been made known, to which the Law and the Prophets testify" (Rom. 3:21). This has both historical and experiential applications. In Jesus, "the LORD Our Righteousness" actually came among us as the Son of Man in history, fulfilling the promise made in Jeremiah 23:5–6. In Him "the radiance of God's glory and the exact representation of His being" (Heb. 1:1–3; cf. John 14:7–9), who from everlasting was Himself the embodiment of the covenant, came among us "in righteousness...a covenant for the people" (Isa. 42:6; Mic. 5:3). In Him we saw the righteousness of God revealed in a manner that could not be surpassed. In Him the moral law of God was fulfilled, embodied, magnified (Matt. 5:17–20). Thus in Jesus, from a historical perspective, "a righteousness from God, apart from law, has been made known."

This is also true from an experiential perspective. For if the law increased people's awareness of their sin and drew them to God for His forgiving and cleansing grace, then the revelation of righteousness in Jesus would do so to an even greater degree. The closer we draw to Jesus, the more we see our own sinfulness—not in a condemning way, but in a redeeming way.

When Paul lived by the letter of the law, he believed that "as for legalistic righteousness, [he was] faultless" (Phil. 3:6). But once he came to Jesus, the veil was taken away, and he saw himself as the worst of sinners, yet fully accepted by God (1 Tim. 1:15–16). Paul was "found in him [Christ], not having a righteousness of my own that comes from the law, but that which is through faith in Christ—the righteousness that comes from God and is by faith" (Phil. 3:9). And as Paul's relationship with Jesus deepened, God continued writing His law in Paul's heart. This led to an experience of "obedience that comes from faith." And Paul answered God's call to "call people from among all the Gentiles to the obedience that comes from faith" (Rom. 1:5). This is the new covenant experience. Through the ministry of the Spirit, the revelation of God's law and perfect righteousness in Jesus is meant to lead Christians to a life of Spirit-enabled obedience that calls others to the same.

In the old covenant historical period, the Holy Spirit operated through the law itself to bring conviction of sin—not simply conviction of the sinfulness of our immorality but also the conviction that "all our righteous acts are like filthy rags" (Isa. 64:6). The law and the prophets present the utter hopelessness that anyone can do any good whatever, or to have any righteousness whatever, apart from the forgiving, converting, transforming grace of God.[26] Once the sense of sin was aroused, the Spirit operated through animal sacrifices and the Levitical priesthood to point to the provision God had made for their forgiveness and to direct them to trust in "the LORD our Righteousness" as the basis for their own righteousness and acceptance before God (Jer. 23:6; cf. Ezra 9:15; Zech. 3:1–7). Through that continual and deepening experience with God, God continued to write His law in their hearts that they might delight to do His will in their inward being—which is precisely the new covenant experience (Deut. 6:5; 30:6; Ps. 40:8; Isa. 51:7).

## New Covenant Freedom vs. the Yoke that Neither We nor Our Fathers Could Bear

What about the "freedom" proclaimed in the new covenant (Gal. 4:24–5:1)? Is not new covenant freedom a release from at least some of the moral laws God gave at Sinai, as some would have us think?

Hardly so, as the even higher standard set by the New Testament commands makes clear. It was, rather, deliverance by the Holy Spirit from slavery to sin and empowerment by that same Spirit for obedience unto righteousness. Paul eloquently makes this case in Romans 6: "When you were slaves to sin, you were free from the control of righteousness." "Don't you know that…you are slaves to the one whom you obey—whether you are slaves to sin, which leads to death, or to obedience, which leads to righteousness? But thanks be to God, that though you used to be slaves to sin,…you have been set free from sin and have become slaves to righteousness…slaves to God" (Rom. 6:20, 16–18, 22).

Not the commandment itself but one's own experience determines whether the law of God engenders slavery or freedom. Those with an old covenant experience will convert any law, even the great commandment itself, into a legalistic code that binds them in slavery. Conversely, those with a new covenant experience view God's law as a tool in the hands of the Spirit to set them free. Thus the psalmist could write: "I will always obey your law, for ever and ever. I will walk about in freedom, for I have sought out your precepts" (Ps. 119:44–45). And James could refer to the Ten Commandments as "the law that gives freedom" (James 2:10–12). Jan Lochman calls the Ten Commandments a "charter of freedom" and the "Ten Great Freedoms."[27] "For where the Spirit of the Lord is, there is freedom" (2 Cor. 3:17).

> Those with an old covenant experience will convert any law, even the great commandment itself, into a legalistic code that binds them in slavery.

## The Unbearable Yoke

But didn't Peter have in mind the Sinai covenant when he questioned those who were "putting on the necks of the disciples a yoke that neither we nor our fathers have been able to bear" (Acts 15:10)? After the deliberations by the delegates at that Jerusalem council, James announced the consensus that there would be only four commandments initially required of Gentile Christians: "Abstain from food polluted by idols, from sexual immorality, from the meat of strangled animals and from blood" (Acts 15:20). Were the representatives at that council content then to allow Gentiles to murder, steal, and lie? No. But they knew that in time the Gentiles would become educated in those matters, "for Moses…is read in the synagogues on every Sabbath" (Acts 15:21). In other words, as they worshiped each Sabbath, they would get further instruction from the Scriptures.

The "yoke that neither we nor our fathers have been able to bear" could refer to the ceremonial law, represented by circumcision, the primary issue that required the convening of the council in the first place (Acts 15:1). It could also be "the tradition of the elders" (Matt. 15:2) which involved "meticulous rules and regulations governing the daily life of the people" added by Jewish rabbis as "interpretations and applications of the law of Moses,"[28] and which Jesus described as "heavy loads" that had been placed "on men's shoulders" (Matt. 23:4; Luke 11:46). For example, the rabbis had added over 1,500 laws of their own to God's Sabbath commandment in the Decalogue. It could also refer to the legalistic spirit that permeated the ranks of Judaism in their day (Rom. 9:30–32; Gal. 4:10, 21). Peter's very next statement makes it seem likely that he was referring to this third option: "We believe it is through the grace of our Lord Jesus that we are saved, just as they [Gentiles] are" (Acts 15:10–11). Legalism is indeed a yoke that none of us can bear. But we all are vulnerable to it unless we are born of the Spirit and kept by the Spirit.

It seems clear that the "yoke that neither we nor our fathers have been able to bear" is not a reference to the Sinai covenant. God described the entire process of delivering Israel from Egyptian bondage and entering into covenant with them as a process through which "I led them with cords of human kindness, with ties of love; I lifted the yoke from their neck and bent down to feed them" (Hos. 11:4). God's covenant with Israel, rather than placing on them an unbearable yoke, actually *"lifted the yoke"* from their necks. God did not deliver them from the yoke of Egyptian slavery only to impose on them an even more damning yoke of moral and ethical bondage.

Referring to the tendency of many commentators to portray Old Testament religion as tending to bondage, R. L. Dabney writes: "I am persuaded that the strong representations which these writers…give of the bondage, terror, literalness, and intolerable weight of the institutions under which Old Testament saints lived, will strike the attentive reader as incorrect. The experience, as recorded of those saints does not answer to this theory; but shows them in the enjoyment of a dispensation free, spiritual, gracious, consoling."[29]

It is not the number of commandments involved, nor the nature of those commandments, nor whether they were issued in the Old Testament or the New, that determines whether they engender slavery or freedom. Even one divine commandment can be bondage for "the sinful mind" that is by nature "hostile to God. It cannot submit to God's law, nor can it do so" (Rom. 8:7). But the heart that has been renewed by the Holy Spirit finds those same laws to be a yoke that is easy—Christ's own yoke, which He offers to us by grace through faith. "Come to me, all you who are weary and burdened, and I will give you rest. Take my yoke upon you and learn from me, for I am gentle and humble in heart, and you will find rest for your souls. For my yoke is easy and my burden is light" (Matt. 11:28).

The yoke of Christ is easy because He died for our sins and grants/imputes to us the righteousness of His sinless life—the very righteousness we need as our "passport" to eternal life—as a gift which we can receive by faith (1 Cor. 15:3; Rom. 5:10; Eph. 2:8–9). It is also easy because it represents His laws that are an expression of His love for us and which He has promised to write in our hearts.

"Is it hard to do the things with which Jesus illustrates the kingdom heart of love? Or the things that Paul says love does? It is very hard indeed if you have not been substantially transformed in the depths of your being, in the intricacies of your thoughts, feelings, assurances, and dispositions, in such a way that you are permeated with love. Once that happens, then it is not hard. What would be hard is to act the way you acted before."[30] This applies to every believer from the time of Adam's fall to the second coming of Jesus. The true believers listed in Hebrews 11, as well as other faith-filled believers in the Old Testament era, did not bear "the yoke that neither we nor our fathers have been able to bear," but Christ's yoke that is easy and light. By faith they experienced the everlasting gospel through the operation of the Holy Spirit.

All who wear the yoke of Christ perceive His commands as liberating promises rather than burdensome demands. God's new covenant promise to write His laws in our hearts is timeless and universal.[31] Only one with such a perception could declare, "Oh, how I love your law! I meditate on it all day long" (Ps. 119:97; cf. vs. 113, 127, 163). Only one with such a perception could declare, "For in my inner being I delight in God's law" (Rom. 7:22; cf. Ps. 119:47, 70, 77, 92, 143, 174). For these writers, God's law represents a work the Spirit is doing in their lives, preparing them as His ambassadors through whom God's "ways may be known on earth" and His "salvation among all nations" as they "see your good deeds and praise your Father in heaven" (Ps. 67:2; Matt. 5:16).

## Summary

Some have depicted the Old Testament as a book of law in contrast to the New Testament book of love. A careful study of the Old and New Testaments reveals that the emphasis on love exists in both. The New Testament actually contains more direct commandments than did "the law" God gave to His people at Sinai, and these New Testament laws mention equally severe eternal consequences for disobedience. Legalism cannot be correlated with the number of commandments involved. A single commandment, even the commandment to love, is enough to engender legalism in a heart controlled by the sinful nature. Obedience that comes from a heart subdued by a sense of its own sinfulness and overwhelmed by the grace and forgiveness of God is not mere obedience to a commandment. It is a service of love, rendered eagerly to the object of that love.

## Notes

1. E.g., "Instead of the many detailed laws [in the old covenant] the new covenant gives a few basic principles falling under the one chief moral commandment of 'you shall love one another as I have loved you.' [John 13:34] Therefore Paul could say, 'For he who loves his neighbor has fulfilled the law. For this, "You shall not commit adultery, You shall not murder, You shall not steal, You shall not covet," and if there is any other commandment, it is summed up in the saying, "You shall love your neighbor as yourself." Love does no wrong to a neighbor; love therefore is the fulfillment of the law' (Rom. 13:8–10)." Ratzlaff, 208.

2. Ibid., 178.

3. Paulien, *Meet God Again for the First Time*, 79–88, points out that law provides structure and security in a society.

4. Rayburn, "The Contrast Between the Old and New Covenants," 47.

5. R. C. Dentan, *The Knowledge of God in Ancient Israel* (New York: Seabury Press, 1968), 50.

6. Stefanovic, *Revelation of Jesus Christ*, 167–172.

7. Prior to the giving of the Ten Commandments, the term "love" occurs only five times in the Bible, and always in reference to things or people, not God: 1) Jacob asked Esau for the meat he loved (Gen. 27:4, 9 NIV "liked," but it's the Hebrew word for love, *'ahab*); 2) Jacob's seven-year labor for Rachel seemed like a few days, so strong was his love for her (Gen. 29:20); 3) when Leah bore Jacob's son, she hoped she had thereby gained Jacob's love for her (Gen. 29:32); 4) God asked Abraham to sacrifice the son he loved (Gen. 22:2); (5) Joseph's brothers testify to their father's love for Benjamin (Gen. 44:20).

8. E.g., Just before Cain killed his brother Abel, a violation of what was later to be specified as the sixth commandment (Exodus 20), God said to him, "Sin is crouching at your door; it desires to have you, but you must master it" (Gen. 4:7). God later said of Abraham: "Abraham will surely become a great and powerful nation, and all nations on earth will be blessed through him. For I have chosen him, so that he will direct his children and his household after him to keep the way of the LORD by doing what is right and just, so that the LORD will bring about for Abraham what he has promised him....I will make your [Isaac's] descendants as numerous as the stars in the sky and will give them all these lands, and through your offspring all nations on earth will be blessed, because Abraham obeyed me and kept my requirements, my commands, my decrees and my laws" (Gen. 18:18–19; 26:4–5). When a seductive women invited Joseph to commit adultery with her, a violation of what God would later specify as the seventh commandment (Exodus 20), Joseph replied, "How then could I so such a wicked thing and sin against God?" (Gen. 39:9).

9. Rayburn, "The Contrast Between the Old and New Covenants," 49. Cf. M. Weinfeld, "Berith," in G. Johannes Botterweck & Helmer Ringgren, *Theological Dictionary of the Old Testament*, vol. II, trans. John T. Willis (Grand Rapids, MI: Eerdmans Publishing Company, 1975), 278: "The prophets, especially Hosea, Jeremiah, and Ezekiel, expressed the idea of exclusive loyalty by describing the relationship between God and Israel as one between a husband and wife, which itself is also considered covenantal. Although the idea of marital love between God and Israel is not explicitly mentioned in the Pentateuch, it seems to exist there in a latent form. Following other gods is warned against with the statement, 'For I the Lord your God am a jealous God' (Ex. 20:5; Dt. 5:9; cf. Ex. 34:14; Josh. 24:19). The root *qānā'*, 'to be jealous,' is, in fact, used in Nu. 5:14 in the technical sense of a husband who is jealous over his wife. Similarly, the verb used in the Pentateuch for disloyalty is *zānā*, 'to play the harlot, to whore' ('*achre*, 'after'). Furthermore, the formula expressing the covenantal relationship between God and Israel, 'I will be your God, and you shall be my people' (Lev. 26:12; Dt. 29:12[13]; etc.), is a legal formula taken from the sphere of marriage, as attested in various legal documents from the ancient Near East (cf. Hos. 2:4[2])."

10. Ratzlaff, 76.

11. Note the prayer of dependence Solomon prayed in the hearing of God's covenant people on the occasion of the dedication of Solomon's temple: "Praise be to the LORD, who has given rest to his people Israel just as he promised. Not one word has failed of all the good promises he gave through his servant Moses. May the LORD our God be with us as he was with our fathers; may he never leave us or forsake us [abiding in God]. May he turn our hearts to him, to walk in all his ways and to keep the commands, decrees and regulations he gave our fathers" (1 Kings 8:56–58). Compare the similar prayer of David in 1 Chronicles 29:18. Note also the language of Psalm 119:32–40, a historical old covenant psalm expressing a new covenant experience toward God and His law.

12. Pierre Grelot and Jean Giblet, "Covenant," *Dictionary of Biblical Theology*, ed. Xavier Leon-Dufour (New York: Desclée Co., 1970), 95.

13. Samuele Bacchiocchi, *The Sabbath Under Crossfire: A Biblical Analysis of Recent Sabbath/Sunday Developments* (Berrien Springs, MI: Biblical Perspectives, 1998), 108.

14. Ratzlaff, 189, 259.

15. Ibid., 184.

16. Ibid., 189.

17. Rayburn, "The Contrast Between the Old and New Covenants," 95: "If a commandment is given to Christians as something which must be obeyed, the commandment is a law and the obligation thus laid upon Christians is a legal one....Besides the command to love, Paul in several places catalogues activities or forms of behavior which are acceptable and activities and behavior which are unacceptable to God (Gal. 5:19ff.; 1 Cor. 6:9ff.; 1 Tim. 1:9ff.). This is law in the well known Old Testament sense. It is obvious that the principles of the Torah, especially of the decalogue, underlie these lists."

18. In addition, the New Testament commands all followers of Jesus to obey the civil laws of the government of the nations they live in as though they were the laws of God, making special mention of taxes (which in the United States includes thousands of specific tax regulations enforced by the Internal Revenue Service), which would add many thousands of divinely approved commandments to those already specified in the New Testament (Rom. 13:1–7).

19. This is not to suggest that Paul taught perfectionism, or that he in any way compromised the gospel of salvation by grace through faith which he, along with the prophets of the Old Testament, taught consistently. It does, however, reveal the sacred seriousness and radicalness with which he held and applied the law of God to the life of the believer, even as Jesus did in the Sermon on the Mount.

20. McComiskey, *The Covenants of Promise*, 228.

21. Ibid.; cf., Dallas Willard understands Jesus's direct and indirect commands in the Sermon on the Mount not as laws but as illustrations "to bring us to terms with what is in our hearts and, simultaneously, to show us the rightness of the kingdom heart." Jesus did, however, present them as commands, and Willard agrees that Jesus expected His hearers to do what He taught them to do. "Jesus gives us urgent warnings about failing to actually *do* what he calls us to do in his teachings and mentions the specific things that are most likely to trip us up in this regard. Dietrich Bonhoeffer forcefully states, 'The only proper response to this word which Jesus brings with him from eternity is simply to do it....The sermon on the mount is there for the purpose of being done (Matt 7:34ff.).' (Dietrich Bonhoeffer, from *The Cost of Discipleship*, as quoted in *Disciplines for the Inner Life*, by Bob Benson and Michael W. Benson [Nashville: Generoux/Nelson, 1989]), p. 227; and Bonhoeffer's *Ethics*, translated by Neville Horton Smith [New York: Macmillan Collier Books, 1986], p. 43). Remarkably, almost one sixth of the entire Discourse (fifteen of ninety-two verses) is devoted to emphasizing the importance of actually doing what it says" (Willard, *The Divine Conspiracy*, 157, 137).

22. Ratzlaff, 189.

23. Stefanovic, *Revelation of Jesus Christ*, 215–219: "The covenant curses [Leviticus 26; Deuteronomy 28], then, can be explained in the following way: when Israel became unfaithful to the covenant, God would remove his protective power, and the enemy nations would come and afflict the people of Israel as a result. They would bring the sword against them. Wild beasts would rob them of their children and destroy their livestock. Pestilence and famine would complete the desolation of the land. If God's people persisted in their sins, the final consequence would take place: exile from the promised land....Revelation 6 follows the covenant-curses pattern." Cf. Jon Paulien. "The Seven Seals," in *Symposium on Revelation—Book 1*, 223ff. (*Daniel and Revelation Committee Series 6* [Silver Spring, MD: Biblical Research Institute, 1992]).

24. Rayburn, "The Contrast Between the Old and New Covenants," 190–191.

25. Stefanovic, *Revelation of Jesus Christ*, 216.

26. Gen. 8:21; Deut. 9:4–6; Josh. 24:19; 1 Kings 8:46; Ps. 5:9; 10:7; 14:1–3; 36:1; 51:4–5; 53:1–3; 58:3; 59:7–8; Eccl. 7:20. Many of these same texts were quoted by Paul in Romans 3:9–20 as proof that "Jews and Gentiles alike are all under sin" and "under the law, so that every mouth may be silenced and the whole world held accountable to God. Therefore no one will be declared righteous in his sight by observing the law; rather, through the law we become conscious of sin" (3:9, 19–20). This was the message of the old covenant law and prophets. Statements such as "Keep my decrees and laws, for the man who obeys them will live by them" (Lev. 18:5) and "if we are careful to obey all this law before the LORD our God, as he has commanded us, that will be our righteousness" (Deut. 6:25) were no more inclined to bend people toward legalism under the old covenant than statements such as "He who does what is right is righteous" (1 John 3:7) were inclined to do so under the new covenant. It was Rabbinic misinterpretation of such Scriptures, coupled with the legalistic bent of the sinful nature which seizes the opportunity afforded by the good commandment of God and uses it to deceive and

kill, which led Israel to pursue righteousness "not by faith but as if it were by works" (Rom. 7:10–12; 9:31–32).

27. Jan Milič Lochman, *Signposts to Freedom: The Ten Commandmetns and Christian Ethics*, trans. David Lewis (Minneapolis: Augsburg Publishing House, 1982), 19: "The real purpose and goal of this [Sinai] covenant event, and of the Decalogue, too, therefore, also follows clearly from its anchorage in history. This covenant event is the Exodus, i.e., the *history of liberation* of the people of God, that all-important sequence of events on which this people's very existence rested. The divine covenant with Israel established Israel's freedom and set the seal on it. The celebration of the renewal of this covenant was a constantly renewed festival of freedom, the renewal of this freedom. Within this quite specific context Israel was given the Ten Commandments through Moses. The purpose of 'teaching' the Decalogue to the people of the Old Covenant and the New, every seven years at the festival of the renewal of the covenant [cf. Deut. 31:10f.] but also in ordinary daily life, was to maintain and exercise this God-given freedom. This document of the covenant, essentially, is a *charter of freedom*. The Ten Commandments are the 'Ten Great Freedoms.' Only within this decisive setting of the history of Israel's deliverance can their original significance be understood. They have very little to do with legalism and moralism and a great deal to do with the struggle to understand 'the freedom of a Christian.'"

28. *NIV Study Bible* (1427), note on "tradition of the elders" in Matthew 15:2.

29. R. L. Dabney, *Lectures in Systematic Theology* (Grand Rapids, MI: Zondervan, 1972), 457ff.

30. Willard, *The Divine Conspiracy*, 183. Highly instructive is Willard's presentation of the spiritual disciplines (prayer, study, worship, service, fellowship, solitude, frugality, etc.) as activities we can engage in, and through which God works, to bring about this transformation from a heart of stone to a "kingdom heart of love." Ibid., pp. 311–373. For more extensive treatment, see Richard Foster, *Celebration of Discipline*, 2d ed. (San Francisco: Harper Collins, 1978), and *The Spirit of the Disciplines* (San Francisco: Harper Collins, 1988).

31. Deut. 30:6; 1 Kings 8:57–58; Ps. 119:32–40 (cf. 1 John 5:14–15, in the sense that God's commands are His will, and if we ask anything according to His will for us, i.e. that we obey His commandments with an "obedience that comes from faith," [Rom. 1:5] we are assured that He will hear and answer that prayer).

# Chapter 9

# Covenant Signs

In conjunction with the three Old Testament covenants—with Noah, Abraham, and the Israelites—God gave three signs to remind people about key elements in the covenants. These signs were the rainbow, circumcision, and the seventh-day Sabbath. Each sign was also intended to remind later generations of the covenant principles that God had sought to instill in the minds of the recipients of the earlier covenants. Each of these covenants was termed an "everlasting covenant" by virtue of its expression of the primordial everlasting covenant that encompasses the depth and breadth of God's unchanging commitment to His entire created order.

## Rainbow

After the flood God made a covenant with the earth through Noah and created the rainbow as "the sign of the covenant I have established between me and all life on the earth" that He would never again destroy the earth by a flood (Gen. 9:8–17). There appears to be no terminus to this sign. In Ezekiel's vision "the glory of the LORD" had "the appearance of a rainbow in the clouds on a rainy day, so was the radiance around him" (Ezek. 1:28). John's vision of the throne room of God in heaven revealed "a rainbow, resembling an emerald, [which] encircled the throne" (Rev. 4:3). In His glorified state Jesus appeared to John "with a rainbow above His head" (Rev. 10:1). So it seems reasonable to assume

that the rainbow will continue as a symbol of God's faithfulness to His covenant promises throughout eternity.

## Circumcision

Many scholars consider the sign of circumcision as a symbol of a self-maledictory oath: "If I am not loyal in faith and obedience to the Lord, may the sword of the Lord cut off me and my offspring…as I have cut off my foreskin."[1]

When God initiated His covenant with Abraham, He ratified it in a ritual involving slain animals (Gen. 15:6–18). "In ancient times the parties solemnized a covenant by walking down an aisle flanked by the pieces of slaughtered animals (see Jer. 34:18–19). The practice signified a self-maledictory oath: 'May it be so done to me if I do not keep my oath and pledge.'"[2] In a covenant made between unequals, the superior party, such as a victorious king, would require the inferior party, such as a defeated king, to walk between the pieces, pledging loyalty to the victor on pain of death for disloyalty to the terms of the covenant. But in Abraham's case, he saw a vision of a "blazing torch," representing God Himself, the superior party to the covenant, passing between the pieces (Gen. 15:17–18). Thus, in the strongest possible way, God assured Abraham of His commitment to His covenant promises.[3]

God promised to give Abraham a son through whom his descendants would become as numerous as the stars (Gen. 15:1–5). "Abram believed the Lord [specifically, God's promise to give him a son], and he credited it to him as righteousness" (Gen. 15:6). Genesis 15 records the whole story.

The very next chapter, Genesis 16, records the story of Abraham's impatience with God's delay in fulfilling His promise and apparent doubt as to whether He would really do so. So, at the bidding of his wife Sarah, he produced a child himself through her maidservant, Hagar. The chapter describes the grief and estrangement Abraham's action created in his family—grief that reaches to this very day in the Arab/Israeli conflict.

In Genesis 17 God returned to Abraham, renewed His covenant pledge to him as "an everlasting covenant," and introduced circumcision as "the sign of the covenant"—a sign carved into Abraham's physical flesh by which he had taken matters into his own hands to force God's promise to be fulfilled in his own way (Gen. 17:7, 11, 13, 19). Circumcision would be a perpetual reminder to him and his descendants, who were also to undergo the rite (Gen. 17:12–14; 21:2–4), of the utter futility and waywardness of trying to force the fulfillment of God's promises, whether physical or spiritual promises, by our own efforts. It would be a perpetual reminder that our acceptance before God is based solely on our trust in Him, not on our own efforts. It was a symbol that true love and obedience for God come not by human effort but by a heart transformation performed by God when we submit to Him in reverence and trust. It was a sign that all spiritual achievements come not by human might and power but by the Spirit of the Lord Almighty.

When Moses was on the road back to Egypt to fulfill his call from God to demand that Pharaoh set His people free, God met Moses and threatened to take his life, until Moses's wife Zipporah interposed and circumcised their son (Exod. 4:24–26). This drastic action on God's part reminded Moses that the deliverance of His people from bondage in Egypt, which later represented deliverance from spiritual bondage to sin, would not come by Moses's might or power but by God's own Spirit.

Forty years later when the nation of Israel returned to the banks of Jordan and was about to follow Joshua into the promised land, God required that the Israelite men first be circumcised to remind them that the conquest of Canaan would not come by their might or power but by His Spirit (Josh. 5:1–9).

## The Spiritual Meaning of Circumcision

The sign of circumcision was not meant to be merely a physical identity marker to distinguish Jews from non-Jews but even more so a spiritual identity marker. "Other nations also practiced circumcision."[4]

However, circumcision had a different meaning for God's covenant people than it did for the nations around them. By referring back to Abraham's experience, it represented their total dependence on God for every physical and spiritual blessing, that their victory in this life and the next would come by faith in God rather than their own independent efforts, and that God and God alone was their strength and righteousness. The physical sign in the flesh represented a spiritual transformation of the heart, which God was pledged to accomplish in response to their faith in Him: "The LORD your God will circumcise your hearts and the hearts of your descendants, so that you may love him with all your heart and with all your soul, and live" (Deut. 30:6).[5] Embedded in this assurance was the new covenant promise: "I will put my laws in their minds and write them in their hearts." The fulfillment of this promise was assured to all who did not resist the Holy Spirit. Unfortunately, "not all the Israelites accepted the good news" (Rom. 10:16). Stephen said that "uncircumcised hearts" resulted from "always resist[ing] the Holy Spirit" (Acts 7:51).

So the Old Testament emphasis on circumcision was never merely as a physical identity marker, but always connoted spiritual relation to God, of trust in and love for God, and of the holiness of character that would rightly represent Him before others. When Moses expressed doubts that his "uncircumcised lips"[6] (Exod. 6:12, 30 NKJV) could persuade Pharaoh to let God's people go, he doubted his own ability to speak with the power and authority of God that would change Pharaoh's heart. David's query concerning Goliath—"Who is this uncircumcised Philistine that he should defy the armies of the living God?"—had in mind Goliath's rebellious attitude toward God, not simply his physical foreskin (1 Sam. 17:26; cf. v. 36). Jeremiah pines that Israel's "ears are closed" (Hebrew, "uncircumcised") to God's warning appeals, rendering them "uncircumcised in heart" (Jer. 6:8–10; 9:26; cf. Ezek. 44:7–9).

The teaching of the historical old covenant law and prophets regarding circumcision was expressed eloquently by Paul in Romans:

"A man is not a Jew if he is only one outwardly [old covenant experience of spiritually and proudly relying on one's ethnic origin, religious affiliation, or outward conformity to religious regulations], nor is circumcision merely outward and physical. No, a man is a Jew if he is one inwardly [new covenant experience]; and circumcision is circumcision of the heart [an internalized new covenant experience], by the Spirit, and not by the written code [an externalized old covenant experience]"[7] (Rom. 2:28–29).

Salvation was not based on circumcision in the Old Testament. The list in Hebrews 11 of those saved by faith before circumcision was introduced as a covenant sign demonstrates that salvation and righteousness were always dependent on the grace of God and were to be received by faith. Paul testifies that righteousness was not credited to Abraham based on circumcision but on his faith (Rom. 4:10–11). Thus, on behalf of those in every historical era whom the Holy Spirit has brought to conversion, Abraham "is the father of all who believe but have not been circumcised" as well as "the father of the circumcised who not only are circumcised but

> The fact that circumcision was required of God's covenant people does not mean that their salvation was based on circumcision any more than God's appeal to us to be baptized and obey His law would prevent Him from saving the thief on the cross who simply called out to Jesus in faith.

who also walk in the footsteps of the faith that our father Abraham had before he was circumcised" (Rom. 4:11–12).[8]

The fact that circumcision was required of God's covenant people as His missionary nation does not mean that their salvation was based on circumcision any more than God's appeal to us in the New Testament to be baptized and obey His law would prevent Him from saving the thief on the cross who simply called out to Jesus in faith (Mark 16:16; Matt. 5:19; Luke 23:40–43).[9]

## Circumcision in the New Testament

Circumcision was not only a covenant sign but also a ceremonial rite, albeit a ritual outside the sanctuary system. Practiced from the time of Abraham throughout the Old Testament period as the sign of the covenant, circumcision by New Testament times had come to represent not only the whole body of ceremonial laws but even more so the legalistic attitude toward them, and all God's other commandments, held by the Jews at large.[10] The issue that precipitated the church council recorded in Acts 15 was the teaching of some that "unless you are circumcised, according to the custom taught by Moses, you cannot be saved" (Acts 15:1).

But in reality, circumcision in and of itself never saved anyone. "We have been saying that Abraham's faith was credited to him as righteousness. Under what circumstances was it credited? Was it after he was circumcised, or before? It was not after, but before! And he received the sign of circumcision, a seal of the righteousness that he had by faith while he was still uncircumcised" (Rom. 4:9–11).

The Jerusalem council made the decision, "which seemed good to the Holy Spirit and to us," that circumcision would not be among the requirements placed on the Gentiles (Acts 15:23–29). The Holy Spirit guided them to the conclusion that the God-given spiritual meaning signified by the physical act of circumcision had become so laden with legalistic overtones that it had to be discarded as a covenant sign.

The Old Testament rite of circumcision appears to have been replaced by the New Testament ceremony of baptism: "In him [Christ] you were also circumcised, in the putting off of the sinful nature, not with a circumcision done by the hands of men, but with the circumcision done by Christ, having been buried with him in baptism and raised with him through your faith in the power of God, who raised him from the dead" (Col. 2:11–12).

While baptism is the Christian initiation ceremony equivalent to circumcision in the Old Testament, the New Testament does not specifically designate it as a covenant sign. If God declared of the covenant sign of circumcision, "My covenant in your flesh is to be an everlasting covenant" (Gen. 17:13), how could it later be discontinued and replaced with the baptismal ceremony? For one thing, the scriptural use of the Hebrew term *olam*, from which we get the English translations of "everlasting" and "forever," while generally indicating "never ending," does not always mean that.[11] Each use of that term in Scripture must be interpreted in relation to its context.[12] The New Testament clearly states that the physical act of circumcision no longer serves as a covenant sign.

In his Galatian letter alone, Paul refers to circumcision thirteen times, never positively. He even asserts, "If you let yourselves be circumcised, Christ will be of no value to you at all" (Gal. 5:2). Even then, however, it was not so much the physical act of circumcision itself against which he was contending but against the legalistic application made of it by those who "were teaching the brothers: 'Unless you are circumcised, according to the custom taught by Moses, you cannot be saved'" (Acts 15:1).

Paul instructs the Galatians that circumcision for those who "want to be under the law" and "rely on observing the law" represents a disconnect from Christ and the righteousness that comes through faith in Christ (Gal. 4:21; Gal. 3:10). He reminded the Galatians that against the urging of "false brothers" he had refused to have Titus circumcised, because to do otherwise would have emboldened their belief in the meritorious significance of the act itself (Gal. 2:3–5). However, on his second missionary journey Paul did have Timothy circumcised "as a matter of expediency so that his work among the Jews might be more effective,"[13] which further reveals that it was not the physical act of circumcision against which he was contending but its legalistic application.

Many believers in God's new covenant historical period have had their sons circumcised, not as meritorious acts but for health reasons, without any concern that by doing so Christ would become of no value to them. It's not the physical act itself but the motivation behind it that determines its value and significance. Just as surely as one could be circumcised for legalistic motivations, one could also refuse to be circumcised for legalistic, experientially old covenant motivations. It's possible that someone today could refuse to be circumcised, or refuse to have his son circumcised, based on the New Testament statement, "If you let yourselves be circumcised, Christ will be of no value to you at all." But if by doing so he would hope to increase his chances of gaining eternal life, he would be exhibiting an old covenant experience. The bottom line issue in the New Testament is not circumcision or no circumcision but a new covenant experience versus an old covenant experience.

## The Sabbath

"Then the LORD said to Moses, 'Say to the Israelites, "You must observe my Sabbaths. This will be a sign between me and you for the generations to come, so you may know that I am the LORD, who makes you holy.…The Israelites are to observe the Sabbath, celebrating it for the generations to come as a lasting covenant. It will be a sign between me and the Israelites forever, for in six days the LORD made the heavens and the earth, and on the seventh day he abstained from work and rested"'" (Exod. 31:12–13, 16–17).

### Instituted at Creation

Several important observations can be made concerning God's establishment of the Sabbath as "a sign between me and the Israelites forever." First, God anchored the sign significance of the Sabbath in creation—"It will be a sign between me and the Israelites forever, for in six days the LORD made the heavens and the earth, and on the seventh day he abstained from work and rested" (Exod. 31:17). The Sabbath was not limited to Judaism but "was made for man" (Mark 2:27–28) by the Lord Himself at creation as a day for Adam and his descendants to cease their labor and, in the words of Herman Witsius, to engage in "the worship of God, (that is, laying aside the things pertaining to the body and its conveniences, be wholly taken up in those duties which become a soul delighting in God, glorifying him and celebrating his praise,) and that too in the public assembly, for the common joy and edification of all."[14] Indeed, many, if not most, Reformed theologians including Calvin himself recognize this truth and argue for it persuasively.[15]

## Residual Glow of Creation

In 1948 two scientists, Ralph Alpher and Robert Herman, were working with colleague George Gamow on the Big Bang theory of the origin of our universe. Alpher and Herman postulated that if their theory were true, there should be a detectable radioactive residual glow or radioactive "noise" present in the universe from the original explosion. The scientific community in general did not hold this new theory in high esteem, and therefore no experiments were conducted to test it. However, in 1965, two Bell Telephone engineers, Arno Penzias and Robert Wilson, discovered that a horn antenna they had constructed to search for signals coming to earth from space was picking up a low level, constant static from every direction. This frustrated them until a friend told them about Alpher and Herman's theory. Subsequent research confirmed that the signal Penzias and Wilson had discovered had the very pattern of wavelengths that would be expected to persist from the primordial explosion. This discovery has been heralded as "one of the great scientific events of all time," and established scientific credibility for the idea that our universe had an origin.[16]

In a similar manner, the seventh-day Sabbath could be considered the "residual glow" of God's creation of our world as revealed in Genesis 1. When God codified the Sabbath in the fourth commandment, He specifically referenced it to His creation of our world in seven days. "For in six days the LORD made the heavens and the earth, the sea, and all that is in them, but he rested on the seventh day. Therefore the LORD blessed the Sabbath day and made it holy" (Exod. 20:11).

The universally recognized "week of seven days" is most likely rooted in "the original institution of the Sabbath."[17] In over one hundred languages of the world, the name for the seventh day of the week is not "Saturday" as in the English language but rather "Sabbath" or its equivalent, which could possibly to point to an ancient, universal recognition of the seventh-day Sabbath.[18]

## Sign of the Creation Covenant

The Sabbath was instituted at creation both as a blessing ordinance for the benefit of humankind and as a divinely appointed sign of the creation covenant. Meredith Kline explains it thus: "If the Sabbath ordinance serves as a symbolic *sign* of God's covenantal lordship in the holy kingdom of Israel, it is surely because *the original divine Sabbath represented the Creator's covenantal lordship over the world....* The meaning of the original Sabbath (Gen. 2:2) is mirrored in the Sabbath ordinance (Gen. 2:3), the record of which emphasizes that the Sabbath is set apart as sacred to the Creator....Observance of the Sabbath by man is thus a confession that Yahweh is his Lord and Lord of all lords. Sabbath-keeping expresses man's commitment to the service of his Lord"[19] (italics added).

Many theologians have recognized the parallels between God's intervention after the flood and the Genesis creation story. In the list given by Jacques Doukhan, note the parallels, especially the parallel between the covenant signs—the rainbow after the flood and the Sabbath at creation:

1. The wind over the earth and waters. Gen. 8:1; cf. Gen. 1:2.
2. Division of waters. Gen. 8:2–5; cf. Gen. 1:6–8.
3. Appearance of plants. Gen. 8:6–12; cf. Gen. 1:9–13.
4. Appearance of light. Gen. 8:13–14; cf. Gen. 1:14–19.

5. Deliverance of animals. Gen. 8:15–17; cf. Gen. 1:20–23.

6. Animals together with men, blessing, food for men, image of God. Gen. 8:18–9:7; Gen. 1:24–31.

7. Sign of covenant. Gen. 9:8–17 [rainbow, sign of the Noachian covenant]; cf. Gen. 2:1–3 [Sabbath, sign of the covenant of creation].[20]

## Sign That God Makes Us Holy

Instituted at creation, the Sabbath "represented the Creator's covenantal lordship over the world,"[21] intended as a blessing for all humankind. When God reiterated the Sabbath institution to Israel, He elaborated on its sign significance, calling His holy day a representation of His commitment and ability to make His people holy, the great purpose of the covenant of redemption: "[The Sabbath] will be a sign between me and you for the generations to come, so you may know that I am the LORD, who makes you holy" (Exod. 31:12).

At creation "God blessed the seventh day and made it holy" (Gen. 2:3). The day was not intrinsically holy, except by virtue of God's investiture of it as a holy day. Its role as a sign for God's covenant people was to represent to them that 1) they have no holiness at all except through His presence among them and by the work of His Spirit within them, and that 2) a divinely inwrought holiness of character is to be their identity marker as His covenant people.[22] God set them apart from the nations that they might "be holy, because I am holy," and that through the resultant holiness of their lives attained by their connection with God they might leaven the nations with His grace and salvation (Lev. 11:44–45; 19:2; 20:7; Ezek. 36:23; 1 Pet. 2:13–16).[23]

Some would claim that God's Sabbath commandment taught Old Testament believers to limit their worship of God and communion with God to a single day each week, in contrast to the new covenant emphasis on a daily, continual experience with God. This claim is made in an attempt to demonstrate that believers in the new covenant era have expanded spiritual freedom and access to God, compared to those in the old covenant era. Portrayed thus, the new covenant provides an invitation to worship God whenever we choose rather than just one day a week. But this misrepresents both the Sabbath commandment and the teaching of God's historical old covenant. God appealed through Moses: "Love the LORD your God with all your heart and with all your soul and with all your strength. These commandments that I give you today are to be upon your hearts. Impress them on your children. Talk about them when you sit at home and when you walk along the road, when you lie down and when you get up" (Deut. 6:5–7).

The historical old covenant believer's consciousness of God permeated every waking activity day and night: "And on his law [the record of God's redeeming works on his behalf and the totality of God's revealed will for him] he meditates *day and night*" (Ps. 1:2, italics added). Indeed, worship of God on the Sabbath enhanced the believer's consciousness of God throughout the week. The Sabbath freed believing worshipers *from* the distractions of everyday work activities and the guilt of not attending to uncompleted work projects, and freed them *to* focus on spiritual issues that were closest to their hearts.

I've heard some people say in essence, "I'm a new covenant believer and worship God in freedom every day rather than just one day a week as they did in the days of old covenant bondage." This sounds very spiritual. But such a "new covenant believer" misunderstands both the letter and the spirit of God's historical old covenant, and the deep spiritual "new covenant" love-based experience that God provided through it for His Old Testament people.

## The Sabbath and the New Covenant

The applicability of the Sabbath of the fourth commandment to New Testament believers has been a subject of debate for much of the New Testament period. It is beyond the scope of this book to discuss all the biblical, theological, and historical issues involved in that ongoing discussion, except as they relate to the old and new covenants.[24]

## For Israel Only?

One such argument against the continuing application of the Sabbath for believers in the New Testament era focuses on its purported role exclusively as a sign of the covenant between God and the nation of Israel ("It will be a sign between me and the Israelites" Exod. 31:17) during the old covenant historical era from Sinai to Jesus's initiation of the new covenant at the Last Supper. But this ignores three very important points, the first being that the Sabbath was instituted at creation for the benefit of all humankind long before the nation of Israel existed.

Secondly, even when God invested the Sabbath with the significance of "a sign between me and the Israelites" at the time He gave them the law at Sinai, He never intended it to be a sign for the nation of Israel exclusively. One of God's primary purposes in His covenants with Abraham and Israel was to prepare a genuinely converted people with new covenant experiences to be His witnesses to the nations. People from every nation who responded to the gospel invitation by putting their trust in God were to be incorporated into His covenant community. It was written in the law: "You and the alien shall be the same before the Lord. The same laws and regulations will apply both to you and to the alien living among you" (Num. 15:15–16). Zechariah spoke of a remnant of Philistines who could "become leaders in Judah" (Zech. 9:6–7). Isaiah specifically appealed to foreign converts: "Let no foreigner who has bound himself to the Lord say, 'The Lord will surely exclude me from his people.'…For this is what the Lord says:…'foreigners who bind themselves to the Lord to serve him, to love the name of the Lord, and to worship him, all who keep the Sabbath without desecrating it and who hold fast to my covenant—these I will bring to my holy mountain and give them joy in my house of prayer. Their burnt offerings and sacrifices will be accepted on my altar; for my house will be called a house of prayer for all nations'" (Isa. 56:3–4, 6–7).

Becoming a full-fledged member of the covenant community involved circumcision for the males[25] just as becoming a member of the church involves baptism today. Being a full-fledged member of the covenant community also involved participating in the sacrificial services which pointed forward to the Messiah's atoning sacrifice, just as becoming a member of the church today involves participation in the holy communion service. In the same way, the Sabbath, which God designated as "a sign between me and the Israelites," was a sign between Him and the foreign converts to His covenant community (Num. 15:15–16; Isa. 56:3–7).

Throughout God's historical old covenant period from Sinai on, the Sabbath was a sign between God and all who had become spiritual Israelites by faith. Even in its role as a divine sign between God and His covenant people, the Sabbath never exclusively applied to the nation of Israel, but included all people from all nations who became part of the covenant community through faith in God. Paul's statement that "those who believe are children of Abraham" acknowledged a timeless and universal truth (Gal. 3:7; cf. Isa. 56:3–7).

This makes the third point highly significant. The new covenant, like the old, was not made with the nations at large, but specifically with Israel: "I will make a new covenant with *the house of Israel* and with *the house of Judah*....This is the covenant I will make with *the house of Israel* after that time," declares the Lord (Jer. 31:31, 33; Heb. 8:8, 10, italics added).

God's historical new covenant, like the old, only had application to the nations in general through the faithful witness of God's covenant people, namely spiritual Israel—"those who believe" (Gal. 3:7).[26] As the nations responded to the witness of God's new covenant "Israel" by putting faith in God and submitting to the continuing work of His Spirit in their lives to make them a holy people with an "obedience that comes from faith," they would be incorporated into the covenant people, the true Israel of God. This brings new significance to God's statement that the Sabbath "will be a sign between me and the Israelites forever" (Exod. 31:17). If the Sabbath applied to literal Israel only, then so does the new covenant. However, just as the new covenant, which was specifically "for the house of Israel," applied to all "those who believe," it is reasonable to conclude that the Sabbath, which was God's chosen "sign" between Himself and Israel, should likewise still apply to all "those who believe."

Unless God Himself revoked the Sabbath with the same clarity and force as He revoked circumcision,[27] the Sabbath must continue to have significance throughout the new covenant historical era. It is still a sign between God and the true, new covenant, Israel, and will be forever.

> Just as the new covenant, which was specifically "for the house of Israel," applied to all "those who believe," so the Sabbath, which was God's chosen "sign" between Himself and Israel, should likewise apply to all "those who believe."

## Change of Wills?

There are several immediate objections to this conclusion. The first is the claim that the covenants are God's legal will in which He identifies the inheritance His covenant children will receive, as well as stipulating any conditions that may need to be fulfilled to receive the inheritance. Thus, it is claimed, God's historical new covenant represents His updated will that voids and replaces His previous will, the historical old covenant.

The question must be asked, however, did God intend for the New Testament to completely overwrite the Old Testament? The scriptural answer is clearly no.

Paul wrote to Timothy, "From infancy you have known *the holy Scriptures*, which are able to *make you wise for salvation through faith in Christ Jesus*. All Scripture is God-breathed and is *useful for teaching, rebuking, correcting and training in righteousness*, so that the man of God may be thoroughly equipped for every good work" (2 Tim. 3:15–17, italics added). Here Paul strongly affirms that the Scriptures Timothy learned from in his infancy—the Old Testament Scriptures—are "able to make you wise for salvation" and are "useful for teaching ["doctrine" NKJV], rebuking, correcting and training in righteousness"—all the divinely ordained functions of holy Scripture. Furthermore, when Paul preached the gospel, he encouraged his hearers to check the (Old Testament) Scriptures "to see if what Paul said was true" (Acts 17:11).

As the New Testament gospel was being promoted throughout the world, the New Testament evangelists and authors used the Old Testament Scriptures as their authority, as the many Old Testament quotations in the books of Romans and Galatians, and indeed in most of the New Testament books, amply illustrate. While Peter acknowledged that in his own day some of Paul's letters came to be regarded on the same level of authority as the Old Testament (2 Pet. 3:15–16), the Bible of New Testament believers in the days of the apostles was essentially the Old Testament Scriptures. If any teaching in the Old Testament needed to be overwritten in the New Testament era, it would be made unmistakably clear, as it was in the case of circumcision (Acts 15:1–31; 1 Cor. 7:19; Gal. 5:2).

Animal sacrifices and the Levitical priesthood were also abolished, and the author of Hebrews makes it clear that this was done in light of Jesus's completed, once-for-all sacrifice and His eternal priesthood (Heb. 7:11–28; 9:11–28). Major sections of the New Testament are dedicated to overwriting these Old Testament ceremonial practices regarding circumcision, priesthood, and sacrifice. Barring such clear and forthright indications, the default position is that later covenants incorporate and expand on the major elements of previous ones.

There are two places in the New Testament where God's covenant is likened to a will. The first is in Galatians:

> Brothers, let me take an example from everyday life. Just as no
> one can set aside or add to a human covenant [will] that has been

duly established, so it is in this case. The promises were spoken to Abraham and to his seed. The Scripture does not say, "and to your seeds," meaning many people, but "and to your seed" [quoting Gen. 12:7; 13:15; 24:7], meaning one person, who is Christ. What I mean is this: the law [God's covenant at Sinai], introduced 430 years later [than God's covenant with Abraham], does not set aside the covenant previously established by God and thus do away with the promise. For if the inheritance depends on law, then it no longer depends on a promise; but God in his grace gave it to Abraham through a promise....Is the law, therefore, opposed to the promises of God? Absolutely not! (3:15–18, 21)

Paul's point is precisely that God's covenant at Sinai did not overwrite the gospel taught in His previous covenant with Abraham but incorporated it. "*The law*, introduced 430 years later, *does not set aside the covenant previously established by God* and thus do away with the promise [that is, the gospel given to Abraham, and before him to Adam and Noah on behalf of their descendants]" (Gal. 3:17, italics added).

The second New Testament reference comparing God's covenant to a will is in Hebrews:

The blood of goats and bulls and the ashes of a heifer sprinkled on those who are ceremonially unclean sanctify them so that they are outwardly clean. How much more, then, will the blood of Christ, who through the eternal Spirit offered himself unblemished to God, cleanse our consciences from acts that lead to death, so that we may serve the living God!

For this reason Christ is the mediator of a new covenant, that those who are called may receive the promised eternal inheritance—now that he has died as a ransom to set them free from the sins committed under the first covenant.

In the case of a will, it is necessary to prove the death of the one who made it, because a will is in force only when somebody had died; it never takes effect while the one who made it is living. This is why the first covenant was not put into effect without blood (9:15–18).

In fact, the law requires that nearly everything be cleansed with blood, and without the shedding of blood there is no forgiveness (9:22).

But now he has appeared at the end of the ages to do away with sin by the sacrifice of himself (9:26).

The meaning of these texts is straightforward. Just as a human will takes effect when a death occurs, so God's forgiving grace extended to humankind through previous ages anticipated the atoning death of Jesus. All the animal sacrifices during the historical old covenant era pointed forward as mere shadows of this reality. And now that the great sacrifice has been made, sins committed under all God's covenants, previous and present, have been atoned for by the blood of the true Lamb of God. The once-for-all atoning death of Jesus "put an end to sacrifice" forever in the economy of God (Dan. 9:27).

A number of years ago a friend of mine included me in his will. Later I learned that he had made several wills along the way, updating various particulars with each one. It's rare that a new will completely overhauls a previous version. Generally, it adjusts for major changes in circumstances (someone named in the will has died, some item of value has been added or lost to the estate, etc.). In my case, my friend had penciled me in during the last days of his life. The will had not even been retyped. It was essentially the same will, only now with me included.

Similarly, the New Testament incorporates the gospel of the Old Testament. It need not restate a provision of the gospel previously revealed for that provision to be applicable. If such provisions are not repealed, they remain unless the circumstances to which they were addressed no longer exist or have materially changed. Neither is the case with regard to the fourth commandment. Jesus acknowledged such Himself when He affirmed that "the Sabbath was made for man," and "it is lawful to do good on the Sabbath" (Mark 2:27; Matt. 12:12). Jesus never questioned *whether* the Sabbath should be kept, but He had issues with the scribes of His time about *how* and *why* it should be kept.

The gospels record numerous healing miracles Jesus performed on the Sabbath, to which the rabbis objected as improper Sabbath-keeping. They didn't allow carrying a burden on the Sabbath, and Jesus defended His healing acts on the Sabbath as an act of removing the burden of physical ailments from those "bound" by them so they could worship burden-free (e.g., Luke 13:10–16). One can only imagine what

> The New Testament incorporates the gospel of the Old Testament. It need not restate a provision of the gospel previously revealed for that provision to be applicable.

many interpreters would make of it if these same miracles had all been performed on the first day of the week.

## Literal and Spiritual Israel

A second objection sometimes made to the belief that the seventh-day Sabbath still remains for the new covenant people of God focuses on an alleged fundamental difference between the historical old and new covenants. This argument contends that the old covenant initiated by God at Sinai was made with the literal descendants of Israel regardless of whether they exercised faith or obedience of any kind. Thus, the covenant blessings and curses were apparently applicable to the faithless Israelites even as to the faithful ones. Does not this observation establish that God's historical old covenant, which was with all natural descendants of Abraham through Isaac, was significantly and essentially different from His historical new covenant which He made exclusively with true spiritual Israelites who have the faith of Abraham?

The answer is no. For while the historical Sinai covenant *was* indeed with the literal descendants of Israel, it always had in mind their spiritual conversion and growth into a new covenant experience. God designed everything in the covenant to achieve that end.

In a similar way, everyone is in covenant relation to God by virtue of birth into the world, and is subject to the covenant blessings and curses of God's everlasting covenant with all humankind. Thus Isaiah could boldly say, "The earth is defiled by its people; they have disobeyed the laws, violated the statutes and broken the everlasting covenant. Therefore a curse consumes the earth; its people must bear their guilt" (Isa. 24:5). Without a doubt, all the people of the earth are in covenant relation to God in the sense of being held responsible for the knowledge God provides them through nature and the Spirit concerning His nature and laws (John 1:9; Acts 17:26–27; Rom. 1:18–20; 3:19).[28] But only those who respond to Him in faith, a faith which results in the obedience that comes from faith, are considered part of the covenant people of God (James 2:8–26).

The same distinction can be made between those whose Israelite identity in the Old Testament era was simply a matter of having genealogical ancestors who could be traced back to Sinai or Abraham, and those who actually entered into covenant relation with God by faith. "Not all who are descended from Israel [the physical descendants of those who received the covenants] are Israel [those who entered into covenant relation with God by faith and by the Spirit gained a new covenant experience]. Nor because they are his descendants are they all Abraham's children" (Rom. 9:6, 7).

Paul was emphatic: "A man is not a Jew if he is only one outwardly [having simply been born into it genealogically speaking, or perhaps even having meticulously complied with the covenant commandments from a legalistic motivation], nor is circumcision merely outward and physical. No, a man is a Jew if he is one inwardly [with a new covenant experience—genuinely converted, growing in love for God and in the obedience that comes from faith]; and circumcision is circumcision of the heart, by the Spirit, not by the written code" (Rom. 2:28–29).

The same application could be made for those born into a Christian home and perhaps baptized as infants or as young children who did not understand what baptism meant. They may be listed in the official church records as members of the covenant community, even while it is acknowledged that "to all *who received him*, to those *who believed in his name*, he gave the right to become children of God—children born not of natural descent, nor of human decision or a husband's will, but born of God" (John 1:12, italics added).

## Regarding Every Day Alike

A third objection to the applicability of the Sabbath as a new covenant institution is the claim that in Romans 14 and Colossians 2 Paul appeals for Christians not to judge one another with regard to the Sabbath.

Romans 14:5 reads, "One man considers one day more sacred than another; another man considers every day alike. Each one should be fully convinced in his own mind." Paul surely would not have in mind here the Sabbath God instituted at creation, embedded in the Ten Commandments, and which both Jesus and Paul observed throughout their lives.

In Romans 14:1 Paul admonishes Christians against "passing judgment on *disputable matters*." The Sabbath instituted at creation and embedded in the Ten Commandments was never a disputable matter.[29] However, what evidently had come to dispute within the Jewish Christian community was whether Christians could or should observe the ceremonial festivals, feast days, and holy days, such as Passover, which had been fulfilled by Christ's sacrifice, as distinguished from the Sabbath which Christ had instituted at creation.[30] Paul responded in Romans 14: In these *disputable* matters, let each decide for himself. There is no sin in observing such ceremonies as long as one realizes that Christ to whom they pointed has now come. On the other hand, Jewish Christians should not feel that Gentile Christians *have to* attend such feasts or observe the proscribed fast days. Let each be convinced in his own mind about such things. A number of biblical scholars concur with this general interpretation, viewing Paul's discussion in Romans 14:1–5 as an extension of issues he addresses in 1 Corinthians 8–10.[31]

## A Shadow of Things to Come

Colossians 2:16–17 says, "Therefore do not let anyone judge you by what you eat or drink, or with regard to a religious festival, a New Moon celebration, or a Sabbath day. These are a shadow of the things that were to come; the reality however is found in Christ." These verses are often coupled with verses 13–14—"He forgave us all our sins, having canceled the written code, with its regulations, that was against us and that stood opposed to us; he took it away, nailing it to the cross"—to make the point that God nailed the Ten Commandments to the cross, abolishing them, and with them the seventh-day Sabbath. However, "the written code (or 'bond') that was against us" is not a reference to the Ten Commandments *per se* but rather to the death warrant incurred due to sin, as G. R. Beasley-Murray aptly states:

> Christ has "cancelled the bond which stood against us with its legal demands." The "bond" is an I.O.U., a signed statement of indebtedness; if it applies to the Jew through his acceptance of the Law, it also applies to the Gentile who recognizes his obligation to what he knows of the will of God. It means, in the picturesque paraphrase of Moule, "*I owe obedience to God's will, signed Mankind.*" This bond stands "against us," for we have all failed to discharge its obligations (cf. Rom. 7:16, 22f.). By becoming man and accepting the death warrant which the bond constituted, Christ has discharged the debt, erased the writing of the bond, and nailed it to his cross to show that it no longer has any force.[32]

The Sabbaths, or elements of the Sabbath, referred to in Colossians 2:16 were only those that were "a *shadow* of things to come, but the substance is of Christ," which was true only of the ceremonial Sabbaths,[33] or of the ceremonial activities that were performed on the seventh-day Sabbath as part of the Old Testament sanctuary services.[34] In contrast to the seventh-day Sabbath of the Decalogue, both the ceremonial Sabbaths and the specific ceremonial activities carried out on the Sabbath were types pointing forward to the coming Messiah. Once Christ had come, the ceremonial services and activities pointing to Him came to an end, as was already anticipated and prophesied in the Old Testament (Dan. 9:26–27), and were replaced by the holy communion service.

A number of scholars believe that Paul never intended his statement in Colossians 2:16–17 as an abolishment of the Sabbath God Himself instituted at creation. See appendix C (pp. 285–290) for a listing of their comments on this passage.

## Observing Special Days

Those who argue against the continuing sanctity of the seventh-day Sabbath often link Galatians 4:10 with Romans 14:4–5 and Colossians 2:16. Here Paul laments that the Galatians appeared to have backslidden into their former observance of "special days and months and seasons and years." Note the text within its immediate context in Galatians 4:8–11: "Formerly, when you did not know God, you were slaves to those who by nature are not gods. But now that you know God—or rather are known by God—how is it that you are turning back to those weak and miserable principles? Do you wish to be enslaved by them all over again? You are observing special days and months and seasons and years! I fear for you, that somehow I have wasted my efforts on you."

Even if the "special days" referred to in this passage include the seventh-day Sabbath (a conclusion which is highly debatable as we shall see), that does not necessarily argue against the continuing sanctity of the seventh-day Sabbath. Many scholars interpret this text as an attack on a legalistic, heartless observance of religious ritual rather than an attack on the ritual itself.[35]

Marvin Moore sees an important application for seventh-day Sabbath keepers in Galatians 4:10:

> The issue is *how* we keep the Sabbath. Do we keep it by the rule book, with our primary attention given to what is right and wrong to *do*

on the Sabbath? Or is the primary focus of our Sabbath-keeping a relationship with Jesus and our Christian brothers and sisters? If the former, then Galatians 4:10 applies to the weekly Sabbath as much as it does to any of the yearly Sabbaths, new moons, and other festivals in the Jewish year. Sabbath-keeping by the rule book is a reversion to the "weak and miserable" basic principles of the world that Paul spoke about in Galatians 4:9, just before his comments about days and months and seasons and years....He was telling the Galatian Christians to move beyond the rules and regulations to the heart of what it means to keep the Sabbath.[36]

But Troy Martin, professor at Xavier University in Chicago, contends that evidence both external and internal to the text itself supports the conclusion that "when Paul refers to days, months, seasons, and years in Gal 4:10, he lists categories most characteristic of a pagan time-keeping system."[37] Other Bible scholars concur with Martin in this conclusion.[38]

"The immediate context of Gal 4.10 argues for the pagan character of this list. In 4.8, Paul mentions the former pagan life of the Galatian Christians. In 4.9, he asks them how they can desire their former life again. He then proposes their observance of the time-keeping scheme in 4.10 as a demonstrative proof of their reversion to their old life. Considering only the immediate context of Gal 4.10, the list must be understood as a pagan temporal scheme."[39] Thus, as the immediate context supports, Galatians 4:8–11 most likely constitutes Paul's warning for pagans not to revert to their heathen religious customs, which included observing the "special days, months and seasons" of the heathen religious calendar.

## The Sabbath's Relationship to Circumcision and the Lord's Supper

It is a scriptural fact that while the Jerusalem council deliberations recorded in Acts 15 include enormous contention over the applicability of circumcision to Gentile Christians in the New Testament era, there is no discussion whatsoever over the issue of the Sabbath. This fact supports the applicability of the Sabbath of the Decalogue for the New Testament era. Thus, it is precisely against this observation that the third objection to the applicability of the Sabbath as a new covenant observance has been directed. Note the following claim:

> The entrance sign to the old covenant was circumcision, and the continuing, repeatable sign Israel was to "remember" was the Sabbath, [while] the entrance sign of the new covenant is baptism, [and] the continuing sign of the New Testament that we are to "remember" is the Lord's Supper....If circumcision were not required for Gentile Christians, then neither would Sabbath observance be required, for the Sabbath was reserved only for members of the old covenant community....The Jerusalem council settled the issue...not by dealing with the Sabbath directly, but by way of eliminating the entrance sign in the old covenant: circumcision.[40]

The author making this claim summarized it in the following chart:[41]

| [Old Covenant] | | [New Covenant] |
|---|---|---|
| | *Entrance Sign* | |
| Circumcision | | Baptism |
| | *Remembrance Sign* | |
| Sabbath | | The Lord's Supper |

This argument attempts to account for the remarkable lack of controversy in the New Testament over something so radical as a change in one of the Ten Commandments. But it makes the following three grave errors.

The first error lies in the assertion that the validity and applicability of the Sabbath of the fourth commandment was dependant on the observance of circumcision. If the Sabbath relied on circumcision for its applicability, so should the rest of the Ten Commandments. There is nothing in Scripture that even hints at such a connection between circumcision and the fourth commandment. Indeed, the Sabbath (instituted at creation) pre-dated circumcision (instituted in the Abrahamic covenant) by many centuries.

The second error involves the assertion that Jesus instituted the Lord's Supper as a replacement for the Sabbath. What is quite clear from Scripture is that the Lord's Supper replaced the animal sacrificial ceremonial system that pointed forward to the atoning ministry of the Messiah. Jesus's very words on the night He observed the Passover meal with His disciples—"This is my body.... This is my blood of the covenant which is poured out for many"—introduce the communion service as the replacement for the Passover and the entire bloody sacrificial system of the old covenant (Mark 14:22, 24). The blood of animals was being replaced by Christ's own blood, represented by the communion cup. Animal sacrifice was the forward-looking ceremony, while the Lord's Supper is the backward-looking one. The book of Hebrews weighs in heavily against continuing to perform animal sacrifices now that Jesus's sacrifice has been made, but it breathes not a word against God's Sabbath. The more accurate alignment of old and new covenant ceremonies looks like this:

| | Old Testament | New Testament |
|---|---|---|
| **Initiation ceremony** | Circumcision | Baptism[42] |
| **Continuing ceremony** | Animal sacrifices | Communion/Lord's Supper[43] |

The third error in the argument under scrutiny is the failure to distinguish between circumcision as one of the ceremonial provisions of the old covenant, albeit one chosen by God as a covenant sign, in contrast to the Sabbath as one of God's enduring commandments. "Circumcision is nothing and uncircumcision is nothing. Keeping God's commands is what counts" (1 Cor. 7:19). It was God, not Moses, who embedded the Sabbath in His enduring moral code of Ten Commandments, perhaps in part to prevent it from being confused with the provisional ceremonial regulations.

## Jerusalem Council Directives

The Jerusalem council required only four things of Gentile Christians: "It seemed good to the Holy Spirit and to us not to burden you with anything beyond the following requirements: You are to abstain from food sacrificed to idols, from blood, from the meat of strangled animals and from sexual immorality" (Acts 15:28–29).

Why these particular laws and not others? Certainly the council would not consider Gentile Christians in good and regular standing if they committed murder, rebelled against their parents, bore false witness against their neighbors, never gave a penny to support the advancement of God's kingdom or to relieve the suffering of the poor, and never showed love for God or their neighbor as themselves.

It has been suggested that the four requirements the council asked Gentile Christians to observe were so-called Noahic laws that Jewish tradition held had been given to humankind in general prior to Sinai. One searches in vain to find a scriptural commandment to abstain from food polluted by idols or from sexual immorality prior to Sinai. This doesn't mean that such laws were not given or known by people before that time, but simply that they weren't recorded in the early records of Scripture. These laws, and others with them, may have been among those God had in mind when He said to Isaac, "Through your offspring all nations on earth will be blessed, because Abraham obeyed me and kept my requirements, my commands, my decrees and my laws" (Gen. 26:4–5). Nevertheless, the council chose to ignore everything but the four requirements identified in Acts 15:29. Nor did the early Christians require more of Gentile Christians anytime soon. Two missionary journeys later those were still the only requirements expected of Gentile Christians (Acts 21:25).

Concerning these four specific requirements placed on Gentile Christians, Davidson observes: "Particularly striking is that this is the same list, *in the same order*, as the four major legal prohibitions explicitly stated to be applicable to the stranger/alien as well as to the native Israelites in Lev 17–18. In these OT chapters we find (1) sacrificing to demons/idols (Lev 17:7–9); (2) eating blood (Lev 17:10–12; (3) eating anything that has not been immediately drained of its blood (Lev 17:13–16); and (4) various illicit sexual practices (Lev 18)."[44]

While the universal applicability of the moral provisions of the Ten Commandments was never in question by the Jerusalem council, the same was apparently not the case with the ceremonial provisions of the law in a post-resurrection-and-ascension-of-Christ era. Therefore, the council felt the need to specify the importance of these four provisions specifically enjoined upon the stranger/alien/gentile (Hebrew, *ger*), as well as the Israelite, in the law. Because the Ten Commandments were taken for granted as universally applicable, the council had no need to specifically instruct Gentile converts not to murder or steal, to be respectfully obedient to parents, or to observe the Sabbath (which in the law was itself enjoined upon "the alien [Hebrew, *ger*] within your gates," Exod. 20:10; cf. Isa. 56:3–7).

How did the leaders of the Jerusalem council expect the Gentile Christians to grow into spiritual maturity and sacrificial love and care for others? The plethora of ethical commandments that emerged in the New Testament writings suggests that they didn't expect Gentiles to develop a mature Christian experience of holiness and mission exclusively through private prayer and the guidance of the Holy Spirit in isolation from Christian community and Scripture. They undoubtedly expected that more seasoned Jewish Christian communities would provide godly environments wherein Gentile converts fresh out of paganism would be nurtured in faith and service. But equally if not more importantly, the Jerusalem council trusted that Gentile converts would be nurtured through the sanctifying influence of the Holy Scriptures.

Immediately following their announced decision regarding the four requirements expected of Gentile Christians, the council added, "For Moses has been preached in every city from the earliest times and is read in the synagogues on every Sabbath" (Acts 15:21). In other words, they expected that new Gentile Christians would attend a synagogue and hear "Moses" read on the Sabbath. No doubt their reference to "Moses" in this instance had in mind the entire Old Testament including the writings of Moses. The council trusted the influence of the Scriptures of their day, read in corporate worship every Sabbath, to make new Gentile Christians "wise for salvation," providing for them the needed "teaching, rebuking, correcting and training in righteousness" that would be essential for them to mature in their new faith (2 Tim. 3:15–16).[45] They knew that when God's word goes forth from His mouth,

> Because the Ten Commandments were taken for granted as universally applicable, the Jerusalem council had no need to specifically instruct Gentile converts not to murder or steal, to be respectfully obedient to parents, or to observe the Sabbath.

it does not return to Him void, but accomplishes the very purpose for which He sent it—the conversion and sanctification of those who hear in faith (Isa. 55:10–11).

## Testimony for the Ten Commandments and the Sabbath in the Book of Revelation

The book of Revelation is permeated with direct and indirect allusions to the Ten Commandments, showing their enduring nature. Sprinkled throughout the book are references that allude to the specific commandments: 2nd—"worshiping…idols" (Rev. 9:20); 3rd—"have not denied my name" (Rev. 3:8; cf. 21:8); 4th—"the Lord's Day" (Rev. 1:10);[46] 6th—"murders" (Rev. 9:21; cf. 21:8); 7th—"sexual immorality" (Rev. 2:14; cf. 2:20; 9:21; 21:8); 8th—"thefts" (Rev. 9:21); 9th—"liars" (Rev. 21:8).

John was shown a future day when "the time" would "come for judging the dead." He wrote, "Then God's temple in heaven was opened, and within his temple was seen the ark of his covenant. And there came flashes of lightning, rumblings, peals of thunder, an earthquake and a great hailstorm" (Rev. 11:18–19). The heavenly representation of the earthly ark of the covenant, which contained the Ten Commandments, will evidently play some part in the final judgment of the world when all will stand before God and His holy law (James 2:8–13; cf. Eccl. 12:13–14). The reference to "flashes of lightning, rumblings, peals of thunder, an earthquake and a great hailstorm" is borrowed from language used to describe the celestial manifestations on Mount Sinai surrounding God's writing of the Ten Commandments with His own finger (Exod. 19:16–19).

Revelation 13 describes the world's last great crisis, the battle of Armageddon, a great spiritual battle on earth waged by those who have the mark of the beast against God's final covenant people, His remnant. Bracketing both sides of Revelation's portrayal of that great spiritual conflagration is a description of the character of God's final people as those who "keep God's commandments and hold to the testimony of Jesus," and "who obey God's commandments and remain faithful to Jesus" (Rev. 12:17; 14:12). In view of Revelation's many allusions to the Ten Commandments, it would be hard to argue that these texts do not have prominently in mind both the Ten Commandments and the law's characteristic call to obedience (Deut. 6:1–2, 5–6; 11:1, 13–14, 22–24).

Revelation 14:7 is God's response to the world's final spiritual battle and test described in Revelation 13. In Revelation 13 an unholy trinity of the symbolic dragon, sea beast, and land beast metaphorically parallels the roles of the Father, Son, and Holy Spirit. They seek the loyalty, allegiance, and worship of the whole world. Seven times Revelation 13–14 refer to the unholy trinity's claim to the world's worship and the global lemming-like response. By contrast, in Revelation 14:7 God makes a single final appeal to the world for the worship that rightfully belongs to Him: "Worship Him who made the heaven and the earth, the sea, and the fountains of water." This is a direct allusion to the fourth commandment regarding the seventh-day Sabbath recorded in Exodus 20:8–11, particularly the phrase, "In six days the Lord made the heavens and the earth, the sea, and all that is in them." After examining the many verbal, thematic, and structural parallels between these two references, Jon Paulien concludes: "The cumulative evidence is so strong that an interpreter could conclude that there is no direct allusion to the Old Testament in Revelation that is more certain than the allusion to the fourth commandment in Rev 14:7. When the author of Revelation describes God's final appeal to the human race in the context of the end-time deception, he does so in terms of a call to worship the creator in the context of the fourth commandment."[47]

In Revelation 15 John sees a vision of the heavenly "tabernacle of the Testimony" (Rev. 15:5). Once again the Ten Commandments are in view. The *NIV Study Bible* note on "the temple of the Testimony" in this verse says, "It was so named because the ancient tent contained the two tables of the Testimony brought down from Mount Sinai (Ex. 32:15; 38:21; Dt. 10:5)."[48] The vision of Revelation 15 also contains a proleptic snapshot of those from every nation who by the virtue of the "righteous acts" of God have gained the ultimate victory over the spiritual forces of evil and hence stand eternally secure on the heavenly sea of glass. It describes them singing the historically old covenant *and* experientially new covenant "song of Moses the servant of God," and the historically *and* experientially new covenant "song of the Lamb" (Rev. 15:3). Sung by the experientially new covenant believers from both historical eras, the song consists of a triumphant chorus of praise that represents the common passion and focus of them all: "Great and marvelous are your deeds, Lord God almighty. Just and true are your ways, King of the ages. Who will not fear you, O Lord, and bring glory to your name? For you alone are holy. *All nations will come and worship before you*, for your righteous acts have been revealed" (Rev. 15:3–4, italics added).

The phrase "*All nations will come and worship before you*" is borrowed from a similar vision of eternity God gave to the prophet Isaiah: "'As the new heavens and the new earth that I make will endure before me,' declares the Lord, 'so will your name and descendants endure. From one New Moon to another and from one Sabbath to another, *all mankind will come and bow down* [in worship] *before me,' says the Lord*" (Isa. 66:22–23, italics added). Isaiah describes the redeemed of all ages assembling to worship God from one Sabbath to another in eternity. When the book of Revelation pictures those who refuse to receive the mark of the beast, it references Isaiah's description of God's people in the new earth who will worship God throughout eternity from one Sabbath to another.[49]

Revelation 17–18 describes a harlot and city that epitomizes the religious-political system that both opposes and counterfeits God's true covenant people in the last days. Though possessing a near fanatical religious zeal, this system is described as "drunk with the blood of the saints" (Rev. 17:6). This counterfeit system is graphically described as being "dressed in fine linen, purple and scarlet, and glittering with gold, precious stones and pearls!" (Rev. 18:16; cf. 17:3–5). J. Massyngberde Ford, among others, has noted that this garb parallels the high priest's garb in the Old Testament, and thus "this harlot is no 'commoner'; she appears to be of the priestly class," a "priest harlot," for "the garments for the priests have similar colors gold, blue, purple and scarlet, fine linen; cf. Exod 28:5, 15, 23."[50] There was one glaring difference, however—the blue! The high priest's garment was predominately blue: "Make the robe of the ephod entirely of blue cloth" (Exod. 28:31; cf. 39:22–31). And why is the omission of blue on the harlot's garment so significant in Revelation 17? God assigned the color blue a very specific meaning in the covenant garb of the Old Testament: "Make tassels on the corners of your garments, with a blue cord on each tassel. You will have these tassels to look at and will remember all the commands of the LORD, that you may obey them....Then you will remember to obey all my commands and will be consecrated to your God" (Num. 15:37–40). The fact that the counterfeit priest in this symbolic portrayal of the final spiritual conflict wears no blue seems to represent the contrast between this counterfeit religious system and the true covenant people described in Revelation 12:17 and 14:12 as those who not only "hold to the testimony of Jesus" and "remain faithful to Jesus," but who also "obey God's commandments." It warns of a counterfeit religious system with a leader who will pose as the world's spiritual high priest, but without a commitment to the commandments of God. Compare this with a parallel warning in 2 Thessalonians 2:7–9 where Paul calls the antichrist "the man of *lawlessness*"—"the *lawless* one" who works through "the secret power of *lawlessness*" to deceive many.

## The Sabbath—God's Enduring Covenant Sign

The Sabbath was 1) blessed and made holy by God at creation; 2) reiterated by God in Exodus 16 prior to the initiation of the Sinai covenant; 3) embedded in the heart of His Ten Commandments; 4) invested by God with significance as a sign between Him and His covenant people; and 5) observed by the apostles and by Jesus Himself whose numerous miracles on that day revealed its full meaning. And the Sabbath will be among the commandments obeyed by God's final covenant people who experience earth's last great spiritual crisis and are opposed and oppressed by a counterfeit religious system. It is a day when all nations will worship God in the earth made new. The following table of the covenant signs shows the duration of their sign significance indicated by arrows:

| Covenant Sign | Creation | Old Testament Era | New Testament Era | New Earth |
|---|---|---|---|---|
| Rainbow | | → → → → | → → → → | ? ? ? |
| Circumcision | | → → → → | | |
| Sabbath | → → | → → → → | → → → → | → → |

## Responses to Several Practical Concerns
## Regarding the Spiritual Effect of Sabbath Observance

Much of the discussion of the old and new covenants, and most if not all discussion of the continuing applicability of the Ten Commandments, seems ultimately to boil down to a single question—is it necessary to still observe the seventh-day Sabbath? Besides some of the biblical issues that have been discussed above, there are a number of practical concerns and questions that some have regarding whether the observance of the seventh-day Sabbath of the fourth commandment in the new covenant historical era would contribute positively or negatively toward the development of a deepening spiritual experience with Christ (i.e., a new covenant experience). Several of those concerns are addressed below.

There seems to be a concern among some in the Christian world that observing the biblical Sabbath as enjoined in the fourth commandment would discourage a believer from having a worshipful spirit and continual communion with God during the remainder of the week. However, it did not have such a detrimental effect on Moses and the prophets, on the 7,000 who had not bowed the knee to Baal in Elijah's day, and on the many others whom the author of Hebrews 11 said he did "not have time to tell about" in his representative list of Old Testament believers. All of these were seventh-day Sabbath keepers who were honored for exercising faith in God even unto death and became heirs of the righteousness that comes by faith. Jesus's observance of the Sabbath didn't restrict His spiritual experience or limit His time meditating on His heavenly Father and on God's will for Him. It was these Sabbath keepers' "delight" to meditate on spiritual things "day and night," "when you sit at home and when you walk along the road, when you lie down and when you get up" (Ps. 1:2; Deut. 6:7).

Many in the Christian world appear to believe that worshiping God on the seventh day of the week represents legalism and spiritual bondage. But there is no proclivity toward legalism or spiritual bondage built into the seventh-day Sabbath as God instituted it at creation and embedded it in His Ten Commandments. Quite the opposite. The Sabbath, as designed by God and supervised by the Holy Spirit in the life of a believer, is calculated to deliver God's covenant people from workaholism and to contribute toward the development of an ever growing and deepening new covenant experience that finds its greatest joy and freedom in God.

There are some who seem to believe that the Ten Commandments, and the Sabbath in particular, contributed toward the legalism of the Israelites of the historical old covenant era who did not attain to righteousness "because they pursued it not by faith but as if it were by works" (Rom. 9:32). And yet no one would suggest that the gospel taught in the New Testament era should be made responsible for the spiritual lethargy

> Much of the discussion of the old and new covenants and the Ten Commandments ultimately boils down to a single question—is it necessary to still observe the seventh-day Sabbath?

of the "dark ages" or for the general unbelief that will prevail in the final generation as suggested by Jesus's plaintive query: "When the Son of Man comes, will he find faith on the earth?" (Luke 18:8). God would not invite people into a covenant that would prevent them from entering the kingdom of God and growing in sanctification.

It is a delusion to think that by refusing to observe the seventh-day Sabbath believers thereby insulate themselves from faithless legalism. Choosing *not* to observe the Sabbath can be as potentially legalistic in motivation as a choice to observe it could be. Choosing to observe the seventh-day Sabbath according to the fourth commandment can indeed be, and was intended by God to be, an experientially new covenant, loving response to God's grace, an act of "obedience that comes from faith" (Rom. 1:5).

Some seem to consider it more spiritual, more new covenant, to watch videos late into Saturday night, go to church the next morning, and then watch sports events, do chores, go shopping, work at the office, or attend a movie on Sunday afternoon, than it is to observe the seventh-day Sabbath of the fourth commandment. And while the seventh-day Sabbath as a day of worship may indeed be observed legalistically, as may the observance of any other day, there is a spiritual freedom provided in laying aside secular activities at Friday sundown in order to engage worshipful pursuits, with minds directed toward God, family, serving others, and healthful rest until sundown on Saturday as the Sabbath commandment envisions and Jesus's own practice exemplifies.

## Summary

The three covenant signs given in Scripture were initiated by God at various times—the rainbow at the time of Noah, circumcision with Abraham, and the Sabbath at creation. The rainbow appears to have no scriptural terminus point—visions of Ezekiel and John about the rainbow around God's throne suggest that the rainbow may continue through eternity as a sign that God will forever remain true to His covenant promises. Circumcision, though referred to as an everlasting ordinance, clearly had a terminal point in the times of the New Testament. Circumcision as an initiation ceremony into covenant relation with God from the time of Abraham has been replaced in New Testament times with the ceremony of baptism, though baptism is never referred to specifically as a covenant sign. The Sabbath, instituted at creation as a universal blessing for humanity, was invested with special covenant sign significance for Israel, with whom the new covenant was also specifically made. The true Israel of God has been assessed throughout both Old and New Testament periods not on the basis of genealogy but on the basis of faith and "the obedience that comes from faith." Though there is a sharp controversy in the New Testament over the terminus of circumcision, there is no such debate about Sabbath observance. Isaiah and the book of Revelation envision Sabbath observance in the new earth, suggesting that the Sabbath will continue throughout eternity as a covenant sign that God both created and makes holy His eternally redeemed people.

## Notes

1. *NIV Study Bible* (31), comment on "circumcision" in Genesis 17:10.

2. *NIV Study Bible* (29), note on Genesis 15:17.

3. Genesis 15:6–18 also provides a clue to the meaning of the much misunderstood saying of Jesus in Luke 17:34–35: "I tell you, on that night two people will be in one bed; one will be taken and the other left. Two women will be grinding grain together; one will be taken and the other left." This text is often used to support the theory of a rapture that has Jesus taking some people to heaven while leaving others to live seven more years on earth to endure a period of tribulation. However, setting these verses in their proper covenant context reveals the exact opposite to be the case. In the very next verse the disciples asked, "Where, Lord?" In other words, where will those who are "taken" be taken to? And Jesus answered, "Where there is a dead body, there the vultures will appear" (Luke 17:37). During the covenant initiating ceremony recorded in Genesis 15:6–18, note is taken that "the birds of prey came down on the carcasses, but Abram drove them away" (v. 11). Ever after, kings and religious leaders who consistently broke covenant with God were not given a normal burial. Rather, their bodies were thrown out for the dogs and birds of prey to devour (cf. 1 Kings 14:11; 16:4). In Jeremiah's day the leaders of Israel made another covenant with God and ratified it by walking between the pieces of a calf they had cut in two. When they promptly broke this covenant, God said He would treat them "like the calf they cut in two and then walked between its pieces.… Their dead bodies will become food for the birds" (Jer. 34:18–20). Revelation 19 describes the destruction of the wicked at Christ's second coming, "and all the birds gorged themselves on their flesh" (vv. 17–21). So when Jesus's disciples asked Him where those who would be taken at His return would be taken to, and He answered in covenant language, "Where there is a dead body, there the vultures will appear" (Luke 17:37), it is quite clear that He was not describing righteous people being taken to heaven but wicked covenant breakers being taken to destruction. And those who are "left" are the righteous who will inherit the earth and reign with Christ forever (Matt. 5:5).

4. *The Interpreter's Dictionary of the Bible* (Nashville, TN: Abingdon Press, 1962), 629: "Circumcision was widely practiced in antiquity, and was by no means unique with the Hebrews. It was practiced by the Egyptians and by most of the ancient Semites, except the Babylonians and the Assyrians. Of the peoples living adjacent to the ancient Hebrews only the Philistines did not practice it; they were contemptuously referred to by Hebrews as 'the uncircumcised' (Judg. 14:3; 15:18; 1 Sam. 14:6; 17:26, 36; 31:4; 2 Sam. 1:20; 1 Chron. 10:4). It was observed by pre-Mohammedan Arabs and is now generally practiced by Muslims.… The custom has been found among many tribes of Africa, Australia, and America."

5. Cf. 10:12–16; Lev. 26:40–42; Jer. 4:4; 9:23–26; Rom. 2:25–29.

6. "Faltering lips" in the NIV translation, but with the textnote that the original Hebrew reads "uncircumcised of lips."

7. John R. W. Stott makes the same application to baptism in the New Testament: "Moreover, what Paul writes here about circumcision and being a Jew could also be said about baptism and being a Christian. The real Christian, like the real Jew, is one inwardly; and the true baptism, like the true circumcision, is in the heart and by the Spirit. It is not in this case that the inward and spiritual *replace* the outward and physical, but rather that the visible sign (baptism) derives its importance from the invisible reality (washing from sin and the gift of the Spirit), to which it bears witness. It is a grave mistake to exalt the sign at the expense of what it signifies." *The Message of Romans: God's Good News for the World* (Downers Grove, IL: InterVarsity Press, 1994), 94.

8. Paul presses the point home even further to the Jew of his day with remarks that are timeless in their application: "If those who are not circumcised keep the law's requirements, will they not be regarded as though they were circumcised? The one who is not circumcised physically and yet obeys the law will condemn you who, even though you have the written code and circumcision, are a lawbreaker" (Rom. 2:25–26). "(Indeed, when Gentiles, who do not have the law, do by nature things required by the law, they are a law for themselves, even though they do not have the law, since they show that the requirements of the law are written [by the Holy Spirit] on their hearts, their consciences also bearing witness, and their thoughts now accusing, now even defending them.) This will take place on the day when God will judge men's secrets through Jesus Christ, as my gospel declares" (Rom. 2:14–16).

9. Cf. Matt. 7:24–27; Acts 2:37–38; Rom. 2:13; 1 Cor. 7:19; James 1:22; 2:8–12.

10. In Titus 1:10 Paul refers to "those of the circumcision group" and says "they must be silenced." Commenting on "the circumcision group" referred to in this text, the *NIV Study Bible* says they were "like the people of Galatians 2:12, believing that, for salvation or sanctification or both, it was necessary to be circumcised and to keep the Jewish ceremonial law" (1851). In the Jewish mind of Paul's day, circumcision had come to represent both the entire ceremonial law and a meritorious attitude toward obedience to God's commands in general.

11. E.g., Jonah 2:6 where the term *olam* is used to signify the time Jonah was in the belly of the fish.

12. The objection sometimes used against the conditional nature of Hebrew term *olam*, namely, if it doesn't always mean never ending, then how can we know that "everlasting life" will be never ending, is answered by God's assurance that in the new earth "there will be no more death" (Rev. 21:4).

13. *NIV Study Bible* (1676), note on Acts 16:3.

14. Herman Witsius, *The Economy of the Covenants Between God and Man*, vol. 1 (Escondido, CA: den Dulk Christian Foundation, reprinted 1990 from the 1803 English edition of its 1677 original publication in Dutch), 119.

15. E.g., ibid., 117–135; Robertson, 68–74; Kline, *Kingdom Prologue*, 39–41.

16. Robert Jastrow, *God and the Astronomers* (New York: Warner Books, 1984), 17. This story is told on pages 14–22 of this book.

17. Vos, *Biblical Theology*, 139.

18. It is well known to language students that the name of the seventh day of the week is derived from the Hebrew *Shabbath* in many European and Near Eastern languages, not to mention in many other languages around the world that adopted the seven-day week in modern times, borrowing the names of the days from European or Near Eastern languages. Examples include: *sabbata* (Latin), *sabado* (Spanish), *samedi* (French; *same* is a contraction of

Sabbath, *di* signifies day), *Samstag* (German; similar derivation as French, with *tag* meaning day), *sabato* (Italian), *sabado* (Portuguese), *subbota* (Russian), *sobota* (Czech), *subota* (Serbo-Croatian), *sambata* (Romanian), *szombat* (Hungarian), *sebt* (Iraqi Arabic), and *sabi* (Egyptian Arabic). The languages that derive their name for the seventh day from the Hebrew *Shabbat* are all the Romance languages (the languages derived from Latin), all the Slavic languages (like Russian, Czech, and Polish), German, the Semitic languages (Aramaic, Arabic, Syriac, etc.), Hungarian, and doubtless others.

19. Kline, *Kingdom Prologue*, 19, 39.

20. Jacques B. Doukhan, *Daniel: The Vision of the End* (Berrien Springs, MI: Andrews University Press, 1989), 134. "For the connection between Creation and the Flood, see Ps. 74:12–17, cf. 2 Pet. 3:5–13. See also W. A. Gage, *The Gospel of Genesis* ([Winona Lake, IN: Carpenter Books,] 1984), 16–20." See also Paulien, *Meet God Again for the First Time*, 22–27.

21. Kline, *Kingdom Prologue*, 19.

22. It was the unholy lives of His covenant people that brought disrepute on His name and discredited the salvation appeal He was seeking to make to the nations through them: "You who brag about the law, do you dishonor God by breaking the law? As it is written: 'God's name is blasphemed among the Gentiles because of you' [Isa. 52:5]" (Rom. 2:23–24).

23. The significance of the Sabbath as representing deliverance from sin was recognized in the second giving of the law by reference to God's act of deliverance from their slavery in Egypt as a second basis for its observance (besides being a memorial of God as the creator and covenantal Lord of the earth) (Deut. 5:12–15). Note Geerhardus Vos's comment: "The history of Israel was shaped by God intentionally so as to mirror all important situations befalling the people of God in all subsequent ages. When Jehovah appeals to the redemption from Egypt as a motive for obedience, He appeals to something that has its spiritual analogy in the life of all believers. The historical adjustment does not detract from the universal application, but subserves it." *Biblical Theology*, 131.

24. *The Sabbath in Scripture and History*, ed. Kenneth Strand (Washington, DC: Review and Herald Publishing Association, 1982) is an excellent scholarly reference source from the Seventh-day Adventist perspective. For a historical account of the Seventh-day Sabbath, see the five-part video/DVD series, *The Seventh Day: Revelations From the Lost Pages of History* with Hal Holbrook, published by LLT Productions, P.O. Box 205, Angwin, CA 94508.

25. Many converts would have come from nations that already practiced physical circumcision (see footnote 150) and would only need instruction in the new spiritual meaning of the physical mark they already bore.

26. Tim Crosby ("Did the Apostolic Council Set Aside the Sabbath? [part 1]," *Ministry*, vol. 77, no. 2 [February, 2005], 25n6) cites evidence of recent scholarship's emphasis on the New Testament's presentation of a non-ethnic, spiritual Israel. "According to Brent Kinman, 'Lucan Eschatology and the Missing Fig Tree,' *JBL*, 113, no. 4 (1994); 675n23, in recent scholarship on Luke/Acts the essential unity of Israel and the church has been emphasized by defining Israel as an entity consisting of those Jews and Gentiles who believed in Jesus to be the Messiah. Israel has been redefined so as both to incorporate believing Gentiles and to exclude ethnic Jews who do not believe. See J. Jervell, *Luke and the People of God: A New Look at Luke/Acts* (Minneapolis: Augsburg, 1972), 41–74; E. Franklin, *Christ the Lord: A Study in the Purpose and Theology of Luke-Acts* (London: SPCK, 1975), 77–115; D. L. Tiede, *Prophecy and History in Luke-Acts* (Philadelphia: Fortress, 1980), 9–11; idem, 'The Exaltation of Jesus and the

Restoration of Israel in Acts 1,' HTR 79 (1986); 278–286; Fitzmyer, 59; J. T. Carroll, *Response to the End of History: Eschatology and Situation in Luke-Acts*, Society of Biblical Literature Dissertation Series 92 (Atlanta: Scholars Press, 1988)."

27. E.g., Paul's statement, "If you let yourselves be circumcised, Christ will be no value to you at all" (Gal. 5:2), was never said of the Sabbath.

28. Cf. Rom. 1:20, 21, 28; 2:12–16.

29. Rousas John Rushdoony, *Romans and Galatians* (Vallecito, CA: Ross House Books, 1997), 260, commenting on Romans 14:1–5: "If the issue had been the clean and the unclean animals of the Law (Lev. 11:1–45: Deut. 14:3–21; etc.), Paul would have said so. If the issue had been Biblical festivals or the Sabbath, Paul would again have said so. In neither case would he ever have called an earnest desire to obey God's law a matter of 'doubtful disputations.'"

30. R. C. Sproul, *The Gospel of God: Romans* (Ross-shire, Great Britian: Christian Focus Publications, 2000), 234: "Most of the problems that Paul was dealing with were brought into the Christian community by Jewish converts who insisted on keeping the Jewish festivals. The Gentile Christians didn't want to keep the Jewish festivals, they did not mean anything to them. And Paul makes it clear [in Rom. 14:5–6] that they did not have to keep those festivals. He is not referring to the Christian Sabbath, he is talking about specific festivals that were on the Jewish calendar. The Gentile Christians were not required to keep those festivals." Charles R. Erdman, *The Epistle of Paul to the Romans* (Philadelphia: The Westminster Press, 1966), 143: "So, too, one man regards certain days as particularly holy, while another regards all days alike, excepting of course the Sabbath Day." Matthew Henry's commentary on Romans 14:5, 6: "concerning days: (v. 5.) Those who thought themselves still under some kind of obligation by the ceremonial law, esteemed *one day above another*, kept up a respect to the times of the passover, pentecost, new moons, and feasts of tabernacles; thought those days better than other days, and solemnized them accordingly with, particular observances, binding themselves to some religious rest and exercise on those days. Those who knew that all these things were abolished and done away by Christ's coming, esteemed *every day* alike. We must understand it with an exception of the Lord's day, which all Christians unanimously observed; but they make no account, took no notice, of those antiquated festivals of the Jews." Cf. also the note on Romans 14:5, 6 in Robert Jamieson, A. R. Fausset, and David Brown, *A Commentary, Critical and Explanatory, on the Old and New Testaments*, vol. 2 (Hartford: The S. S. Scranton Company, n.d.): "Certainly, if the sabbath was more ancient than Judaism; if, even under Judaism, it was enshrined amongst the eternal sanctities of the Decalogue, uttered, as no other parts of Judaism were, amidst the terrors of Sinai; and if the Lawgiver Himself said of it when on earth, 'The son of man is LORD EVEN OF THE SABBATH DAY' (see Mark 2:28)—it will be hard to show that the apostle must have meant it to be ranked by his readers amongst those vanished Jewish festival days, which only 'weakness' could imagine to be still in force—a weakness which those who had more light ought, out of love, merely to bear with." Numerous other biblical scholars likewise recognize that Romans 14:5–6 does not refer to the Sabbath God instituted at creation, and exempt the creation Sabbath from the "disputable" days at issue in these verses, even though they worship on a day other than the seventh-day Sabbath proscribed by God at creation, a position which we deem indefensible.

31. "If Rom. 14:1–15:13 is to be considered as a generalized adaptation of Paul's previous theological positions, how does one explain the references to 'vegetables' in 14:2 and to 'days' in 14:5? Concurring with Rauer and Dederen, I would argue that 'days' refers to fast days.

Thus, in both instances there is a question of abstinence from food. Furthermore, I would suggest that Paul is generalizing from his discussion in 1 Cor. 8; 10:23–11:1 which dealt with food sacrificed to idols. That is, 'vegetables' is meant to cover all cases of abstinence from food. The reference to 'fast days' is also general, typical. Here Paul may be generalizing from the controversy he had with the Galatians (Gal. 4:10)." Robert J. Karris, "Romans 14:1–15:13 and the Occasion of Romans," a chapter in *The Romans Debate*, ed. Karl P. Donfried (Minneapolis, MN: Augsburg Publishing House, 1977), 89–90. Daniel Harrington likewise acknowledges that "the reference [to 'days' in Rom. 14:5–6] could also be to fast days." *Romans: The Good News According to Paul* (New York: New City Press, 1998), 131. Cf. also the "14th and 15th chapters of Romans demand a comparison with 1 Cor. 8–10." Gunther Bornkamm, "The Letter to the Romans as Paul's Last Will and Testament," in *The Romans Debate*, ed. Karl P. Donfried (Minneapolis, MN: Augsburg Publishing House, 1977), 27; and "[Romans] 14:1–15:13 rediscusses the problems which were earlier considered in 1 Cor. 8–10." T. W. Manson, "St. Paul's Letter to the Romans – and Others," in *The Romans Debate*, ed. Karl P. Donfried (Minneapolis, MN: Augsburg Publishing House, 1977), 15.

32. G. R. Beasley-Murray, "The Second Chapter of Colossians," *Review and Expositor: A Baptist Theological Journal*, vol. LXX, no. 4 (Fall, 1973): 477.

33. Following is a list of seven annual sabbaths (days on which no ordinary work was done) that were part of the services of the Old Testament sanctuary and were observed regardless of the day of the week on which they were kept (they fell on different days each year like our Christmas does): Feast of Unleavened Bread (first day—Lev. 23:7); Feast of Unleavened Bread (last day—Lev. 23:8); Pentecost (Lev. 23:21); Feast of Trumpets (Lev. 23:24); Day of Atonement (Lev. 23:32); Feast of Tabernacles (first day—Lev. 23:35); Feast of Tabernacles (last day—Lev. 23:36). Note the *NIV Study Bible* scholarly note on Colossians 2:16: "The *ceremonial laws* of the OT are here referred to as the shadows (cf. Heb. 8:5; 10:1) because they symbolically depicted the coming of Christ; so any insistence on the observance of such ceremonies is a failure to recognize that their fulfillment has already taken place" (italics added).

34. See Numbers 28:9–10. Note Paul Giem's conclusion on the word *sabbaton* in Colossians 2:16: "The weight of evidence indicates that what Paul actually had reference to was the sacrifices on the seventh-day sabbath prescribed in Num 28:9–10, which pointed forward to Christ and are no longer binding on the Christian since his death. The phrase 'a festival or a new moon or a sabbath' appears to have been a catch-phrase tied to the sacrificial system, and referred to the offerings at the times designated. Whatever else Paul may have had in mind in making his statement in Col 2:16, his primary meaning in that text is that the sacrificial system pointed forward to Christ and therefore is no longer necessary now that Christ has come." "Sabbaton in Col 2:16," *Andrews University Seminary Studies*, vol. 19, no. 3 (Autumn 1981): 195–210. Cf. Kenneth Wood, "The 'Sabbath Days' of Colossians 2:16, 17," *The Sabbath in Scripture and History*, ed. Kenneth Strand (Washington, DC: Review and Herald, 1982), 338–442.

Tim Crosby ("Did the Apostolic Council Set Aside the Sabbath? [part 2]," *Ministry*, vol. 77, no. 4 [April 2005]: 15n5): "Some Pauline passages regarded as referring to Sabbath observance refer instead to sacrifices, such as Colossians 2:16: 'Do not let anyone judge you by what you eat or drink, or with regard to a religious festival, a New Moon celebration or a Sabbath day.' Whenever these phrases ('festival, new moon, Sabbath') are used together in the Old Testament, they refer to the burnt offerings on those days (1 Chron. 23:31; 2 Chron. 2:4; 8:13; 31:3; Isa. 1:13, 14; Ezek. 45:17; 46:4–11; Neh. 10:33; Hos. 2:11). Nehemiah 10 is particularly interesting, because this chapter speaks of both Sabbath keeping (verse 31) and of Sabbath sacrifices (verse 33), but only in verse 33 in reference to the sacrifices do we find the threefold phrase used in Colossians. This phrase refers to the annual, monthly, and weekly sacrifices of Numbers 28 and 29. Numbers 28:2 reads, 'My offering, my food for my offerings by fire, my pleasing odor, you shall take heed to offer to me in its due season.' There follows a description of the daily sacrifices (9–10), the monthly new moon sacrifices (11–15), and the annual festival sacrifices (28:16–29, 38). This interpretation is the only one that makes sense of Colossians 2:17, 'Which are a shadow of things to come, but the body (*soma*) is of Christ.' It is the sanctuary service that is a shadow (Heb. 8:5). The closest parallel is Hebrews 10:1–9, which uses many of the same phrases: 'The law is only a *shadow of the good things that are coming*—not the realities themselves. For this reason it could never, by the same sacrifices repeated endlessly year after year, make perfect those who draw near to worship…therefore, when Christ came into the world, he said: "Sacrifice and offering you did not desire, but a *body (soma)* you prepared for me"…he sets aside the first to establish the second.' Colossians 2:16, 17, then, is a condensed version of the argument of Hebrews 10. Even the '*food and drink*' of Colossians 2:16 relate to the sacrificial service (Cf. Heb. 9:9, 10; Num. 28:24)."

35. Cf. NIV scholarly note on Galatians 4:9–10: "Legalistic trust in rituals, in moral achievement, in law, in good works, or even in cold, dead orthodoxy may indicate a relapse into second childhood on the part of those who should be knowing and enjoying the freedom of full-grown sons. **4:10** *special days*. …which had never been, and can never be, in themselves means of salvation or sanctification…*months and seasons… years*.…The Pharisees meticulously observed all these to gain merit before God." Kenneth S. Wuest, *Galatians in the Greek New Testament* (Grand Rapids, MI: Eerdmans Publishing Company, 1946), 122: "The word *observe* is from *paratereo*. The word denotes careful, scrupulous observance, an intent watching lest any of the prescribed seasons be overlooked. A merely legal or ritualistic system of religion always develops such scrupulousness. Paul, a former Pharisee, was well acquainted with the meticulous care with which the Pharisees kept all the appointed feasts and fasts." Kenneth Grayston, *The Epistles to the Galatians and to the Philippians* (London: The Epworth Press, 1957), 55: "Presumably the well-developed system of Jewish feasts and fasts which Paul did not object to in themselves (some of them he certainly kept, e.g. Acts 20:16, 1 Cor 16:8) but only when they were made a requirement for full salvation." William Hendriksen, *New Testament Commentary: Exposition of Galatians* (Grand Rapids, MI: Baker Book House, 1968), 166: "Paul is saying [in Gal. 4:10] that strict observance of such days and festivals has nothing whatever to do with securing the divine favor. As a foundation upon which to build one's hope of being justified in the sight of God such a superstition is utterly futile, nothing but sinking sand!"

36. Marvin Moore, *The Gospel vs. Legalism: How to Deal With Legalism's Insidious Influence* (Hagerstown, MD: Review and Herald Publishing Association, 1994), 123–124.

37. Troy Martin, "Pagan and Judeo-Christian Time-Keeping Schemes in Gal. 4:10 and Col. 2:16," *New Testament Studies*, vol. 42:1 (January 1996): 112.

38. Cf. Mark D. Nanos, *The Irony of Galatians: Paul's Letter in First-Century Context* (Minneapolis: Fortress Press, 2002), 267, 270: "Paul ridicules the addressees as former idolaters: 'turn back again [ἐπισρέφετε] to the weak and beggarly elements [στοιχεια], of which you again want to be slaves. You observe days, and months, and seasons, and years' (4:10). Troy Martin has argued, against the consensus, that what the addressees are turning back to are not Jewish practices but pagan ones. I find his case convincing, and it is useful for evaluating the matter

at hand....And it would make sense of his call to freedom from a former ('and do not submit again') 'yoke of slavery' (5:1), which for these former pagans is not Jewish Law observance but observance of pagan practices such as are expressed by participation in the imperial cult and other idolatrous festivities that are part of pagan civic life." St. Thomas Aquinas, *Commentary on St. Paul's Epistle to the Galatians*, trans. F. R. Larcher (Albany, NY: Magi Books, 1966), 122–124: Aquinas believed that in this passage Paul warns former "heathens" not to return to "the distinction of days, months, years and times [which are] based on the course of the sun and moon [because] those who observe such distinctions of times are venerating heavenly bodies and arranging their activities according to the evidence of the stars." R. A. Cole, *The Epistle of Paul to the Galatians* (Grand Rapids, MI: Eerdmans Publishing Company, 1965), 118: While Cole acknowledges the possibility that the special days of Gal. 4:10 could have reference to "the liturgical calendar of orthodox Judaism," he adds, "they could equally refer to the quasi-magical observances that we know to have been rife in Ephesus and, presumably, in other parts of Asia Minor (Acts xix)." Philip Mauro, *Our Liberty in Christ* (New York: Fleming H. Revell Company, n.d.), 110: "As heathen worshippers of idols they had observed 'days, and months, and times, and years.' And now, notwithstanding their deliverance from that and every other form of 'bondage' through the cross of Christ, they are returning to it again!"

39. Troy Martin, "Pagan and Judeo-Christian Time-keeping Schemes," 112–113.

40. Ratzlaff, 180–183, 215.

41. Ibid., 182.

42. "In [Christ] you were also circumcised, in the putting off of the sinful nature, not with a circumcision done by the hands of men but with the circumcision done by Christ, having been buried with him in baptism and raised with him through your faith in the power of God, who raised him from the dead" (Col. 2:11–12).

43. Mark 14:22–24; Matt. 26:27; Luke 22:19–20.

44. Richard M. Davidson, "Divorce and Remarriage in Deuteronomy 24:1–4," *Journal of the Adventist Theological Society* 10 (1999): 7. Regarding an intertextual connection between the fourth requirement ("abstain...from sexual immorality," Acts 15:29) with Leviticus 18, see especially H. Reisser, "*porneuo*," in *New International Dictionary of New Testament Theology* (1975), 1.497–501, F. Hauck and S. Schulz, "πόρνη, πόρνς, πόρνεία, πόρνεύω, εκπορνεύω," *Theological Dictionary of the New Testament*, 6:579–595; and Hurley, 95–106, 129–137.

45. The appeals of New Testament writers for historical new covenant believers to live righteous lives were not infrequently based directly on Old Testament teaching. Note an example from Paul, who quotes from the law and the prophets in his admonition to live pure and holy lives: "What agreement is there between the temple of God and idols? For we are the temple of the living God. As God has said: 'I will live with them and walk among them, and I will be their God, and they will be my people' [provision 2 of the new covenant as quoted in Lev. 26:12]. 'Therefore come out from them and be separate, says the Lord. Touch no unclean thing and I will receive you' [Isa. 52:11; Ezek. 20:41]. 'I will be a Father to you, and you will be my sons and daughters, says the Lord Almighty' [2 Sam. 7:14]. Since we have these promises, dear friends, let us purify ourselves from everything that contaminates body and spirit, perfecting holiness out of reverence for God" (2 Cor. 6:16–7:1). In his appeal for us historical new covenant Christians to "purify ourselves," Paul used the same word (*katharizo*, "cleanse, purify") as was used in the Greek translation of Leviticus 16:30 and Daniel 8:14 in reference to the typical and antitypical Day of Atonement.

46. Cf. Isaiah 58:13 where God calls the Sabbath "My holy day;" Mark 2:28 where Jesus says, "the Son of man is Lord of the Sabbath"; Rev. 10:5–6 where an angel takes an oath in the name of "Him…who created the heavens and all that is in them, and the earth and all that is in it, and the sea and all that is in it" which borrows language directly from the fourth commandment that identifies the One who made the Sabbath as "the LORD [who] made the heavens and the earth, the sea, and all that is in them" (Exod. 20:11). The earliest reference attaching the term "the Lord's Day" to Sunday in early-Christian literature occurs more than a decade after the most accepted date for when John wrote Revelation.

47. Jon Paulien, "Revisiting the Sabbath in the Book of Revelation," *Journal of the Adventist Theological Society* 9, nos. 1 & 2 (1998): 185.

48. *NIV Study Bible,* 1943, comment on "tabernacle of the Testimony" in Revelation 15:5.

49. Note comments on Isaiah 66:22–23 by Roy Gane, "The Sabbath and the New Covenant," *Journal of the Adventist Theological Society* 10 (1999): 311–332. Also published online at www.sdanet.org/atissue. A longer version is published at www.biblicalresearch.gc.adventist. org, "The Role of God's Moral Law, Including Sabbath, in the 'New Covenant'":
"Evidence that the Sabbath will continue as a day of worship into the eschatological era is found in Isaiah 66:22–23: [verses quoted].

"The context of these verses shows that Isaiah envisioned the *Eschaton* through the lens of God's plan to use literal Israel to gather all nations to himself at Jerusalem (cf. Isa 66:18–21). As shown by comparison with the book of Revelation, God will still gather all nations to himself (Rev 7:9–10). Since the Sabbath was universal from the beginning, there is no reason why it should be regarded as an obsolete element in Isaiah's eschatological description.

"Isaiah 66:23 mentions on-going eschatological worship on new moon days along with worship on sabbaths. Like sabbaths, new moons were honored by extra sacrifices in the Israelite ritual system (Num 28:11–15). But this does not mean that new moon days cannot be worship days apart from the ritual system even as the Sabbath was. According to Genesis 1:14, before sin or the ritual system existed, God created and appointed the sun and the moon 'to separate the day from the night; and let them be for signs and for seasons and for days and years.' The term 'seasons' here is *mo'adim,* which refers to 'appointed times' (see Brown, Driver and Briggs 1979: 417). In passages such as Leviticus 23:2,4,37,44, this word refers to regular, cyclical times of worship. In Genesis 1:14, the term could not include the Sabbath because the weekly cycle is not marked by movements of the sun or moon in relation to the earth as are days, months, and years. But new moons would fit well into the category of *mo'adim* in Genesis 1:14. Thus, eschatological observance of regular worship at new moons could revive a potential which was recognized at Creation (compare the monthly cycle of the tree of life, Rev 22:2). But we must make two qualifications here:

"1. Isaiah 66:23 mentions sabbaths and new moons as days of worship. But whereas sabbaths by definition are days of rest, new moons are not. Sabbaths are constituted as sabbaths by cessation of ordinary weekly activity. New moons are constituted as such by the position of the moon in relation to the earth (see Gen 1:14). So Isaiah 66:23 does not inform us that new moons will be observed as eschatological days of *rest.*

"2. Since God sanctified the Sabbath and instituted cessation of labor on this day by his example (Gen 2:2–3), which he subsequently reinforced by his command (Ex 20:8–11), the Sabbath is naturally a day of worship. But the Bible does not give us this kind of indication that we should observe new moons as days of worship in the Christian era. It is true that new moons were honored by additional sacrifices at the Israelite sanctuary (Num 28:11–15), but that appears to be all the attention they received. In fact, while the cultic calendar or Numbers 28 includes new moons because it lists the sacrifices, the list of cyclical appointed worship times in Leviticus 23 passes directly from seventh day sabbaths (verse 3) to yearly festivals (verses 4ff), without mentioning new moons at all. The implication seems to be that the new moons did not function as special days of worship except for the addition of some sacrifices."

50. J. Massyngberde Ford, *Revelation* (New York: The Anchor Bible, Doubleday, 1975), 303, 287–288, cf. 278–9, 285, 287–288, 298.

# Chapter 10

# Covenant Rest

The book of Hebrews contains extensive discussions on the two covenants and covenant-related themes. The most extensive discussion in the New Testament on the historical old and new covenants occurs in Hebrews 7–10 (see appendix A on pages 251–266 for an analysis of these chapters). The Bible's most thorough discussion of another important covenant theme—covenant rest—occurs in Hebrews 3 and 4. This study of the covenants would not be complete without exploring the biblical theme of covenant rest, especially as it is presented in Hebrews 3 and 4.

## The Spiritual Rest Offered God's Covenant People

God the Father, Son, and Holy Spirit rest in one another's love. The angels trust God and rest in His love for them. Faith itself is a resting in God, trusting in Him and His promises. This rest of faith is covenant rest. Covenant rest is nourished by an assurance of God's presence and the trustworthiness of His promises. Covenant rest manifests itself in an obedience that comes from faith.

When Moses implored God to lead His covenant people and teach them His ways, God responded, "My Presence will go with you, and I will give you rest " (Exod. 33:14). God Himself is His people's true rest. As they would put their faith in Him, and through the empowerment of His Spirit would obey His commandments, they would experience covenant rest—a confident rest in His love and promises to provide for

their temporal necessities and eternal salvation. "Let the beloved of the LORD rest secure in him, for he shields him all day long, and the one the LORD loves rests between his shoulders" (Deut. 33:12). Covenant rest is the experience that results from resting in God and internalizing the gospel of salvation by grace through faith.

The faith experiences of God's covenant people of old were expressions of this covenant rest in Him:

- Created in God's image, Adam, before he fell, rested in God's love for him, and after he fell rested in God's promise that He would provide One who would crush the head of the serpent (Gen. 1:27; 3:15).
- Enoch by faith rested in God when he "was taken from this life, so that he did not experience death" (Heb. 11:5).
- Noah rested in God "when [he was] warned about things not yet seen, [and] in holy fear built an ark to save his family…and became heir of the righteousness that comes by faith" (Heb. 11:7).
- Abraham was resting in God by faith "when called to go to a place he would later receive as his inheritance, [he] obeyed and went, even though he did not know where he was going, [making] his home in the promised land like a stranger in a foreign country;… for he was looking forward to the city with foundations, whose architect and builder is God" (Heb. 11:8, 10).
- Moses also experienced covenant rest when "by faith…he regarded disgrace for the sake of Christ as of greater value than the treasures of Egypt, because he was looking ahead to his [eternal] reward [promised by God]…[and] saw him who is invisible" (Heb. 11:24–27).

While the Bible nowhere explicitly states that any specific Old or New Testament believer entered this deep, spiritual rest promised by God, it may be safely assumed that all true believers did. It was this covenant rest that God spoke of through Isaiah—"This is what the Sovereign Lord, the Holy One of Israel, says: 'In repentance and *rest* is your salvation, in quietness and trust is your strength,...'"—and through Jeremiah: "This is what the Lord says: 'Stand at the crossroads and look; ask for the ancient paths, ask where the good way is, and walk in it, and you will find *rest* for your souls'" (Isa. 30:15; Jer. 6:16, italics added).

## The Sabbath—Sign of Covenant Rest

The Sabbath represents this covenant rest in God. The word "Sabbath" is not a word that has been translated from an original Hebrew or Greek term in the Bible, but rather one that's been transliterated. A translated word brings the meaning of the original language into the new language. A transliterated word simply brings the sound of the original word into the new language. The English word "Sabbath" comes from the Hebrew word "*shabaat*" and the Greek word "*sabbaton*." Translated, they mean "rest." Thus at creation "God blessed the seventh day and made it holy, because on it he rested [Hebrew, *shabaat*] from all the work of creating that he had done" (Gen. 1:3).

When God codified the Sabbath commandment in the Decalogue at Sinai, He invested it with both temporal and spiritual significance. On the one hand, it provided much needed physical rest and restoration from the labor of the week. On the other, it was to continually remind His covenant people that He Himself was their true rest—they could trust Him, their Creator, to make provision for their temporal needs on this earth, and to make provision also for their every spiritual necessity to secure their place in His eternal kingdom. This truth must never be lost from view. The Sabbath represented not merely physical rest but even more importantly spiritual rest—"so you may know that I am the Lord who makes you holy" (Exod. 31:12–13). The rest envisioned in the Sabbath provided physical rest from labor in order to promote deeper spiritual rest in God. Sabbath rest, with its attendant temporal and spiritual blessings, was not offered exclusively to the nation of Israel, but to all humankind—"the Sabbath was made for man" (Mark 2:27). The only true rest for all humanity is in God. The Sabbath of the fourth commandment represents that universal, timeless truth. The Sabbath always pointed beyond itself to Him who is humanity's true rest. God intended that in observing the Sabbath, humanity would be drawn by His Spirit more deeply into rest in Him.

## The "Rest" Israel Did Experience, and the "Rest" They Didn't

When God brought Israel out of Egypt, He promised to lead them into Canaan and give them rest from their enemies that they might worship Him, be groomed by His Spirit into a holy people who "keep his precepts and observe his laws," and fulfill their missionary purpose unhindered (Ps. 105:42–45; cf. Deut. 12:8–11). He performed mighty acts on their behalf, providing them with abundant evidence that they could trust Him and rest in His promises to provide for their every physical and spiritual necessity. He worked miracles to deliver them from Egypt, opened the Red Sea before them, fed them with manna from heaven, brought water from a rock to quench their thirst, and gave them His law amidst wondrous displays of His power. And yet, when He brought them up to the borders of Canaan to take the land He had promised them, they rebelled, refusing to go in for fear of being impotent against the fortified cities and well-armed inhabitants of the land who appeared to them as giants (Num. 14:2–11). As a result, they were required to return to the wilderness where they wandered around for forty years until a new generation grew up who would exercise greater faith (Num. 14:26–33). This refusal to trust God and enter Canaan at the first opportunity He gave them became known as "the rebellion." Ever after it would symbolize their failure to rest in God and trust in His covenant commitment to enable them to do everything He would ever ask of them. It symbolized the truth that those who do not exercise faith in God will never enter His rest.

Once, during the forty years the Israelites subsequently wandered in the wilderness, they again came to a place with no water. Earlier, at a place they afterward appropriately called Massah (meaning "testing"), they had run out of water and accused God of betraying them. At that time God brought water from a rock to quench their thirst, demonstrating that they could trust Him and rest in Him (Exod. 17:1–7). Now again, years after "the rebellion," they again ran out of water and complained against God, showing that they still did not fully trust Him and were not resting in His love and provision for them. They appropriately named that place Meribah, which means "quarreling" (Num. 20:1–13).

Forty years after "the rebellion," when they had refused to enter Canaan under Moses's leadership, Joshua successfully led Israel into Canaan that they might receive rest from their enemies and be able to love and obey God unhindered. "Now that the LORD your God has given your brothers rest as he promised,…be very careful to keep the commandments and the law that Moses the servant of the LORD gave you: to love the LORD your God, to walk in all his ways, to obey his commands, to hold fast to him and to serve him with all your heart and all your soul" (Josh. 22:4–5; cf. 23:1, 6, 11). In other words, now that God has given you physical rest from your enemies, strive to enter the spiritual rest of complete trust in God that will manifest itself in love for God and obedience to His commandments. As a general rule, however, the physical rest Joshua gave Israel from their enemies never translated into the spiritual rest of complete trust in God, love for God, and obedience to His commandments.

Thus the nation of Israel on the whole failed to trust God who alone could be their true rest and Sabbath. And it is the nature of God's covenant that no matter how many physical blessings He may shower on us, if we do not trust Him, we will never experience the deep spiritual rest He invites us into in covenant relation with Him. Only those who through the Spirit accept the gospel and enjoy a new covenant experience in loving relationship with God will enter that rest.

Though Israel as a whole did not enter that rest, God never gave up. Centuries later we find God, through the psalmist, appealing for the people of Israel to stop hardening their hearts (doubting and disobeying God) so that they might enter into the spiritual rest and security God had promised them: "Today, if you hear his voice, do not harden your hearts as you did at Meribah, as you did that day at Massah in the desert, where your fathers tested and tried me, though they had seen what I did. For forty years I was angry with that generation; I said, 'They are a people whose hearts go astray, and they have not known my ways.' So I declared on oath in my anger, 'They shall never [while remaining in that condition of unbelief and disobedience] enter my rest'" (Ps. 95:7–11).

Yet, even though God continued His appeals through the prophets, the majority of Israel failed to enter God's rest. One senses a deep blend of hope, frustration, and anguish permeating God's appeals to His people through the prophets Isaiah, Jeremiah, and Ezekiel:

- "This is what the Sovereign LORD, the Holy One of Israel, says: 'In repentance and rest is your salvation, in quietness and trust is your strength, but you would have none of it'" (Isa. 30:15).
- "This is what the LORD says: 'Stand at the crossroads and look; ask for the ancient paths, ask where the good way is, and walk in it, and you will find rest for your souls. But you said, "We will not walk in it"'" (Jer. 6:16).
- "Turn! Turn from your evil ways! Why will you die, O house of Israel" (Ezek. 33:11).

However, it is vitally important to keep this truth in mind: no one was precluded from entering God's true rest simply because that person happened to be born and live during the old covenant historical era. While "not all the Israelites accepted the good news [gospel]" (Rom. 10:16), and thus not all entered the deep spiritual covenant rest God offered them, many in the Old Testament period did. As Hebrews 11 testifies, countless thousands of Old Testament believers did through the Spirit's enabling put their trust in God, manifest the obedience that comes from faith, and thereby enter and enjoy God's covenant rest. God Himself was their true rest, their true Sabbath. The rest offered to believers in the new covenant era may be deeper, just as Christ's sacrifice surpasses the sacrifices of animals, but the experience of entering God's rest was no less real for the Old Testament believer than for the New.

Continuing the appeal to enter His rest that God had extended through the law and the prophets, Jesus appealed to those in the historical new covenant era: "Come to me, all you who are weary and burdened, and I will give you rest. Take my yoke upon you and learn from me, for I am gentle and humble in heart, and you will find rest for your souls. For my yoke is easy and my burden is light" (Matt. 11:28–30).

> No one was precluded from entering God's true rest simply because that person happened to be born and live during the old covenant historical era.

The Messiah had come into human history. Covenant rest was now found in Jesus during the historical new covenant era even as it had been found in the LORD[1] during the historical old covenant era. In both eras the Lord Jesus was the true Sabbath rest of His people as they put their trust in Him, relied on Him, and rested in Him.

## The Sabbath-Rest That Remains for the People of God

This thematic backdrop of covenant rest, as developed in the law and the prophets and the subsequent appeal through Jesus to enter that rest, must be kept in mind if we hope to properly understand two critical chapters: Hebrews 3 and 4.

## What the Bible Says

These chapters will first be quoted, followed by brief explanatory notes.

*Hebrews 3:7–19*

Therefore, holy brothers, who share in the heavenly calling, fix your thoughts on Jesus, the apostle and high priest whom we confess. He was faithful to the one who appointed him, just as Moses was faithful in all God's house. Jesus has been found worthy of greater honor than Moses, just as the builder of a house has greater honor than the house itself. For every house is built by someone, but God is the builder of everything. Moses was faithful as a servant in all God's house, testifying to what would be said in the future. But Christ is faithful as a son over God's house. And we are his house, if we hold on to our courage and the hope of which we boast. So, as the Holy Spirit says: "Today, if you hear his voice, do not harden your hearts as you did in the rebellion, during the time of testing in the desert, where your fathers tested and tried me and for forty years saw what I did. That is why I was angry with that generation, and I said, 'Their hearts are always going astray, and they have not known my ways.' So I declared on oath in my anger, 'They shall never enter my rest'" [Ps. 95:7–11]. See to it, brothers, that none of you has a sinful, unbelieving heart that turns away from the living God. But encourage one another daily, as long as it is called Today, so that none of you may be hardened by sin's deceitfulness. We have come to share in Christ if we hold firmly till the end the confidence we had at first. As has been said: "Today, if you hear his voice, do not harden your hearts as you did in the rebellion" [Ps. 95:7–8]. Who were they who heard and rebelled? Were they not all those Moses led out of Egypt? And with whom was he angry for forty years? Was it not with those who sinned, whose bodies fell in the desert? And to whom did God swear that they would never enter his rest if not to those who disobeyed? So we see that they were not able to enter, because of their disbelief.

*Hebrews 4:1–16*

Therefore, since the promise of entering his rest still stands, let us be careful that none of you be found to have fallen short of it. For we also have had the gospel preached to us, just as they did; but the message they heard was of no value to them, because those who heard did not combine it with faith. Now we who have believed enter that rest, just as God has said, "So I declared on oath in my anger, 'They shall never enter my rest.'" And yet his work has been finished since the creation of the world. For somewhere he has spoken about *the seventh day* in these words: "And *on the seventh day God rested from all his work.*" And again in the passage above he says, "They shall never enter my rest." It still remains that some will enter that rest, and those who formerly had the gospel preached to them did not go in, because of their disobedience. Therefore God again set a certain day, calling it today, when a long time later he spoke through David, as was said before: "Today, if you hear his voice, do not harden your hearts." For if Joshua had given them rest, God would not have spoken later about another day. *There remains, then, a Sabbath-rest for the people of God*; for anyone who enters God's rest also rests from his own work, just as God did from his. Let us, therefore, make every effort to enter that rest, so that no one will fall by following their example of disobedience. For the word of God is living and active. Sharper than any double-edged sword, it penetrates even to dividing soul and spirit, joints and marrow; it judges the thoughts and attitudes of the heart. Nothing in all creation is hidden from God's sight. Everything is uncovered and laid bare before the eyes of him to whom we must give account. Therefore, since we have a great high priest who has gone through the heavens, Jesus the Son of God, let us hold firmly to the faith we profess. For we do not have a high priest who is unable to sympathize with our weaknesses, but we have one who has been tempted in every way, just as we are yet was without sin. Let us then approach the throne of grace with confidence, so that we may receive mercy and find grace to help us in our time of need. (italics added)

These chapters begin (in 3:1–6) with references to Moses as the representative of God's grace-based, gospel-bearing, faith-inducing, and mission-directed historical old covenant and Jesus as the representative of the new. Both are honored as faithful stewards in God's house, but Jesus is as much more honored than Moses as His role is superior in the plan of salvation.

Psalm 95 is quoted (in 3:7–12), warning worshipers in the historical new covenant era against the faithless response to God that Israel demonstrated in "the rebellion" and during their experience in the wilderness. Those in the new covenant era who lack ultimate trust in God will as surely fail to enter God's covenant rest as did faithless Israel of old. This warning to new covenant worshipers appears all the more relevant and ominous in light of Jesus's warning question to the New Testament generation: "However, when the Son of Man comes, will he find faith on the earth?" (Luke 18:8).

Note how obedience and faith, disobedience and unbelief are used interchangeably throughout these chapters. For example, see Hebrews 3:18–19: "And to whom did God swear that they would never enter his rest if not to those who *disobeyed*? So we see that they were not able to enter, because of their *disbelief*" (italics added). God never intended that faith and obedience be separated in the new covenant experience that "enters God's rest." Resting in God—trusting Him, growing in Him, relying on Him to empower us by His Spirit to love Him and obey Him—this is what it means to "enter God's rest."

Note that God's rest is equated with the gospel in chapter 4: "Therefore, since the promise of entering *his rest* still stands, let us be careful that none of you be found to have fallen short of it. For we also have had *the gospel* preached to us, just as they did; but the message they heard was of no value to them, because those who heard did not combine it with faith" (vv. 1–2, italics added). The same everlasting gospel that was preached through God's historical old covenant is being preached through the new. It must also be true that all those who accepted the gospel by faith in the historical old covenant era entered God's rest, just as those who accept the gospel by faith in the historical new covenant era do.

Though Joshua led Israel into Canaan so that they experienced the physical rest from their enemies God promised them, he was not able to lead them as an entire nation into the deeper spiritual rest God offered them in Himself, through faith in Him. If he had, God would not have continued appealing through David (Psalm 95) for them to enter His rest (Heb. 4:8).

*"There remains, then, a Sabbath-rest for the people of God"* (4:9). All eight previous uses of the word "rest" in Hebrews 3 and 4 are a translation of the Greek word *katapausis*. But in this verse (4:9) the author deliberately used the Greek word, *sabbatismos*, a word not used elsewhere in the Bible, but used in extrabiblical sources to mean observance of the seventh-day Sabbath.[2] Even someone who doesn't understand Greek can tell from the sound of this word that it makes reference to the Sabbath. The author of Hebrews himself leaves no doubt, for in this same context he links God's continuing appeal to enter His rest to the origin of the Sabbath at creation when "on the seventh day God rested from all his work" (4:4). By declaring that a Sabbath rest remains for the covenant people of God, Hebrews rescues true Sabbath observance from the faithless legalism of Judaism into which it had fallen and restores it to its true covenant role as a sign between God and His people that He is their Creator and the only One who can make them a holy people who can enter His rest.

There were many in Israel who ceased from work on the Sabbath and attempted to abide by the more than 1,500 additional laws the rabbis had added to the Sabbath, but who failed to enter God's rest "because they pursued it not by faith but as if it were by works"—an old covenant experience (Rom. 9:32). However, it is equally true that all those in the historical old covenant period who through the Spirit enjoyed a new covenant experience and thereby entered God's rest were observing the Sabbath according to the commandment. For them

> By declaring that a Sabbath rest remains for the covenant people of God, Hebrews rescues true Sabbath observance from the faithless legalism of Judaism into which it had fallen.

Sabbath observance achieved the purpose God designed for it, pointing beyond itself to Him who is their true rest. By observing it they were drawn by His Spirit more deeply into true covenant rest in Him.

I was taught from childhood to observe the Sabbath of the fourth commandment. I know from personal experience what a burdensome yoke Sabbath observance can be when it's applied legalistically, and also what an incredible blessing it can be when it's observed in a new covenant experience. I have no doubt in my mind but that by the agency of His Spirit God has worked through the Sabbath to draw my heart out more fully toward Him and to increase my love for Him. I have no doubt that the dedication of the Sabbath hours to worship, rest, and service has resulted in great spiritual blessing not only to my own spirit but to many others as well. If not for the time provided by the Sabbath hours I would probably not have taken time to minister to these people. I tend to be a fairly high-end type-A person who totes around shamefully long to-do lists. God has used the Sabbath to help keep me in balance and focused on people to the extent that I am. I am convinced that if any damage has accrued to me or to others in my sphere of influence relative to the Sabbath, it has not resulted from my attempts to observe the Sabbath but from my failure to observe it more fully as God originally gave it and as Jesus magnified it through His own example in His Sabbath miracles. For me it points beyond itself to Him. He is my true Sabbath.

"For anyone who enters God's rest also rests from his own work, just as God did from his" (4:10). Anyone who has experienced conversion from an immoral life or from legalism knows what it means to "rest from his own work." It is rest from the hopelessness engendered by immorality and from the insecurity and dry formality engendered by legalism. Isaiah said it well: "But the wicked are like the tossing sea, which cannot rest.…'There is no peace,' says my God, 'for the wicked'" (Isa. 57:20–21). To which the psalmist answers: "Great peace have they who love your law" (Ps. 119:165). No heart knows such peace and love except one that rests in God as its true Sabbath. The heart that has been set free knows the meaning of Jesus's offer: "Come to me, all you who are weary and burdened, and I will give you rest."

Sabbath rest is exemplified in the testimony of Seminar speaker Shelley J. Quinn, who began observing the seventh-day Sabbath as an adult:

> I grew up in a family that demanded perfection from me. The church I attended as a youth painted a picture of a wrathful God who also demanded perfection. I thought the Heavenly Father was watching over me, ready to zap me when I missed the mark.
>
> All of my life I was performing for acceptance—for my family's and my God's. It wasn't until the Lord taught me His Sabbath truth that I was cut free from the cord of this performance mentality.
>
> The first time I ever experienced complete *freedom from performance* was on the first Sabbath I celebrated. I sensed I had been given permission to sit back, relax and enjoy—no work, no daily duties, no demands. But most of all, I had the whole day to spend with God.
>
> I suddenly knew *that I knew* He would sanctify me—causing me to be all that He called me to be. Talk about entering into His rest! There is nothing like it. That's why Exodus 31:13 is my favorite Scripture about the Sabbath. It's a sign for me to remember that it is God who works in me to sanctify me—developing Christ's character of holiness.
>
> Still, towards the end of the week, I sometimes find I'm slipping back into a *performance mentality*—thinking I'm not doing enough for God. But as I welcome the Sabbath, God reminds me of Galatians 3:3, "Are you so foolish? Having begun in the Spirit, are you now being made perfect by the flesh?" The Sabbath reminds me that apart from Christ, I can do nothing.
>
> My life experience with God went through a radical transformation when I began celebrating His seventh-day Sabbath. I became aware that His grace is sufficient—His power is made perfect in my weakness.
>
> I learned obedience is the pathway to blessing. And it's so much easier to obey, now that I know to depend totally upon Him for all things. Celebrating the Sabbath has taught me to receive God's love in a new dimension.[3]

"Let us, therefore, make every effort to enter *that* rest, so that no one will fall by following their example of disobedience" (4:11, italics added). The appeal here is to not be content with that form of religion that is external only and a continual burden. Sabbath-keeping that experiences nothing deeper than mere cessation from physical labor will not enter the true covenant rest of God. The striving to enter the true rest of God called for in this text is "the good fight of faith" to be fought with "the sword of the Spirit, which is the word of God" and prayer, learning to trust Him and lean on Him and rest in Him through all circumstances, "for he who promised is faithful" (1 Tim. 6:12 NKJV; Eph. 6:17–18; Heb. 10:23). Anyone who responds to Jesus's invitation, "Come to me, all you who are weary and burdened," trusting His promise, "and I will give you rest" (Matt. 11:28), will not fail to enter that rest, for He has also promised, "Whoever comes to me I will never drive away" (John 6:37).[4] And those who sincerely and persistently ask God to show them His glory, that they might increasingly "grasp how wide and long and high and deep is the love of Christ, and to know this love that surpasses knowledge—that you may be filled to the measure of all the fullness of God" (Eph. 3:18–19), will not fail to experience more and still more of His rest. Furthermore, this great truth is universal and timeless, experienced by believers of every people group and in every era of human history.

Another wonderful assurance has been granted in Hebrews 4:12–13 to all who earnestly desire a new covenant experience with God: "For the word of God is living and active. Sharper than any double-edged sword, it penetrates even to dividing soul and spirit, joints and marrow; it judges the thoughts and attitudes of the heart. Nothing in all creation is hidden from God's sight. Everything is uncovered and laid bare before the eyes of him to whom we must give account." Under the supervision of the Spirit, the Word of God in Scripture received by faith searches out and destroys anything in the heart that inclines toward an old covenant experience, and will continue to produce more and still more of the fruit of righteousness that will enable the believer's witness to influence the lives of others toward the kingdom of God and true covenant rest in Him. For He has promised: "As the rain and the snow come down from heaven, and do not return to it without watering the earth and making it bud and flourish, so that it yields seed for the sower and bread for the eater, so is my word that goes out from my mouth: it will not return to me empty, but will accomplish what I desire and achieve the purpose for which I sent it" (Isa. 55:10–11).

Finally, this extended passage ends (4:14–16) as it began with a focus on Jesus. He who came among us, as one like us, understands our weaknesses and can sympathize with our suffering. Being without sin, He is able to do for us everything that is necessary to secure our place in His eternal kingdom. Because He ministers constantly on our behalf from His position in heaven as our great high priest, we are called to "hold firmly to the faith we profess" and "approach the throne of grace with confidence, so that we may receive mercy and find grace to help us in our time of need" (4:14–16). Those who by the Spirit enter God's rest will not be without temptations and trials. They may experience some failures in temporal and spiritual matters. But through eyes that have been opened by the Spirit, they discern God's throne as a throne of grace—not an indulgent, patronizing grace, but a forgiving, cleansing, and empowering grace that will supply all our needs "in our time of need." That throne of grace represents to them the constancy of His promise given long ago: "My Presence will go with you, and I will give you rest" (Exod. 33:14).

## Summary

God's covenant provides spiritual rest and security for all who trust Him. God provided Israel with physical rest from their enemies and invited them to experience the deeper spiritual rest in Him through their trust in Him and confident reliance on Him to supply every need, both temporal and eternal. On the whole, due to their unbelief and disobedience, Israel failed to experience the spiritual rest God offered them in His covenant. Many, however, did experience that rest as Hebrews 11 testifies. God offers that same spiritual rest to all in the New Testament era who trust Him and exercise an obedience that comes from faith. This covenant rest has been signified in both Old and New Testament eras by the Sabbath of the fourth commandment which points beyond itself to Him who is our Creator, our Sanctifier, our true Rest, our Sabbath. "There remains, then, a Sabbath rest [Greek, *sabbatismos*] for the people of God."

## Notes

1. "Yahweh" is the Hebrew Old Testament name for God. It appears in most English translations as "Lord" (in small caps). New Testament authors sometimes identified Jesus with Yahweh of the Old Testament. For example, Hebrews 1:10–12 ascribes to Jesus the hymn sung to Yahweh in Psalm 102. In his commentary on John's vision of the glorified Christ walking among the symbolic lampstands, proclaiming, "I am the first and the last" (Rev. 1:17), Ranko Stefanovic (*Revelation of Jesus Christ*, 101–102) comments: "The statement 'I am the first and the last' is very significant. It mirrors the statement in Isaiah's account of the God of the covenant: 'I am the first and the last, and there is no God apart from Me' (44:6; cf. 41:4; 48:12). In using this Old Testament description of God, Jesus is identifying himself as none other than the Old Testament Yahweh of the covenant. At the outset of this vision, the resurrected Christ is 'one like a son of man' fulfilling God's covenant promise to ancient Israel: 'I will also walk among you and be your God and you will be My people' (Lev. 26:12). Through the symbolic walk among the lampstands, Christ signifies his presence and ministry to the churches. This concluding portion [Christ's statement, 'I am the first and the Last'] makes clear that in the resurrected and exalted Jesus Christ, the very God of the covenant has come down, and he is with his New Testament people. He is their only hope as the end draws near, for 'there is no God apart from him.' God spoke through Isaiah: 'You are My witnesses,' declares the Lord, 'and My servant whom I have chosen, so that you may know and believe Me and understand that I am He. Before Me there was no God formed, and there will be none after Me. I, even I, am the Lord, and there is no savior besides Me. It is I who have declared and saved and proclaimed, and there was no strange god among you, so you are My witnesses,' declares the Lord, 'and I am God. Even from eternity I am He, and there is none who can deliver out of My hand; I act and who can reverse it?' (Isa. 43:1–13) The resurrected and exalted Christ is none other than the God of the covenant."

2. Samuele Bacchiocchi, *The Sabbath Under Crossfire* (Berrien Springs, MI: Biblical Perspectives, 1998), 124: "*Sabbatismos*…was used by pagans and Christians as a technical term for Sabbathkeeping. Examples can be found in the writings of Plutarch, Justin, Epiphanius, the Apostolic Constitutions, and the Martyrdom of Peter and Paul." He footnotes Plutarch, *De Superstitione* 3 (Moralia 1660); Justin Martyr, *Dialogue with Trypho* 23, 3; Epiphanius, *Adversus Haereses* 30, 2, 2; *Apostolic Constitutions* 2, 36; cf. Andrew Lincoln, also quoted by Bacchiocchi (p. 125): "The term [*Sabbatismos*] denotes the observance or celebration of the Sabbath. This

usage corresponds to the Septuagint usage of the cognate verb *sabbatizo* (cf. Ex 16:23; Lev 23:32; 26:34f.; 2 Chron 36:21) which also has reference to Sabbath observance." Andrew T. Lincoln, "Sabbath, Rest, and Eschatology in the New Testament," in *From Sabbath to the Lord's Day*, ed. Donald A. Carson (Grand Rapids, MI: Zondervan, 1982), 213.

The King James and New King James translations do not distinguish between the meaning of *katapausis* and *sabbitismos*, and mistakenly translate both words simply as "rest." This is misleading, for it does not convey the author's intention to remind Hebrew Christians of the full meaning God invested in the Sabbath when He instituted it at creation (Heb. 4:4) and embedded it in the Ten Commandments.

3. Danny Shelton and Shelly J. Quinn, *The Ten Commandments Twice Removed* (n.a.: Remnant Publications, 2005), 88–89.

4. Ellen G. White, commenting on the rest to be found in Jesus through His promise in John 6:37, wrote the following: "The Message of God to me for us is 'Him that cometh to Me, I will in no wise cast out' (Jn. 6:37). If you have nothing else to plead before God but this one promise from your Lord and Savior, you have the assurance that you will never, never be turned away. It may seem to you that you are hanging upon a single promise, but appropriate that one promise, and it will open to you the whole treasure house of the riches of the grace of Christ. Cling to that promise and you are safe. 'Him that cometh unto me I will in no wise cast out.' Present this assurance to Jesus, and you are as safe as though inside the city of God" (*Ms. Release*, vol. 10, 175, as quoted in the week of prayer edition of the *Adventist Review* [October 28, 1993], 8).

# Chapter 11

# Ten Timeless Truths

This study of the covenant(s) has prayerfully and carefully examined the new covenant, identified four major promises or provisions that constitute its DNA markers, and traced those markers back through time. Examining the Old Testament record in light of the new covenant DNA markers revealed that God had either implicitly or explicitly embedded the new covenant promises in every previous covenant He had made with humankind, and had reiterated them here and there in clearly identifiable clusters throughout the whole of the Old Testament as well as the New.

Another finding of this study was the emergence of a set of timeless, universal, gospel truths taught throughout both Old and New Testaments. True believers living in every era of human history have experienced these gospel truths, and as such are considered new covenant believers whether they lived in the historical Old or New Testament eras.

There was a historical old covenant and a historical new covenant represented respectively by the Old Testament and New Testament historical eras.[1] Both the historical old and new covenants taught these same timeless, gospel truths, for there is only one true gospel. At the same time those who have responded in faith to this universal, timeless gospel, and within whom the gospel has become internalized and ingrained, have been recognized in Scripture as having a new covenant

experience, no matter whether they lived in the Old or New Testament historical era (Heb. 4:2; 11). By the same token, those who have rejected this gospel, or who have perverted it into a religious system of works, relying on their own good works for righteousness, have been recognized in Scripture as having experienced an external religion, carved in stone, in granite only—an old covenant experience.

As expressed in Jeremiah, with very minor adaptations in Hebrews, the new covenant reads:

> "The time is coming," declares the LORD, "when I will make a new covenant with the house of Israel and with the house of Judah. It will not be like the covenant I made with their forefathers when I took them by the hand to lead them out of Egypt, because they broke my covenant, though I was a husband to them," declares the LORD. "This is the covenant I will make with the house of Israel after that time," declares the LORD. "I will put my law in their minds and write it on their hearts. I will be their God, and they will be my people. No longer will a man teach his neighbor, or a man his brother, saying, 'Know the LORD,' because they will all know me, from the least of them to the greatest," declares the LORD. "For I will forgive their wickedness and will remember their sins no more." (Jer. 31:31–34)

Following are the four promises/provisions (the DNA markers) God embedded in His new covenant:

**Promise/Provision 1** (Sanctification)—"I will put my laws in their minds and write them on their hearts" (Jer. 31:33; Heb. 8:10).

**Promise/Provision 2** (Reconciliation)—"I will be their God and they will be my people" (Jer. 31:33; Heb. 8:10).

**Promise/Provision 3** (Mission)—"No longer will a man teach his neighbor, or a man his brother, saying, 'Know the Lord' because they will all know me, from the least of them to the greatest" (Jer. 31:34; Heb. 8:11).

**Promise/Provision 4** (Justification)—"I will forgive their wickedness and will remember their sins no more" (Jer. 31:34; Heb. 8:12).

These promises have been accepted, internalized, and ingrained in people of every era who through the operation of the Holy Spirit have by grace through faith gained a new covenant experience. They have been rejected or perverted by all who have lived an old covenant experience. Keeping these four promises/provisions in mind, we can identify the following ten timeless, universal truths of the gospel that are taught in both the Old and New Testaments:

## 1. Adam was created within God's everlasting covenant of love with God's law written on his heart.

God created Adam in His image (Gen. 1:26–27) as an expression of the everlasting covenant of intra-Trinitarian love that extends out from God to embrace all of creation. Thus God's covenant with Adam at creation, while it required his obedience for him to live forever, was also a covenant of grace (2 Tim. 1:9). Since Adam was created perfect, we can assume that God wrote His law in his heart (sanctification: promise/provision 1 of the new covenant). God was Adam's God and he was God's child (reconciliation: promise/provision 2 of the new covenant). Adam had no need for anyone to teach him about God, for he knew God personally and intimately (mission: promise/provision 3 of the new covenant). God had made provision to forgive and redeem Adam should he fall into sin (justification: promise/provision 4 of the new covenant) (1 Cor. 1:23–24 with 2:7–8; 2 Cor. 5:19; 1 Pet. 1:18–20; Rev. 13:8).

## 2. Adam sinned against God and His covenant, subjecting all humanity to a sinful nature and death.

Due to Adam's sin, all of his descendants are born with a sinful nature—at enmity against God, incapable of even seeking God without His intervention, bound over to disobedience, and made subject to death (Gen. 8:21; Ps. 51:5; Jer. 13:23; John 3:6; Rom. 3:10–17; 5:12, 15; 8:7–8; 11:32). Not only are we born with sinful natures due to Adam's sin, but each of us also sins personally and stands guilty before God in judgment, destined to die "the second death" (1 Kings 8:46; Isa. 24:5; Rom. 3:23; 5:12; 6:23; Rev. 20:14–15). Sin is identified as works of the flesh, which can be manifest either as rebellion against God or as attempts to gain righteousness by good works (Rom. 9:31–32; 14:23; Gal. 3:2–3, 10; 5:22–23; Phil. 3:4–6; 1 John 3:4).

### 3. The sinful nature manifests itself in an old covenant experience toward God and His law.

Under the influence of Satan and the sinful nature, God's holy law becomes a mere written code engraved in granite. It becomes an instrument of sin, bondage, condemnation, and death leading to an old covenant experience—something we must die to in order to find true life (Romans 7; 2 Corinthians 3; Galatians 3–4).

### 4. God's everlasting-covenant response to sin was the covenant of redemption.

Immediately after Adam sinned, God's covenant of redemption—His "secret wisdom, a wisdom that has been hidden and that God destined for our glory before time began," His "grace given us in Christ Jesus before the beginning of time"—went into effect (1 Cor. 2:7; 2 Tim. 1:9). He promised to produce a Savior who would defeat Satan and bring salvation (Gen. 3:15). In so doing, God treated sinful humanity as He would want to be treated Himself if our situation and His had been reversed—an expression of His everlasting covenant of sacrificial love for the good of the other, which "sums up the Law and the Prophets" (Matt. 7:12).

### 5. God's covenant of redemption encompasses His four promises/ provisions of the new covenant, the gospel.

In the new covenant God gave four promises or provisions (enumerated above) which express His goals for all humankind and constitute the essence of the gospel, which was proclaimed throughout both the New Testament and the Old, including the Sinai covenant (Deut. 30:11–14 with Rom. 10:10–16; Jer. 31:31–34; Heb. 4:2, 6; 8:8–12). Through these four promises/provisions God reaffirmed His love for humankind and pledged to restore all people to their original estate in God's image. Throughout the history of the covenant of redemption God has been working to accomplish these four promises/provisions in every heart, and is indeed accomplishing them in the hearts of those who are receptive and believe. Their full realization, however, awaits the second coming of Jesus when "face to face" the saved "shall know [Him] fully," "will be his people, and God himself will be with them and be their God"; there will no longer be any need to teach anyone about God, for all will know Him, from the least of us to the greatest (1 Cor. 13:12; Rev. 21:3; Jer. 31:34; Heb. 8:11). Until then, even though we now "see but a poor reflection" and "know [Him only] in part," God "through us spreads everywhere the fragrance of the knowledge of him…among those who are being saved and those who are perishing" (2 Cor. 2:14). Every believer throughout history has experienced a "now/not-yet" fulfillment of these four covenant promises/provisions.

## 6. God has prepared every heart to receive the gospel and be reconciled to Him as a new covenant believer.

God has planted in every heart an enmity against Satan, a God-shaped vacuum that hungers for a loving relationship with God, a vacuum that cannot be filled in an enduring, satisfying way by anything other than God Himself, from whom we came and to whom we belong (Gen. 3:15; Acts 17:24–28). By this every heart has been prepared to receive the gospel and be reconciled to God.[2] This corresponds to promise/provision 2 of the new covenant (reconciliation). The ultimate fulfillment of this promise/provision will take place at the second coming of Jesus—"I will be their God and they will be my people" (Jer. 31:33; Heb. 8:10).

## 7. Through His death and resurrection, Jesus gained and extends forgiveness and justification to every sinner.

Through the righteousness displayed in the perfect life of Jesus, and by the shedding of His blood, forgiveness of sin and salvation have been purchased for the whole world, to be received by faith: "We have put our hope in the living God, who is the Savior of all men, and especially of those who believe" (1 Tim. 4:10; cf. Isa. 53:1–11; Zech. 3:1–7; John 1:29; Rom. 3:22–24). The theological term for this divine gift is *justification*. This corresponds to promise/provision 4 of the new covenant and anticipates its ultimate fulfillment at the second coming of Jesus: "I will forgive their wickedness and will remember their sins no more" (Jer. 31:34; Heb. 8:12).

## 8. The Holy Spirit is the divine agent in the conversion of sinners.

Yielding to the work of the Holy Spirit, the sinner appropriates God's gifts of forgiveness, righteousness, and eternal salvation by faith (Eph. 2:1–8). This is the meaning of conversion—being "born again" or "born of the Spirit"—and is the work of God in the hearts of those who respond to His saving initiative (1 Sam. 10:6, 9; John 3:3–6; Phil. 2:13; Titus 3:3–7). No person in history has ever been converted apart from the ministry of the Holy Spirit. Under the influence of the Holy Spirit, God's law fulfills its intended purpose as an instrument of righteousness, alerting us to our sin and need of forgiveness, and leading us to true spiritual freedom in dependence on Christ as our only righteousness (Rom. 5:20–21; 7:13; 8:2).

## 9. The Holy Spirit is the divine agent in the sanctification of believers.

The Holy Spirit works to write God's law in the heart of believers, teaching them to love God and His law as Adam once did, and to live by faith like Jesus—a new covenant experience (Deut. 30:6; Ps. 40:8; Jer. 31:33; Rom. 7:22, 25; Phil. 2:13; Heb. 8:10). The theological term for this process is *sanctification*. Sanctification is the work of God in the hearts of those who willingly respond in faith to His saving initiative to make them holy as He is holy (Exod. 31:12; Lev. 20:7–8 with 1 Pet. 1:15; Acts 26:18). Faith in God and obedience to His commandments have always been linked in the divine economy (Gen. 15:5–6; 26:4–5; Hebrews 11; James 2:17–26; Rev. 14:12). God's invitation to love Him and keep His commandments was never intended as a call for lost people to do this to be saved, but always as an enabling call to those who are being saved (Deut. 30:6, 11–14; Rom. 10:5–8, 16). In Christ we are proleptically sanctified and glorified even while we are in the process of being saved (Rom. 4:17; 8:30; 1 Cor. 1:2; 6:11). This corresponds to promise/provision 1 (sanctification) of the new covenant and anticipates its ultimate fulfillment at the second coming of Jesus: "I will put my laws in their minds and write them on their hearts" (Jer. 31:33; Heb. 8:10).

## 10. Every believer has been called to share in God's mission to seek the lost.

Converted people share Christ's passion for the salvation of lost people (Gen. 12:3; 28:14; Psalm 67; Matt. 28:19–20; 2 Cor. 2:14; 5:20). They live as spiritual priests and kings whose works show forth the praises of Him who called them out of darkness into His marvelous light (Exod. 19:5–6 with 1 Pet. 2:9–10; Isa. 49:6; Matt. 5:14–16; Eph. 2:10). Working through the loving lives and witness of His children, God purposes to reach the hearts of unbelievers and restore them to Himself (Matt. 5:16; James 5:19–20). "Thanks be to God, who always leads us in triumphal procession in Christ and through us spreads everywhere the fragrance of the knowledge of him" (2 Cor. 2:14). This corresponds to promise/provision 3 (mission) of the new covenant and anticipates its ultimate fulfillment at the second coming of Jesus: "No longer will a man teach his neighbor, or a man his brother, saying, 'Know the Lord' because they will all know me, from the least of them to the greatest" (Jer. 31:34; Heb. 8:11).

In summary, the four divine promises/provisions that constitute the new covenant DNA were expressions of God's everlasting covenant of love which embraced His creation before the beginning of time and continue to do so into eternity. Applied to humankind, they represent God's total commitment in grace to the eternal happiness and security of His children. The following table briefly depicts the applicability of these divine promises/provisions to humankind's past, present, and future:

| The Covenant of Creation | The Covenant of Redemption | New Covenant Promises Fully Realized[3] |
| --- | --- | --- |
| Adam before sin | Adam's Sin to Second Coming | New Earth |
| • New Covenant promises/provisions 1–3 (sanctification, reconciliation, and mission) were realized in Adam at creation.<br>• New Covenant promise/provision 4 (justification) was already a commitment in God's heart and plan if needed. | • New Covenant promises/provisions 1–4 (sanctification, reconciliation, mission, and justification) constitute the everlasting gospel and have been in the process of being realized by the agency of the Holy Spirit in the hearts and minds of all who have accepted these divine promises by faith. | • New Covenant promises/provisions 1–3 (sanctification, reconciliation, and mission) will be fully realized in the experiences of God's covenant people throughout eternity.<br>• New Covenant promise/provision 4 (justification) will be unnecessary as sin will not rise up a second time, but this provision will never be absent from God's heart and everlasting covenant commitment to His creation. |

## Notes

1. Vos, *Biblical Theology*, 26: "When the Bible speaks of a two-fold *berith* [Hebrew Old Testament term for 'covenant'], a two-fold *diatheke* [Greek New Testament term for 'covenant'], it means by the 'old' covenant not the entire period from the fall of man to Christ, but the period from Moses to Christ. Nevertheless, what precedes the Mosaic period in the description of Genesis may be appropriately subsumed under the 'Old Covenant.'"

2. Thus, John Stott encourages Christians who witness to unbelievers: "Conscience is our ally. In all evangelism, I find it a constant encouragement to say to myself, 'The other person's

conscience is on my side.'" Stott, *The Message of Romans*, 89.

3. See LaRondelle, *Our Creator Redeemer*, chapter 11, "The Consummated Covenant in the Book of Revelation," for a detailed discussion of this subject. Representative are the following statements:

Page 154: "John integrates all God's previous covenants into one glorious consummation in the New Jerusalem, thus demonstrating that essential unity of God's work in creation, redemption, and restoration."

Page 157: "We may say that Revelation 21–22 unite all God's covenant promises in one magnificent apotheosis. John's prophetic language refers many times to the Old Testament covenants of God in redemption history. Its apparent purpose is to reassure the churches that God's covenants are in the process of being fulfilled through Christ, the divine Son of David, and in His people. Those covenants will be consummated with unimaginable splendor in the New Jerusalem on the earth made new for all God's covenant peoples.

"God's ideal for Israel—that all Israelites be 'kings and priests' (Exod. 19:6)—will finally be realized (see Rev. 20:6; 22:5). All the redeemed will see God's 'face' and worship Him without any human intermediary (22:4).

Page 160: "This is the lofty goal of all salvation history, the climax of all covenant promises."

# Chapter 12

# Living the Covenants

"Avoid foolish controversies and genealogies and arguments and quarrels about the law, because these are unprofitable and useless" (Titus 3:9). Paul's caveat is certainly applicable to this current work. If a discussion of the law and covenant(s) results in nothing more than an exchange, sometimes a clash, of ideas, then we may be among those indicted by the prophet Isaiah: "Your fasting ends in quarreling and strife, and in striking each other with wicked fists. You cannot fast as you do today and expect your voice to be heard on high" (Isa. 58:4).

That warning must haunt every discussion of theology and every evangelistic presentation. Theology and evangelism that are true to their names should draw the theologians and evangelists themselves nearer to the true heart of God and should engage them in His true fast:

> Is not this the kind of fasting I have chosen: to loose the chains of injustice and untie the cords of the yoke, to set the oppressed free and break every yoke? Is it not to share your food with the hungry and to provide the poor wanderer with shelter—when you see the naked, to clothe him, and not to turn away from your own flesh and blood? Then your light will break forth like the dawn, and your healing will quickly appear; then your righteousness will go before you, and the glory of the LORD will be your rear guard. Then you will call, and the LORD will answer; you will cry for help, and he will say, Here am I. (Isa. 58:6–9)

It is one thing to study the covenants, but it is another to let our study impact our lives, leading us to be more Christlike, living to bless others through acts of selfless service. If it does not, then we have become "a resounding gong or a clanging cymbal" that Paul warned against (1 Cor. 13:1).

How living the new covenant experience will express itself in our lives will vary from person to person. Here is what living an old covenant versus a new covenant experience means to me relative to the four promises/provisions of God's covenant.

## Promise/Provision 1 (Sanctification): "I will put my law in their minds and write it on their hearts."

### Old Covenant Experience

- I treat the commandments of God lightly and am willing to settle for less than full, uncompromising commitment to God and His will.
- I rely on church attendance, tithe paying, and abstinence from pornography, tobacco, alcohol, etc. as that which will put me in good standing before God in the final judgment.
- I serve in a church ministry to put icing on the merit cake.

### New Covenant Experience[1]

- I rely completely on the mercy and grace of God as the only sufficiency for my salvation and all that attends it.
- I rejoice that by His grace my name is written in heaven.
- I seek and rely on God's presence moment by moment to enable me to love Him with all my heart and soul and strength, and my neighbor as myself.
- I am content with nothing less than perfect conformity to God's will, but I realize that such conformity can only be attained by Jesus living and abiding in me constantly.

- I trust God to finish in His own time and way the good work He has begun in me.
- I believe that as I behold Him daily through prayer and meditation on His word, God is at work by His Spirit to restore His image in me, bringing every thought and action into obedience to Christ.
- I trust that He will lead me by His Spirit into a life of wholehearted "obedience that comes from faith" as a natural, spontaneous expression of the love that He has poured out into my heart.
- I pray, "Turn my heart to You, that I might walk in all Your ways."

## Promise/Provision 2 (Reconciliation): "I will be their God and they will be my people."

### Old Covenant Experience

- I think of my spiritual life as a set of rules that I must strive to comply with.
- I consider devotional exercises as tasks that need to be done to gain acceptance with God and a place in heaven.
- I am content with a lifetime of meaningless and lifeless episodes of Bible study, prayer, and religious activities.

### New Covenant Experience[2]

- I approach my spiritual life as a developing and growing relationship with God in which I constantly seek to know Him better and to grant Him deeper access to my heart and thinking through prayer and meditation on His word.
- I take seriously those times when my religious experience feels like a spiritual funk. I will pray about it, continue to attend religious services, seek help from spiritual mentors, join a group, or do whatever it takes to refocus my attention and hope on Christ.
- I trust Him, and by His enabling grace remain faithful to Him and to those things He has asked me to do, whether or not I ever "feel"

accepted by God.

- I commit my feelings, my daily life and needs, and my ultimate salvation to Him who is able to guard whatever I commit to Him against that Day.
- I rest, by God's grace, ever more fully in Him who is my true Sabbath, and in His love for me and commitment to me.
- I trust that He who authored my faith will also finish it by that Day.
- I pray and desire to be led by the Spirit to "grasp how wide and long and high and deep is the love of Christ, and to know this love that surpasses knowledge—that [I] may be filled to the measure of the fullness of God."

### Promise/Provision 3 (Mission): "No longer will a man teach his neighbor or a man his brother, saying, 'Know the Lord,' because they will all know me, from the least of them to the greatest."

### Old Covenant Experience

- I no longer hunger or crave to know more and still more of Him whom to know is eternal life.
- I am content with a *laissez-faire* attitude toward others who do not yet know Jesus and may be confused, hurting, and drifting toward destruction.

### New Covenant Experience[3]

- I ask God to show me His glory.
- I ask God to endow me with His passion for sharing the transforming knowledge of God with others—that through acts of selfless service, loving generosity, and healing words I might share His love with everyone I meet, beginning with my own family and extending out as far as God gives me influence.
- I pray that I, my family, and my spiritual network might be among those through whom God "spreads everywhere the fragrance of

the knowledge of him," so that we might be "to God the aroma of Christ among those who are being saved and those who are perishing."

## Promise/Provision 4 (Justification): "For I will forgive their wickedness and will remember their sins no more."

### Old Covenant Experience

- I deny that I, a long-time Christian, am still a sinner and still sinning, and have specific sins to confess and repent of.
- I take the forgiving grace of God for granted, presuming on it flippantly, not appreciating what it cost Him to provide it, and not taking seriously the truth that "He himself bore our sins in his body on the tree, so that we might die to sins and live for righteousness; by his wounds you have been healed."

### New Covenant Experience[4]

- I live so close to Jesus, by His enabling grace, that I become increasingly aware of how far I fall short of being like Him.
- I confess my known sins to God, asking Him to forgive and cleanse me from all known and unknown sin.
- I trust God's promise to forgive me and cleanse me of my sin.
- I grow in, and express, gratitude to God for the incredible sacrifice He made through Jesus to win back my allegiance and secure my place in His eternal kingdom.
- I recognize that there is absolutely nothing I can possibly add to the work God has already done for me and the salvation He has secured for me through Jesus's death and resurrection; I can only accept His incredible gift by faith.
- I pray, "Lord, I believe, help my unbelief."
- I pray that the purpose for which Christ died might be fulfilled in me by the mighty working of His Spirit within me: "He died for

all, that those who live should no longer live for themselves but for him who died for them and was raised again."

## Benediction

"May the God of peace, who through the blood of the eternal covenant brought back from the dead our Lord Jesus, that great Shepherd of the sheep, equip you with everything good for doing his will, and may he work in us what is pleasing to him, through Jesus Christ, to whom be glory for ever and ever. Amen" (Heb. 13:20–21).

## Notes

1. See Exod. 33:14; Deut. 6:5; 1 Kings 8:58; Isaiah 55; Ezek. 36:25–28; Luke 10:20; 11:11–13; John 15:4–5; Rom. 1:5; 5:5; 6:17; 8:14; 2 Cor. 3:18; 10:5; Gal. 5:18, 22–25; Phil. 1:6; 1 Pet. 1:14–16, 22; 1 John 4:11–12.

2. See Jer. 9:23–24; Matt. 7:7–11, 21–23; Eph. 1:17; 3:16–19; Phil. 1:6; 2 Tim. 1:12.

3. See Exod. 33:18; Isa. 45:22; Matt. 5:14–16; Luke 19:10; John 17:3; 2 Cor. 5:14–20; Eph. 3:17–19; James 2:14–17; 1 Pet. 2:9; 1 John 3:16–18; Rev. 12:10–11.

4. Ps. 51:5–12; 139:23–24; Isa. 1:18–20; 53:4–6; Mark 9:24; 2 Cor. 5:14–15; Eph. 1:3–8; 2:1–10; 1 Pet. 1:17–21; 2:24–25; 1 John 1:9.

# Appendix A: Comparisons of the Old and New Covenants as Presented in Hebrews 7–10

References to the old covenant and new covenant in many of the New Testament epistles are primarily, if not exclusively, to be understood from an experiential perspective. The old covenant represents a rebellious or legalistic response "of the flesh" to God's covenant of grace (Gal. 4:21–31) and the new covenant represents a response of faith, a new birth "of the Spirit," resulting in a life obedience to God's covenant of grace and an eternal inheritance in the kingdom of God (Gal. 4:21–31; John 3:3–6). By God's initiating and sustaining grace, the saved of every historical era exhibited a new covenant experience.

In the book of Hebrews, however, references to the two covenants do not always follow this pattern. In Hebrews 7–10 specifically, the two covenants are primarily understood as God's progressive way of working in the two major dispensations of spiritual history—the Old Testament and New Testament eras. This discussion of Hebrews 7–10 begins with a side-by-side table comparing the two covenants, followed by a discussion of what Hebrews means by describing the second or new covenant as a "better covenant," "superior to the old one," with "better promises," "better sacrifices," and a "better hope," making the first or old covenant "obsolete" and "set aside" (7:18–22; 8:6, 13; 9:23).

| First Covenant/Old | New Covenant |
| --- | --- |
| **1.** Administered by human, imperfect, weak priests (7:11, 28). | **1.** Administered by the "Jesus Son of God," "a great high priest" who is "holy," "perfect," "seated at the right hand of the throne of the Majesty in heaven" (4:14; 7:26, 28; 8:1). |

| First Covenant/Old | New Covenant |
|---|---|
| **2.** The law/regulation establishing the Aaronic/Levitical priesthood on the basis of genealogy was weak and useless, made nothing perfect, and has been changed/set aside (7:11–12, 14, 18–19). | **2.** Christ became a "high priest forever, in the order of Melchizedek" not by genealogy but by the call and oath of God "on the basis of the power of an indestructible life." He thus became "the guarantee of a better covenant" that represents "a better hope through which we draw near to God" (6:20; 7:12–22). |
| **3.** Aaronic/Levitical priests died and had to be succeeded. (The quality of the priestly ministry was always dependent on the character of the one in office at the time, good or bad) (7:23). | **3.** "Because Jesus lives forever, he has a permanent priesthood. Therefore he is able to save completely [alternate translation, "forever," e.g., NRSV] those who come to God through him, because he always lives to intercede for them" (7:24–25). |
| **4.** The high priest needed "to offer sacrifices day after day, first for his own sins, and then for the sins of the people" (5:3; 7:27; 9:7). | **4.** Being "without sin"—"one who is holy, blameless, pure, set apart from sinners, exalted above the heavens"— Jesus did "not need to offer sacrifices… for his own sins,…He sacrificed for their sins once for all when he offered himself" (4:15; 7:26–27; 9:14). |
| **5.** Administered through "an earthly sanctuary" made "by man…according to the pattern shown [to Moses] on the mountain"—"a copy and shadow of what is in heaven" (8:2, 5; 9:1–5). | **5.** "Christ did not enter a man-made sanctuary that was only a copy of the true one; he entered heaven itself, now to appear for us in God's presence" (8:1–2; 9:11, 24). |
| **6.** There was something "wrong with that first covenant," for "God found fault with the people…'because they did not remain faithful to my covenant, and I turned away from them,' declares the Lord" (8:7–9). | **6.** "The covenant of which [Christ] is mediator is superior to the old one, and it is founded on better promises" (8:6). |
| **7.** "The first" covenant is "obsolete" and has been "set aside" (8:13; 10:9). | **7.** "He sets aside the first to establish the second" (10:9). |

| First Covenant/Old | New Covenant |
|---|---|
| **8.** Made by God with Israel (8:9). | **8.** Made by God with Israel (8:8, 10). |
| **9.** Made when God led Israel out of Egypt (8:9). | **9.** "'It will not be like the covenant I made with their forefathers when I took them by the hand to lead them out of Egypt, because they did not remain faithful to my covenant, and I turned away from them,' declares the Lord" (8:9). |
| **10.** Promises: Not specified in Hebrews because the new covenant promises identified in the adjoining column are restatements of covenant promises God made to His covenant people throughout the Old Testament period (see chart 1, page 304: "The DNA of the Covenant[s]"). | **10.** Promises:<br>a. "I will put my laws in their minds and write them on their hearts."<br>b. "I will be their God, and they will be my people."<br>c. "No longer will a man teach his neighbor, or a man his brother, saying, 'Know the Lord,' because they will all know me, from the least of them to the greatest."<br>d. "I will forgive their wickedness and will remember their sins no more" (8:8–10; 10:16–17). |
| **11.** "The way into the Most Holy Place had not yet been disclosed as long as the first tabernacle was still standing" (9:6–8). | **11.** "We have confidence to enter the Most Holy Place by the blood of Jesus, by a new and living way opened for us through the curtain, that is, his body" (10:19). |
| **12.** Levitical priests entered the first compartment of the sanctuary daily, and the high priest entered the second compartment once a year, offering sacrifices that were "an annual reminder of sins" (9:6–7; 10:1–3, 11). | **12.** Christ "entered the Most Holy Place once for all by his own blood, having obtained eternal redemption for us" (9:12, 24–28). |

| First Covenant/Old | New Covenant |
|---|---|
| **13.** "The first covenant was not put into effect [ratified] without blood." The things pertaining to the earthly sanctuary were "purified with [animal] sacrifices." "In fact, the law requires that nearly everything be cleansed with blood, and without the shedding of blood there is no forgiveness" (9:16–23). | **13.** "The heavenly things [were purified] with better sacrifices than these [animal sacrifices]." Christ "has appeared once for all at the end of the ages to do away with sin by the sacrifice of himself." "And where [sins] have been forgiven, there is no longer any sacrifice for sin" (9:23, 26; 10:18). |
| **14.** "The gifts and sacrifices being offered [in connection with the earthly sanctuary] were not able to clear the conscience of the worshiper," but only to make each one "outwardly clean." For these gifts and sacrifices "are only a matter of food and drink and various ceremonial washings—external regulations applying until the time of the new order." "It is impossible for the blood of bulls and goats to take away sins" (9:9, 13, 10; 10:4, 11). | **14.** Christ "entered the Most Holy Place once for all by his own blood, having obtained eternal redemption." "The blood of Christ [will]…cleanse our consciences from acts that lead to death, so that we may serve the living God." By His "one sacrifice he has made perfect those who are being made holy." "For this reason, Christ is the mediator of a new covenant, that those who are called may receive the promised eternal inheritance—now that he has died as a ransom to set them free from the sins committed under the first covenant" (9:12, 14–15; 10:10, 14). |
| **15.** God had no pleasure in the animal sacrifices that were required by the law (10:5–6, 8). | **15.** Christ's obedience in offering up His body was the once-for-all sanctifying sacrifice that brought an end to the sacrificing of animals under the first covenant. In so doing, Jesus "set aside the first to establish the second" (10:5–10). |
| **16.** The Old Testament believer's confession and confidence: "I trust in your unfailing love; my heart rejoices in your salvation." "[The Lord] fulfills the desires of those who fear him; he hears their cry and saves them" (Ps. 13:4; 145:19). | **16.** Christ's sacrifice in history and continuing priestly ministry on our behalf should give new covenant believers confidence and assurance with God, if we hold fast our confession, trust Him who has promised, and encourage each other in love, good works, and fellowship (10:19–25). |

| First Covenant/Old | New Covenant |
|---|---|
| **17.** "Your iniquities have separated you from your God." "Turn, turn from your evil ways! Why will you die, O house of Israel?" (Isa. 59:2; Ezek. 33:11). | **17.** Continuing in sin is no less serious now than it was under the first historical covenant (10:26–31). |
| **18.** Appeal: "Choose life, so that you and your children may live." "Surely this is our God; we trusted in him, and he saved us. This is the LORD, we trusted in him; let us rejoice and be glad in his salvation" (Deut. 30:19; Isa. 25:9). | **18.** Appeal: Endure in faith and in doing the will of God that you may receive the new covenant promise— "salvation to those who are waiting for him" (9:28; 10:32–39). |

Concerning the comparative list above, the following three observations are in order:

## 1. Hebrews 7–10 focuses on two historical covenants divided by Jesus's victorious life and sacrificial death, and discusses the obsolete role of the ceremonial ritual system of the first covenant now that the new has come.

Even a quick reading of Hebrews 7–10 reveals that the dominant focus in these chapters is the transition from the sanctuary, priesthood, animal sacrifices, ceremonial offerings, and ritual of the historical first or old covenant to those of the new. The former were "weak," imperfect, temporary, "useless," effective only to make one "outwardly clean," but "can never take away sins" or "clear the conscience of the worshiper" (7:11, 18, 23, 28; 8:5; 9:9,13; 10:4, 11). "This is why Moses was warned when he was about to build the tabernacle: 'See to it that you make everything according to the pattern shown to you on the mountain'" (Exod. 25:40), because the sanctuary of the first historical covenant, including its ritual and priesthood, was always and only "a copy of what is in heaven" (8:5). The first historical covenant always pointed beyond itself to spiritual realities in the heavens and to God's future invasion into history through His Messiah to make effective the salvation that covenant represented and proclaimed.

By contrast, Jesus's life in the flesh, His victory over sin and the devil, His obedience through suffering, and His once-for-all atoning sacrifice for the sins of the world initiated the historical new covenant. Jesus accomplished everything the historical old covenant represented and proclaimed but was powerless to achieve. He is "without sin," "holy, blameless, pure, set apart from sinners, exalted above the heavens," humankind's "high priest forever...on the basis of the power of an indestructible life," "able to save completely those who come to God through him, because he always lives to intercede for them" (4:15; 6:20; 7:16, 25–26). By His sacrifice "once for all by his own blood" Jesus "[does] away with sin" and "cleanse[s] our consciences from acts that lead to death, so that we may serve the living God." He "has made perfect forever those who are being made holy," and "obtained eternal redemption" for all believers in every historical age (9:12, 14, 26; 10:10, 14).

Phrases such as "we have been made holy" and "he has made perfect forever those who are being made holy" mean that Jesus's victorious life and atoning death made possible and brought about everything believers in every age have dreamed about and hoped for in their relationship with God. Everything the sanctuary, priests, sacrifices, and ceremonies of the historical first covenant represented and proclaimed about the salvation from sin to an eternal inheritance has been ratified and made effectual by Jesus's historical life and death.

This is the context in which Hebrews 7–10 speaks of the first historical covenant being "obsolete," "set aside," "changed" (7:11–18; 8:13). This seems quite clearly to mean that the earthly sanctuary, the priesthood, the sacrifices and ceremonies, the ritual elements of the law that pointed upward to the timeless, universal spiritual issues involved in God's saving work on humankind's behalf, and forward to the decisive role His Messiah would play in history to make it effective, have done their work and fulfilled their mission. Jesus's victorious life and atoning death have ushered in a new historical phase of God's timeless, universal covenant with humankind. In this sense, "Christ is a mediator of a new covenant" (9:15). The grace-based, gospel-bearing, faith-inducing, mission-directed covenant God progressively revealed in increasing detail through the ages has entered a new and ultimate stage of revelation because the Messiah, the embodiment (literally, in-body-ment) of the covenant, has come among us and ratified the covenant with His own blood. This made the former rituals obsolete because what they symbolized had been realized in Jesus.

Some have taken the passing reference in Hebrews 9:4 to "the stone tablets of the covenant" (i.e., the Ten Commandments) to mean that the author of Hebrews taught that the Ten Commandments were included in those laws that became "obsolete" and were "set aside" and "changed" by virtue of Jesus's victorious life and atoning death. However, these interpreters do not believe that all ten have in fact been set aside. Rather, they hold that only the fourth, which specifies the observance of the seventh-day Sabbath, has been set aside. Yet it is only logical that if the Ten Commandments have indeed been declared obsolete, set aside, and changed, then all ten of the commandments should be just that—obsolete, set aside, and changed. It is hard to understand how a declaration that "the stone tablets of the covenant" have become obsolete, set aside, and changed could mean that one commandment became such while the others remained intact.

Rather, it was the Old Testament sanctuary, the priesthood based on the genealogy of Aaron and Levi, and the animal and other ritual sacrifices and offerings that became "obsolete" and were "set aside" and "changed" once Christ had come and defeated Satan where Adam failed, died as the sacrifice God had made provision for "from the creation of the world" (Rev. 13:8), and was established as humankind's high priest forever.

Hebrews 9:2–4 contains a list of articles of temple furniture that accompanied the earthly sanctuary or temple of the first historical covenant during the Old Testament period, including "the lampstand, the table and the consecrated bread…the golden altar of incense and the gold-covered ark of the covenant." Hebrews 9:4–5 adds that the gold-covered ark placed in the Most Holy Place of the temple "contained the gold jar of manna, Aaron's staff that had budded, and the stone tablets of the covenant," and then states, "but we cannot discuss these things in detail now" (9:4–5). It is a serious mistake to interpret this passing reference to "the stone tablets of the covenant" having been kept in the ark of the covenant to mean that Jesus's victorious life and atoning death made the Ten Commandments obsolete, thereby setting them aside and changing them. James certainly didn't think they had been set aside. He quoted directly from the Ten Commandments, referring to them as integral components of "the law that gives freedom" (James 2:8–12).

In 1 Corinthians 6:9–10 Paul appears to have the continuing validity of the Ten Commandments in mind with his list of unrighteous acts that if persisted in will exclude one from the kingdom of God.[1] Jesus Himself didn't consider them changed. When asked, "Teacher, what good thing must I do to get eternal life?" He answered, "If you want to enter life, obey the commandments," and then quoted directly from the Ten Commandments (Matt. 19:16–19). As legalistic as these statements of James and Jesus may sound to some interpreters, they are consistent with Jesus's emphasis throughout His ministry that those who are true citizens of His eternal kingdom are those who not only hear His word but obey it (Matt. 7:24–27; John 14:15, 21). At the same time, however, Jesus never elevated obedience to the commandments to a level of importance above faith. Nor did He appeal for obedience as something that could occur apart from faith or prior to faith. Rather, He presented obedience to the commandments as it had been presented throughout God's covenantal relations with Adam's descendents, as a sure result of faith in God and a natural expression of love for God in response to His saving acts on humankind's behalf. The author of Hebrews maintained that same balanced emphasis between faith and obedience when he appealed, "Let us hold firmly to the *faith* we profess" in "Jesus the Son of God" as our "great high priest," "the source of eternal salvation for all who *obey* Him" (Heb. 4:14; 5:9; italics added).

It is often asked on what basis a distinction can be made between the ceremonial and moral law. God Himself distinguished the timeless and universal nature of His moral law when He wrote the Ten Commandments with His own finger and spoke them audibly to the people (Exod. 31:18; Deut. 4:12–13). In contrast, in God's instructions to Moses regarding the earthly sanctuary and the rituals attending it, He specifically instructed him to "see that you make them according to the pattern shown you on the mountain," which indicated that these were "a copy and shadow of what is in heaven" (Exod. 25:40; Heb. 8:5).[2] Daniel prophesied that the "cut[ting] off" of "the Anointed One" [Messiah] would "put an end to sacrifice and offering" (Dan. 9:26–27). Though the extent to which the average believers during the historical old covenant era understood that the ceremonial ritual they were familiar with would cease with the death of the Messiah is unclear, this truth was divinely revealed and prophetically anticipated.

When Moses instructed the people, "these commandments that I give you today are to be upon your hearts," neither he nor they understood that to mean that God would write instructions on their hearts regarding the dimensions of the temple furniture, the materials and colors for the priests' garments, or the recipe for a firstfruits grain offering (Lev. 23:13). Rather, it was the moral law that was clearly in view in such passages as the following:

- "The LORD your God will circumcise your hearts and the hearts of your descendants, so that you may love him with all your heart and with all your soul...[enabling you to] obey the LORD and follow all his commands" (Deut. 30:6–7).
- "Oh, how I love your law! I meditate on it all day long" (Ps. 119:97).
- "I desire to do your will, O my God. Your law is within my heart" (Ps. 40:8).

The law God promised to write on their hearts was His moral law which reflected His own character. When it was integrated into their lives it would establish them before the nations as "holy to me because I, the LORD, am holy" (Lev. 20:20). Dallas Willard observed that Jesus's own teachings continued "the long-established prophetic emphasis in Israel which always weighted the moral over the ritual. 'Behold, I would have mercy and not sacrifice' (Hos. 6:6)."[3] The distinction between the moral and ritual elements of the law, and the continuing authority of the Ten Commandments for New Testament Christians, has long been recognized in the Reformed tradition of Christianity.[4]

What must be stressed again is the clear emphasis in Hebrews 7–10 on the transitory nature of the earthly sanctuary, priesthood, and sacrifices of the historical old covenant. These ceremonial provisions continually pointed upward to eternal, heavenly realities and forward to the coming of the Messiah in history to fulfill and accomplish what the ritual elements of the first covenant proclaimed and prefigured. Now that Messiah Jesus has come in the flesh, ratifying and sealing the everlasting gospel/covenant with His own blood, the ceremonial rituals of the historical old covenant era have served their glorious purpose and need no longer be observed. They have been "change[d]," "set aside," and are "obsolete" (Heb. 7:12, 18; 8:13).

## 2. The everlasting, new covenant gospel spans both Old and New Testament historical eras, and believers living in both eras were saved by that one unchanging gospel.

The author of Hebrews left no doubt that there is only one gospel that spanned both Old and New Testament eras. In doing this he cited Jeremiah's new covenant prophecy which defined the one timeless, universal, everlasting gospel in terms of four succinct divine promises— the core teaching and purpose of God's covenants in both historical eras. "[Promise 1] I will put my laws in their minds and write them on their hearts. [Promise 2] I will be their God and they will be my people.

[Promise 3] No longer will a man teach his neighbor, or a man his brother, saying, 'Know the Lord,' because they will all know me, from the least of them to the greatest. [Promise 4] For I will forgive their wickedness and will remember their sins no more" (8:10–12; cf. Jer. 31:31–34).

These promises were not presented for the first time when Jesus came. They had been given repeatedly throughout the Old Testament era (see chart 1, page 304: "The DNA of the Covenant[s]"). This gospel constitutes the unifying thread of God's covenantal expressions in both Old and New Testament historical eras.

Jesus's victorious life and atoning death ratified the gospel presented in the historical first covenant and achieved in history the forgiveness promised and granted during that era. "For this reason Christ is the mediator of a new covenant, that those who are called may receive the promised eternal inheritance—now that he has died as a ransom to set them free from the sins committed under the first covenant" (9:15).

This new covenant gospel is the only true gospel there has ever been. It was the gospel introduced to fallen Adam (Gen. 3:15). It was the gospel delivered to Abraham and all of his descendants who are not merely genealogical descendants but who "walk in the footsteps of the faith that our father Abraham had" (Gen. 15:6; Rom. 4:12; Gal. 3:7–9). It was the gospel Paul preached and about which he warned, "Even if we or an angel from heaven should preach a gospel other than the one we preached to you, let him be eternally condemned!" (Gal. 1:8). It is the only gospel by which any believer in any historical age ever has been, or ever will be, saved. It is the gospel "which we [in the historical new covenant era] have had…preached to us, just as they [in the historical old covenant era] did" (Heb. 4:2).

Note the wondrous effects this new covenant gospel achieves in the life of the believer: "a better hope is introduced, by which we draw near to God" (7:19); "save[d] completely" (7:25); "[sins] have been forgiven" (8:18); "consciences [cleansed] from acts that lead to death, so we may serve the living God" (9:14); "made perfect…being made holy" (10:14);

and "receive the promised inheritance" (9:15). A full salvation to be sure, including justification, sanctification, glorification, and whatever else might be conceived as a constituent of a full salvation.

Again, lest the reader of Hebrews conclude that this salvation, effected by the new covenant gospel, is limited to those living during the historical new covenant era, the author immediately presents a representative list of Old Testament believers (beginning with Abel, Adam's second child, and extending through the prophets) who experienced this full salvation, enjoying a new covenant experience while living in the old covenant historical era (11:1–40). Through the sanctuary, priesthood, and ceremonial rituals God had provided for their era. Their minds had been directed by faith to that priest who was higher than the earth and to that once-for-all sacrifice which God would provide to make atonement full and complete. They were forgiven of their sins. God counted them righteous on the basis of their faith in Him, thereby considering them perfect. God was cleansing their consciences from acts that lead to death so they could serve Him. He was writing on their hearts that sacred and holy law that He seeks to write on the hearts of His New Testament believers to make them "holy." He instilled in them the same heavenly hope enjoyed by believers in our own era. "They were longing for a better country—a heavenly one. Therefore God is not ashamed to be called their God, for he has prepared a city for them" (11:16). They were new covenant believers living in the historical old covenant era—Old Testament examples that "[Christ] is able to save completely those who come to God through him, because he always lives to intercede for them" (Heb. 7:25).

## 3. Hebrews reveals the reality and nature of the two historical covenants, and presents the new covenant as a better covenant than the first covenant.

The fact that the gospel by which people are saved in the New Testament era is the same gospel by which they were saved during the Old must not blur the reality of the existence of the two historical covenants or the fact that the historical new covenant was a "better covenant" than the historical old covenant. It could even be said that the everlasting gospel itself became something "new" and "better" in its own right once Jesus had come among us and "shared in [our] humanity, so that by his death he might destroy him who holds the power of death—that is, the devil" (2:14).

At that point in history when Jesus's victorious life and atoning death defeated the devil and "free[d] those who all their lives were held in slavery by their fear of death" (2:15), the timeless, universal promises of the gospel, while materially the same as the promises of old, became "better promises" (8:6). The timeless, universal hope offered to humankind through the gospel, the hope "for a better country—a heavenly one" (13:16), became "a better hope" (7:19). God's covenant of redemption, the face of His everlasting covenant turned to sinful humanity, became "a better covenant" (7:22). Because Jesus had come and won, everything that ever was in God's good universe was now even better. Even those things that had remained the same since the creation of the world became "new." The decisive, in-the-flesh victory of Jesus over Satan made things that have always been true even more so.

The book of Hebrews demonstrates this profound truth in several ways. For example, through the historical old covenant God offered people a real salvation, a real eternal hope that all who would turn to Him were promised they would ultimately and really receive (Deut. 30:19–20; Isa. 45:22; Heb. 11:13–16). He commissioned His new covenant people living during the historical old covenant era to share this offer of eternal salvation with the whole world (Exod. 19:5; Ps. 67:1–2; Isa. 49:3, 6). Hebrews identifies Jesus as "the author of their salvation" (2:10; cf. Rev. 13:8). In other words, long before Jesus ever entered our world He authored, superintended, and administered that divine initiative of grace and promise which we call the plan of salvation. This salvation was that gospel by which believers living in the historical first or old covenant era were saved, and by which we in the historical new covenant era are saved. And yet Hebrews also says "this salvation… was first announced by the Lord," meaning, in context, first announced by Jesus when He came among us in the flesh (2:3). And again, it testifies that it was only after "he learned obedience from what he suffered and, once made perfect, [that] he became the source of eternal salvation for all who obey him" (5:8–9).

So, as Hebrews presents it, 1) Jesus authored the gospel of salvation embedded in the historical old covenant and by which believers were saved throughout the Old Testament era; 2) but He "first announced" this salvation when He came among us in the flesh; and 3) He did not become "the source of eternal salvation" until after His obedience and death (5:3, 8–9). In other words, the grace and salvation "given us in Christ Jesus before the beginning of time" became in some way a new and even better salvation once it was realized in Jesus's victorious life and atoning death (2 Tim. 1:9). In the same way, there is a real sense in which the covenant of redemption with its guaranteed promises and hope of salvation, first announced to Adam in Genesis 3:15 and reiterated in subsequent covenants, became a new and even better covenant with new and better promises and a new and better hope once Jesus had come and won.

Thus, God's everlasting covenant of redemption, while shedding only the ritual elements of "the first covenant" and thus remaining the same grace-based, gospel-bearing, faith-inducing, mission-directed covenant first introduced to fallen Adam and progressively amplified throughout the Old Testament era, is presented in Hebrews as a historically "new covenant." Though the two historical covenants shared the same holy law which reflected the moral/spiritual character of its Giver, and though they shared the same gospel that provided forgiveness for the lawbreakers and the same promise that He would write His law in the hearts of the signatures to His covenant, they were nonetheless designated in Hebrews as "the first [or old] covenant" and "the new covenant." Jesus's incarnation and momentous, vicarious victory over Satan by His obedience, death, and resurrection at a singular point in human history made everything that came before it "old," and everything that came after it "new."

The same is true in the life of the believer. At that point when Jesus comes into someone's life, whether at a defining moment or over a period of time, life itself becomes new (2 Cor. 5:17). And it doesn't stop there. It's meant to be progressively true of even good people, obedient people, securely heaven-bound people. Through times of prayer, meditation on God's word, diligence in service, and faithfulness through trials, Jesus progressively enters the life, thereby making the believer's testimony continually new. His promises become ever more precious, the hope He offers ever more real, His grace and mercy ever more appreciated, and His covenant of love ever a greater treasure and ever new. Jesus's presence enables His covenant people to experience for themselves the reality of John's testimony: "He who has the Son has life," and has it ever new (1 John 5:12).

## Notes

1. "[Paul] takes the occasion to remind [the Corinthians] that the unrighteous shall not inherit the kingdom of God. He lists for us a catalogue of sins, thereby illustrating the unrighteousness which excludes from the kingdom of God—fornication, idolatry, adultery, effeminacy, sodomy, thievery, covetousness, drunkenness, reviling, extortion (1 Corinthians 6:9, 10)....The point of particular interest for our present study is the criterion, presupposed in Paul's teaching here, by which this antithesis [between the kingdom of God and the world] is to be judged. We need but scan the sins which Paul mentions to discover what this criterion is; the precepts of the Decalogue underlie the whole catalogue. Idolatry—the first and second commandments; adultery—the seventh commandment; theft and extortion—the eighth; reviling—the ninth and possibly the third; covetousness—the tenth. Hence it is only too apparent that the criteria of the equity which characterizes the kingdom of God and the criteria of the iniquity which marks off those who are without God and without hope in the world are those norms of thought and behaviour which are epitomized in the ten commandments. And it is Paul's plea that the operations of grace (cf. verse 11) make mandatory the integrity of which these precepts are the canons. It is not grace relieving us of the demands signalized in these precepts, but grace establishing the character and status which will bring these demands to effective fruition." John Murray, *Principles of Conduct: Aspects of Biblical Ethics* (Grand Rapids, MI: William B. Eerdmans Publishing Company, 1957), 193.

2. Walter C. Kaiser, Jr., "The Place of Law and Good Works in Evangelical Christianity," eds. A. James Rudin and Marvin R. Wilson, *A Time to Speak: The Evangelical-Jewish Encounter* (Grand Rapids, MI: William B. Eerdmans Publishing Company and Center for Judaic-Christian Studies, Austin, Texas), 124: "Admittedly, some of the civil and ceremonial legislation, especially related to the ministry and service of the tabernacle and its successor, the temple, had an expiration date attached to its original legislation. This built-in obsolescence is fairly served when the real to which its offices, services, and ministries pointed superannuated it. Thus, the word *pattern* (*tabnit*) in Exodus 25:9, 40 was one such signal to readers of all ages."

3. Willard, *The Divine Conspiracy*, 156. Cf. C. G. Montefiore, *Rabbinic Literature and Gospel Teaching* (New York: Ktav, 1970), 316–317, quoted in Kaiser, "The Place of Law and Good Works," 123: "The Rabbis…were familiar with the distinction between ceremonial and moral commands, and *on the whole* they regarded the 'moral' as more important and more fundamental than the 'ceremonial.'…On the whole the 'heavy' commands are the moral commands….The distinction between 'light' and 'heavy' commands was well known, and is constantly mentioned and discussed."

4. "The importance attached to the Decalogue in Christian education by such Reformed catechism as the Geneva of 1541, the Heidelberg of 1563, the Westminster Larger and Shorter of 1648, is well known….And in this matter of the place of the law in the life of Christians the Church of England has stood alongside the Reformed churches, as may be seen from the fact that in the 1662 Book of Common Prayer (as also in the 1552 Prayer Book) the rehearsing of the Ten Commandments has its place in the order of the Lord's Supper (note the repeated response, 'Lord, have mercy upon us, and incline our hearts to keep this law'), while both in Rite A and in Rite B of the Alternative Service book of 1980 provision is made for either the Summary of the Law (itself, of course, including two quotations from the law) or the Ten Commandments to be read." C. E. B. Cranfield, *On Romans: and Other New Testament Essays* (Edinburgh: T&T Clark, 1998), 123.

# Appendix B: "Under Law" vs. "Under Grace"

In eleven texts in English translations of the Bible, the phrases "under the law" or "under law" are used fourteen times to translate the Greek terms "*hupo nomon*" (literally, "under law"), "*en nomon*" (literally, "in law" but translated "under law" in the English translations I consulted), and "*en to nomon*" (literally, "in the law" but translated "under the law" in the English translations I consulted[1]). In some of these same passages, the terms "under law" or "under the law" are set in contrast to the term "under grace" (Greek, *hupo charin*).

Some interpreters understand the phrases "under law" and "under grace" to refer to two historical periods divided by Christ's institution of the new covenant in the days of His sojourn among us in the flesh. They believe the term "under law" represents God's requirement that those in covenant relation with Him (particularly the Jews) during the Old Testament historical period had to live by all the laws He gave at Sinai. They interpret the term "under grace" to mean that in the New Testament historical period new covenant believers have been liberated from those "bondage-producing" Old Testament laws and set free in Christ to live by faith with an eye single to the great commandments of love to God and others.

This study concludes that rather than referring to the historical divide separated by the coming of Jesus, the New Testament terms "under law" and "under grace" testify primarily to *experiential* truths that are timeless and universal.

The following discussion will first note each of the texts in question with brief comments on their meaning, experientially understood. Then the contributions of these texts to understanding of the spiritual life will be described by integrating them into a suggested model of the plan of salvation.

## The "Under Law" / "Under Grace" Texts
### Romans 2:12

> All who sin apart from the law will also perish apart from the law, and all who sin *under the law* will be judged by the law. (italics added)

In this passage those to whom God has given His special revelation in Scripture, those who are "under the law,"[2] are compared to those who have not been privileged to have God's word in Scripture available to them, those "apart from the law." A few verses later Paul testified to the "advantage [possessed]…in every way" by those who have "been entrusted with the very words of God" (Rom. 3:1–2). But he also left no doubt that when people who have God's revelation in Scripture, those "under the law," fail to live up to the righteous standard revealed therein, they are under the same, if not greater, condemnation than that deserved by the abject heathen who transgress the Spirit's witness to their consciences as to what is right and wrong (Rom. 3:1–2). "For it is not those who hear the law who are righteous in God's sight, but it is those who obey the law who will be declared righteous" (Rom. 2:13). Merely being acquainted with—"hearing" or possessing a copy of—the scriptural revelation of God's righteous standard for eternal life is not enough. One must either perfectly live up to it, or have a faith that "submit[s] to God's righteousness" and "obtain[s] it by faith" (Rom. 3:22; 9:30–32; 10:3). This truth is timeless and universal.

### Romans 3:19

> Now we know that whatever the law says, it says to those who are *under the law*, so that every mouth may be silenced and the whole world held accountable to God. (italics added)

The extended passage that includes this text begins this way: "We have already made the charge that Jews and Gentiles alike are all under sin" (Rom. 3:9). It then proceeds with a long list of Old Testament texts that graphically depict the sinner's hopeless condition apart from divine intervention (3:10–18). And it ends with these words: "Therefore no one will be declared righteous in his sight by observing the law [the teachings of Scripture³]; rather, through the law [Scripture] we become conscious of sin" (3:20).

The phrase "those who are under the law" as used in Romans 3:19 applies to "the whole world held accountable to God." God's law reveals His perfect standard of righteousness which we cannot attain on our own. All humankind is hopelessly and eternally lost without God's gracious intervention on our behalf. This is a timeless and universal truth.

## Romans 6:14–15

> For sin shall not be your master, because you are not *under law*, but *under grace*. What then? Shall we sin because we are not *under law* but *under grace*? By no means! (italics added)

The two uses of the term "under law" in these texts occur in an extended passage that calls baptized believers to live the new quality of life that they were raised up out of the baptismal waters to live—"no longer slaves to sin" (Rom. 6:1–9). The verses immediately preceding these two texts read: "The death [Jesus] died, he died to sin once for all; but the life he lives, he lives to God. In the same way, count yourselves dead to sin but alive to God in Christ Jesus. Therefore do not let sin reign in your mortal body so that you obey its evil desires. Do not offer the parts of your body to sin, as instruments of wickedness, but rather offer yourselves to God, as those who have been brought from death to life; and offer the parts of your body to him as instruments of righteousness" (Rom. 6:10–13).

After affirming the Old Testament revelation that all humankind stands "*under the law*, so that every mouth may be silenced and the whole world held accountable to God" (Rom. 3:19, italics added), Paul dedicated the next two and a half chapters of Romans to amplifying the even more dominant Old Testament revelation that the righteousness all sinners need to attain to God's perfect standard and its consequence, eternal life, would be provided by God. In Romans 5:19 he assured his readers that this righteousness can, by faith, be credited to their account "through the obedience of the one man," Jesus Christ.

Our justification before God by grace through faith begs the question, "Shall we sin because we are not *under law* but *under grace*?" (Rom. 6:15, italics added). In other words, is it necessary for us to be concerned about obedience anymore, now that Jesus's perfect obedience has been graciously credited to our account and we have accepted it by faith?

Paul's answer: Absolutely! Don't you realize that God has not only granted you justifying grace, but sanctifying grace as well. God not only credits you with Jesus's perfect righteousness. He also enables and empowers you to live a life patterned after Jesus's life.[4] "Just as Christ was raised from the dead through the glory of the Father, we too may live a new life" (Rom. 6:4).

There is no question but that Paul used the terms "under law" and "under grace" in Romans 6:14–15 to convey a spiritual message that is applicable and essential to the covenant people of God in every age.

## 1 Corinthians 9:20–21

> To the Jews I became like a Jew, to win the Jews. To those *under the law* I became like one *under the law* (though I myself am not under the law), so as to win those under the law. To those not having the law I became like one not having the law (though I am not free from God's law but am *under* Christ's *law*), so as to win those not having the law. (italics added)

Many have used this text as the key to interpret Paul's uses of the term "under law" to mean "obligated to keep all the laws of the Old Testament" and more specifically "all the laws given to Moses on Mount

Sinai." This, they contend, shows that Paul, a new covenant believer who boasts, "though I myself am not under the law," did not consider himself accountable to laws God gave His covenant people during the Old Testament period. Some have further attempted to suggest that Paul's use of the terms "God's law" and "Christ's law" in this text reveals a distinction he recognized between the laws given to Israel at Sinai ("God's law") and the New Testament emphasis on love ("Christ's law"). However, the attempt to create two different laws out of the New Testament references to the law of God and the law of Christ is as artificial as attempting to create two different spiritual kingdoms from the New Testament references to "the kingdom of God" (e.g., Gal. 5:21; 2 Thess. 1:5) and "the kingdom of Christ" (e.g., Eph. 5:5; 2 Pet. 1:11)."[5] "There is only one Lawgiver and Judge" (James 4:12).

In 1 Corinthians 9:20–21 Paul uses "under law" to include the practices of Jews who still observed ceremonial provisions of Old Testament law that had been fulfilled with the substitionary living and dying of Christ on our behalf. Paul taught that nothing in his understanding of the gospel forbade Jewish Christians from continuing such practices (Romans 14). In Jerusalem he, as a Jewish Christian himself, observed ceremonial "purification rites" to deflect Jewish criticism "by living in obedience to the law," even though he may have felt under no spiritual obligation to do so before God, other than the obligation of love to those he was trying to reach (Acts 21:24). He who taught, "If you let yourselves be circumcised, Christ will be of no value to you at all," himself had Greek-born Timothy circumcised at Lystra "because of the Jews who lived in that area" (Acts 16:1–3). When Paul preached to "a group of Epicurean and Stoic philosophers" in Athens, he did not quote Scripture to those who did not acknowledge its authority (thus, "not having the law"), but gave a philosophical presentation of the gospel with the result that "a few men became followers of Paul and believed" (Acts 17:16–34). Paul would do whatever it took, apart from disobedience to God, to reach people, all kinds of people, with the gospel.[6]

But while these examples match the context of Paul's use of the term "under law" in this passage, they do not exhaust its meaning. Paul lived "under grace," under the justifying position and sanctifying power of God. Thus he could say, "I myself am not under the law." His obedience, even to the great commandments of love to God and others, was no longer motivated as it once was by an anxious desire to gain a positive verdict from God in the judgment, but by a love for all that God had done, and was doing, for him through Christ. Living "under grace," Paul could render wholehearted obedience to "God's law" and "Christ's law" as a service and allegiance of love because "God has poured out his love into our hearts by the Holy Spirit, whom he has given us" (Rom. 5:5).

## Galatians 3:23

> Before this faith came, we were held prisoners by the law [literally, "under the law"], locked up until faith should be revealed.

If the references in this text to "under law" and "until faith should be revealed" are construed to represent two spiritual dispensations, namely the Old and New Testament historical periods respectively, then it must be concluded that faith did not come until the New Testament era. That would leave the entire Old Testament era without faith, something Scripture does not do. This dilemma is resolved when this text is understood experientially. "Until faith should be revealed" in the life of anyone who has ever lived, that person remains "under law" as the only means of pursuing salvation, and thus hopelessly under the curse.

## Galatians 4:4–5

> But when the time had fully come, God sent his Son, born of a woman, born *under law*, to redeem those *under law*, that we might receive the full rights of sons. (italics added)

Jesus was "born under law." "Since the children have flesh and blood, he too shared in their humanity…made like his brothers in every way" (Heb. 2:14, 17). He, like us, was "under law" as a fellow brother of "the whole world [that is] held accountable to God" and to the perfect standard of righteousness revealed in God's character and His holy word (Rom. 3:19). And yet, unlike the rest of us, "he committed no sin, and no deceit was found in his mouth" (Isa. 53:9; 1 Pet. 2:22). This qualified Him "to redeem those under law"—all Adam's descendants of every historical era who are unable to fulfill the righteous requirement of God, who futilely pursue "the hope of eternal life…promised before the beginning of time" "until faith should be revealed" in their experience and they "be found in him, not having a righteousness of [their] own that comes from the law, but that which is through faith in Christ—the righteousness that comes from God and is by faith" (Titus 1:1; Gal. 3:23; Phil. 3:9). "God made him who had no sin to be sin for us, so that in him we might become the righteousness of God" (2 Cor. 5:21). Thus Christ who was Himself "born under law" redeemed "those under law."

## Galatians 4:21

> Tell me, you who want to be *under the law*, are you not aware of what the law says?" (italics added)

Paul here chides legalists ("you who want to be under the law") for misunderstanding and misconstruing the essence of the gospel as taught in the Old Testament Scriptures as well as in the New ("are you not aware of what the law says?").

Paul's gospel of salvation by grace through faith was rooted and grounded in the Old Testament, as the numerous references in his epistles to those Scriptures on this subject attest (e.g., Rom. 4:6–7; 10:6–16; Gal. 3:6–11). "For we also [in the New Testament era] have had the gospel preached to us, just as they [the Israelites of old] did" (Heb.

4:2). It was unthinkable to Paul that anyone could have the Scriptures at their disposal and still "want to be under the law." The only way Paul could make any sense of it was to conclude that these people remained unconverted—"the god of this age has blinded [their] minds" to the point that "when Moses [God's grace-based, gospel-bearing, faith-inducing, mission-directed covenant with Israel] is read, a veil covers their hearts. But whenever anyone turns to the Lord, the veil is taken away" (2 Cor. 4:4; 3:15–16).

Paul warned that those who continue to live "under law" (Gal. 4:21) are "born in the ordinary way" (literally, "according to the flesh," 4:23, 29), and "will never share in the inheritance with the free woman's son" (4:30), which put even more straightforwardly and bluntly means that they are not converted and will not be saved (John 3:3–6; Rom. 8:5–8; Phil. 3:4–6; Gal. 5:19–21). This is not a dispensational issue, wherein the people who lived "under law" in the Old Testament period were saved while those who live "under law" in the New Testament period will not be. It is a salvation issue that is timeless and universal. There is no salvation "under law" and no one since the fall of Adam has been saved "under law" (Jesus perhaps excepted). "For it is by grace you have been saved, through faith—and this not from yourselves, it is the gift of God"—only and always (Eph. 2:8).

## Galatians 5:18

But if you are led by the Spirit, you are not *under law*. (italics added)

Were believers in the Old Testament led by the Spirit? If not, by what means were they convicted of sin, led to repentance, convinced of the gospel, gifted with faith in the Messiah to come, converted and born again? Without this experience no one will see the kingdom of God (John 3:3–5). And by what means did God expect them to become a nation of priests (Exod. 19:5–6), to "be holy because I, the LORD your

God, am holy" (Lev. 19:2), to become a people through whom His "ways may be known on the earth, [His] salvation among all nations" (Ps. 67:1–2) and through whom He, as He expressed His intention, could "show myself holy through you before [the surrounding nations'] eyes" (Ezek. 36:23)? By what means if not by His Spirit? Galatians 5:18 cannot be understood dispensationally. If a child of Adam has been born again of the Spirit and is being led by the Spirit, he or she is no longer "under law," that is, no longer dependent on living a life of perfect righteousness to merit life in the kingdom of God and no longer condemned for failure to have done so. That person has been accepted on the basis of faith in Jesus and has been set free to live a life of holiness— likeness to Jesus—by the power of the Spirit, as God writes His law on his or her heart.[7] This is a timeless, universal truth.

Old Testament believers were surely "led by the Spirit." And it is a spiritual law, universal and timeless, that "if you are led by the Spirit, you are not under law." Scripture rightly read does not teach, nor even suggest, that if you are led by the Spirit as an Old Testament believer you are under law, but if you are led by the Spirit as a New Testament believer you aren't. The same grace-based, gospel-bearing covenant prevailed throughout.

## A Suggested Model of the Plan of Salvation from an Experiential "Under Law" / "Under Grace" Perspective

God's timeless and universal standard for His creation is perfect love, perfect righteousness, perfect holiness—patterned after God's own character (Matt. 5:48). When God created the angels, and subsequently humankind, He placed them under the jurisdiction of His law: "obey and live, disobey and die" (Gen. 2:17; Ezek. 28:14–19). He also inclined and enabled them to live in harmony with the spiritual laws of His kingdom. This moral/spiritual endowment included a human nature "in the image and likeness of God" (Gen. 1:26–27)—naturally loving God and obedient to His will.

At the moment He created Adam and Eve, God embedded His law in their hearts (provision 1 of the new covenant—sanctification), established Himself as theirs and them as His (provision 2 of the new covenant—reconciliation), and made Himself known to them as their Creator/Sustainer who loved them (provision 3 of the new covenant—mission).[8] This is in part what it means that God created them "in our image, in our likeness" and "very good" (Gen. 1:26–31). At that point they no doubt understood God's law as the loving way He related to them rather than as a list of specific commandments. They were created with a love song already playing in their souls—a love song for God and their fellow creatures. Their "hope of eternal life which God, who does not lie, promised before the beginning of time" (Titus 1:2) depended on their continued obedience, motivated by a deep love for God and others that had been implanted in their "very good" natures (Gen. 1:31). Because they were both accountable to God and His standard of perfect righteousness and equipped by God with a nature that loved and obeyed Him, Adam and Eve were "under law." In their sinless state they could live "under law" in loving relationship with their Creator and one another forever.

God never changes. His standard for His kingdom children is the same today as ever—perfect righteousness, perfect holiness, enabled by and through a loving relationship with Himself.

But *something* has changed, and drastically so. "Sin entered the world through one man, and death through sin, and in this way death came to all men, because all sinned" (Rom. 5:12). Adam's sinful choice, violating his sinless nature through disobedience to God, fundamentally changed human nature, bending it away from God. Sin rendered humankind incapable, apart from divine intervention, of acting out the great principle of divine love with perfectly righteous, holy lives. Humanity is still "under the law," under the jurisdiction of God's law, accountable to the divine standard of perfect love, perfect righteousness, and perfect holiness to have eternal life (Rom. 3:19). But subsequent to Adam's fall, all of his children have been born into this world without the enabling endowment bequeathed to Adam at creation to live up to the divine standard of perfect righteousness to gain eternal life. They are in need, in a way that sinless Adam was not, of "the grace that brings salvation" (Titus 2:11)—the unmerited interposition of God to grant them a perfect righteousness not of their own making, a righteousness wrought by God Himself living and dying in Christ on humanity's behalf.

Jesus came among us as one "born under law" (Gal. 4:4). The Lawgiver subjected Himself to the jurisdiction of His own law ("obey and live, disobey and die"—cf. Lev. 18:5). In Gethsemane He subjected Himself to the condemnation of the law as "the LORD...laid on him the iniquity of us all" and He became "a curse for us" (Isa. 53:6; Gal. 3:13). Though He was "tempted in every way, just as we are"[9] (Heb. 4:15), He lived a sinless life so that by His substitutionary life of righteousness and His sacrificial death on our behalf, He might "redeem those under law" (those still held accountable to a perfect standard of righteousness but condemned for having failed to achieve it), "that we might receive the full rights of sons" (Gal. 4:5). Through Him "the grace of God that brings salvation has appeared to all men" (Titus 2:11). The perfect righteousness, perfect holiness, without sin, that Jesus lived out in the flesh was credited to every human being to be received by faith "so that in him we might become the righteousness of God," inheritors of the "eternal life which God, who does not lie, promised before the beginning of time" (Titus 1:1; 2 Cor. 5:21; cf. Rom. 3:22–24). "Consequently, just as the result of one trespass was condemnation for all men, so also the result of one act of righteousness was justification that brings life for all men" (Rom. 5:18). "For as in Adam all die, so in Christ all will be made alive" (1 Cor. 15:22). "We have put our hope in the living God, who is the Savior of all men, and especially of those who believe" (1 Tim. 4:10).

"The whole world" is "under the law" in the sense of being "held accountable to God" and His standard of perfect righteousness that has never changed for the subjects of His eternal kingdom (Rom. 3:19; Matt. 5:48). But since no human being has lived such a life, all who attempt to live "under law"—"rely[ing] on observing the law" as a basis for their eternal salvation unto eternal life—"are under a curse" and condemnation for their failure to observe it perfectly (Gal. 3:10).

Those who have not been born again—born of the spirit into the spiritual kingdom of God—have no alternative than to rely on their own good works, that is, to live "under law." Those who do "not know the righteousness that comes from God" and do not "submit to God's righteousness" by the reception of the vicarious perfect life and atoning death of Jesus Christ on their behalf have no alternative than to try to "establish their own" righteousness by the good things they do, or the bad things they refrain from doing, and then hope for the best (Rom. 10:3).[10] Unless we are converted, born again by God's Spirit into the spiritual kingdom of God, we must "rely on observing the law" (Gal. 3:10), rely on the good we do and the bad we refrain from doing, as our hope of eternal life. "Before this faith came, we were held prisoners by the law [literally, '*under the law*']" (Gal. 3:23).

The New Testament speaks of people "who want to be *under the law*" (Gal. 4:21, italics added). Much of the world fits into this category today. Many secular, professed non-believers boast about living a sufficiently morally-upstanding life to merit a positive verdict on their behalf in a final judgment, "should there even be such." Most, if not all, non-Christian religions assume that people are born with an innate goodness that needs only to be nurtured by religious practices in order to live a sufficiently moral life to gain a store of good karma that will serve them well in the afterlife. Even Israel, God's covenant people, "pursued a law of righteousness [the perfect righteousness required by God for eternal life]…not by faith but as if it were by works," and thus "has not attained it" (Rom. 9:31).

The Old Testament prophets characterized all such human-generated righteousness as worthless, even sinful—"all our righteous acts are like filthy rags…our sins sweep us away"—the remedy for which was reliance on God alone and His righteousness: "[God] has clothed me with garments of salvation and arrayed me in a robe of righteousness" (Isa. 61:10; 64:6; cf. Zech. 3:1–5). Similarly, the New Testament characterizes people who fail to rely on the righteousness of God as people who are living "under law," "slaves to sin, which leads to death" (Rom. 6:14, 16). The apostle Paul himself was educated as a Pharisee to consider his own "legalistic righteousness" as "faultless" before God (Phil. 3:6). Only after conversion did he regard such a life as having been lived "in the flesh," the same term he used to describe immoral, idolatrous people who "will not inherit the kingdom of God" (Phil. 3:3–4; Gal. 5:19–21). Before they are converted, "good" people have "a veil [that] covers their hearts," rendering them incapable of assessing their own righteousness or morality as "filthy rags" insufficient of meeting God's standard (Isa. 64:6; 2 Cor. 3:15). "But whenever anyone turns to the Lord, the veil is taken away" (2 Cor. 3:15–16). Through the conversion process the Holy Spirit convicts them that to "rely on observing the law" is to be "under a curse," i.e., lost! (Gal. 3:10).

When people are converted, born again of water and the spirit, they are no longer "under law" in the sense of having to rely on their own goodness or lack of badness as the basis of their hope for the future. Rather, those who yield to the converting power of the Holy Spirit live by faith, "under grace." Living "under grace" means 1) being credited with the perfect righteousness, perfect holiness, and forgiveness of sins wrought out by Jesus's life and death as the basis of one's salvation, and 2) being divinely endowed with the inclination and ability to live lives of love and "obedience that comes from faith," as "slaves…to obedience, which leads to righteousness" (Rom. 1:5; 6:15–16). And "if you are led by the Spirit, you are not under law" (Gal. 5:18). The freedom thus provided grace-based, Spirit-led believers allows, enables, and motivates them to adapt to the nonbinding religious scruples of others for the purpose of identifying with them and reaching them with the gospel (1 Cor. 9:20–21).

This understanding provides an integrated and coherent interpretation of the "under law" and "under grace" texts of the New

Testament. The theological truths represented by the phrases "under law" and "under grace" are timeless and universal, with application to all humankind from Adam's fall to the second coming of Jesus.

In summary, the differentiated shades of meaning represented by the New Testament phrases "under law," "under the law," and "under grace" are best understood in the context of the unified thematic development of the plan of salvation throughout Scripture. There is not an Old Testament/"under law" plan of salvation or sanctification, and a different, New Testament/"under grace" plan. There is one timeless, universal plan.

Living "under law" for "the first man Adam" in his sinless state signified a divinely bestowed moral and spiritual endowment bequeathed to him at creation. This endowment enabled him to live and love according to the perfect standard of righteousness and holiness seen in the character of God and required for everlasting life (Gen. 1:27, 31; 2:15–17; Matt. 5:48; Titus 1:2). Jesus, "the last Adam," was born "under law" and lived as Adam had originally been endowed to live; thus, He "committed no sin" and "went around doing good" every day of His life on earth (Acts 10:38; 1 Cor. 15:45; Gal. 4:4; 1 Pet. 2:22). (Whether Jesus was born with the pre-fall or post-fall nature of humanity is beyond this study to explore. The clear and undebatable revelation essential for this study is that He was "tempted in every way, just as we are—yet was without sin" [Heb. 4:16].)

What living "under law" means for Adam's descendants follows this same soteriological thematic development. Just as Adam was at the beginning, so "the whole world" is still "under the law," that is, "held accountable to God" and His standard of perfect righteousness (Rom. 3:19; Matt. 5:48). The sinful nature bequeathed to us by sinful Adam bends us away from God, rendering us incapable of attaining perfection apart from God's gracious interposition on our behalf. Our natural bent to sin expresses itself primarily in the following two ways: in defiance of God's law wherein sin reigns as our "master," making us "slaves to sin" (Rom. 6:14–16; cf. Gal. 5:19–21), and in a legalistic religion that makes one feel fully capable within oneself of living a sufficiently moral life that will put him or her in good stead in the afterlife, and that thereby inclines one to "rely on observing the law" and to "want to be under the law" (Gal. 3:10; 4:21; cf. Phil. 3:3–6).

For Adam's descendants to live "under law" also means that they are "under a curse" and condemnation, namely, the loss of eternal life (Gal. 3:10). This curse seems certainly justifiable with regard to those who live in open defiance of God and His law. But the curse also rests on the most moral among us who do "not submit to God's righteousness" but rather seek "to establish their own" (Rom. 10:3). "For all have sinned and fall short of the glory of God," His perfect standard of righteousness, and are thereby deserving of "the wages of sin [which] is death" (Rom. 3:23; 6:23).

It was precisely from this curse and eternal condemnation that Jesus came "to redeem those under law, that we might receive the full rights of sons"—under grace (Gal. 4:5). "God made him who had no sin to be sin for us, so that in him we might become the righteousness of God"—under grace (2 Cor. 5:21). "You are all sons of God through faith in Christ Jesus, for all of you who were baptized into Christ have clothed yourselves with Christ"—under grace (Gal. 3:26–27; cf. Isa. 61:10; Zech. 3:1–6). Living "under grace" means to depend on the righteousness of God as our only sufficiency for our inclusion in God's eternal kingdom, and on His presence with us and within us as that alone which makes it possible for us to love and live according to His perfect righteousness (Rom. 6:14; 8:4).

All children of Adam came into this life "under law"—under the law's jurisdiction, under condemnation for disobeying it, and under the illusion that they could rely on their own goodness and decency and obedience to secure a place in the afterlife. And through conversion by the Spirit, every believer has been redeemed from the curse of the law to live "under grace." The New Testament terms "under law," "under the law," and "under grace" convey these timeless and universal experiential truths of the plan of salvation.[11]

There is but one true gospel. It is the gospel for which Paul contended, for he warned against those who preached "a different gospel—which is really no gospel at all" (Gal. 1:6). This is that gospel about which it was said, "We also have had the gospel preached to us, just as they did" (Heb. 4:2). It is called "the everlasting gospel" (Rev. 14:6). This gospel is not, nor ever has been, the "gospel" of "under law." It is, and always has been, the gospel of "under grace."

## Notes

1. E.g., KJV, NKJV, NIV, NRSV, ASV, NASB, ESV.

2. "That each reference to law [in Rom. 2:12] is to the Old Testament is not to be doubted." C. E. B. Cranfield, *Romans: A Shorter Commentary* (Grand Rapids, MI: Eerdmans, 1985), 49.

3. "Since [Romans 3:10–18] come from the Writings and the Prophets, and not from the Pentateuch, 'the law' must be used here, as it is also in 1 Cor 14.21; Jn 10.34; 15.25, and as the equivalent Hebrew word was quite often used by the Rabbis, to denote the Old Testament as a whole." Ibid., 67.

4. "In Romans 6:14, 'Ye are not under law but under grace,' there is the sharpest possible antithesis between 'under law' and 'under grace,' and that in terms of Paul's intent in this passage these are mutually exclusive. To be 'under law' is to be under the dominion of sin; to be 'under grace' is to be liberated from that dominion....It is this impossibility to alleviate the bondage of sin that is particularly in view in Romans 6:14. The person who is 'under law,' the person upon whom only law has been brought to bear, the person whose life has been determined exclusively by the resources and potencies of law, is the bondservant of sin." To be "under grace" means to "come *under* all the resources of redeeming and renewing grace which find their epitome in the death and resurrection of Christ and find their permanent embodiments in him who was dead and is alive again....Grace is deliverance from the dominion of sin and therefore deliverance from that which consists in transgression of the law." Murray, *Principles of Conduct*, 184–186. Cranfield understands Paul's reference to "under law" in Rom. 6:14 to mean "under God's disfavor or condemnation" from which we have been delivered by Christ (cf. Rom. 8:1). However, in his comment on the meaning of "under grace" in this text, Cranfield agrees with Murray that deliverance from sin's dominion is involved: "The fact that we have been set free from God's condemnation and are now objects of His gracious favour confirms the truth of the promise that sin shall no more be lord over us. The man who knows that he is free from God's condemnation finds himself beginning to be free to resist the tyranny of sin with boldness and resolution." Cranfield, *Romans*, 140.

5. Cf. Ephesians 5:5 and Revelation 11:15 where the kingdom of God and the kingdom of Christ are presented as one kingdom, as should references to the law of God and the law of Christ be presented as one law. Is it not an insult to the Father and the Son to suggest that the law of one is different from the law of the other, or that the law of one is more advanced and spiritually mature than the law of the other? Any law that comes from God is the law of Christ, and vice versa, for "I and the Father are one" (John 10:30). "There is only one Lawgiver and Judge" (James 4:12).

6. "Paul in 1 Corinthians 9:20, 21...must be using the expression 'under law' in some

sense other than that of Romans 6:14. And the precise meaning is not obscure. He means 'under law' in the sense in which Jews who had not yet understood the significance of the death and resurrection of Christ for the discontinuance of the Mosaic rites and ceremonies considered themselves to be under law, and therefore obliged to keep the rites and customs of the Mosaic economy....'Under law' in this latter instance carries the import of being under the rites and ceremonies of the Mosaic economy....He is reflecting simply upon what a certain group of people considered to be their obligation. And when he says that he was for such as one under law, he means that he accommodated himself to the customs and rites which these people observed and to which they considered themselves obligated." Murray, *Principles of Conduct,* 187–188. That Murray has in mind the ceremonial rites and customs of the law in 1 Corinthians 9 and not the moral law of the Ten Commandments is clear from his comment a few pages later on Romans 13:9: "The commandments, 'Do not commit adultery,' 'Do not murder,' 'Do not steal,' 'Do not covet,' and whatever other commandment there may be, are summed up in this one rule: 'Love your neighbor as yourself.'" "What is of particular interest to us at present is to note that Paul regards these precepts of the Decalogue, four of which he quotes, as relevant to the behaviour which exemplifies the Christian vocation....But if love fulfills them, we must still bear in mind that they are fulfilled; and if they are fulfilled they exist as precepts which call for fulfillment: and if they are summarized in one word, the summary does not obliterate or abrogate the expansion of which it is a summary. It is futile to try to escape the underlying assumption of Paul's thought, that the concrete precepts of the Decalogue have relevance to the believer as the criteria of that behaviour which love dictates." Ibid., 193.

7. "In Romans 6:14 [Paul] wrote that 'you are not under law, but under grace.' Here the antithesis between law and grace indicates that he is referring to the way of *justification*, which is not by our obedience to the law, but by God's sheer mercy alone. In Galatians 5:18, however, he wrote that 'if you are led by the Spirit, you are not under law'. Here the antithesis between law and Spirit indicates that he is referring to the way of *sanctification*, which is not by our struggling to keep the law, but by the power of the indwelling Spirit. So for justification we are not under law but under grace; for sanctification we are not under law but led by the Spirit.

"It is in these two senses that we have been 'freed' or 'released' from the law. But this does not mean that we have been divorced from it altogether, in the sense that it has no more claims on us of any kind, or that we have no more obligations to it. On the contrary, the moral law remains a revelation of God's will which he still expects his people to 'fulfill' by living lives of righteousness and love (8:4; 13:8, 10). This is what the Reformers called 'the third use of the law.'" John R. W. Stott, *The Message of Romans* (Downers Grove, IL: InterVarsity Press, 1994), 191.

8. See Chapter 3, "How God Defined the New Covenant" for a discussion of the provisions of the new covenant.

9. That Jesus was tempted as Adam's descendants are tempted does not mean that He needed to be "born again" as we need to be to enter the kingdom of God (John 3:3–6). The sinful traits listed in Romans 3:10–19 were not characteristic of Him in the same way they are of the rest of us. Yet Jesus lived by faith and total dependence on His Father even as we are invited to do. His own testimony assures us of this. He who told His disciples, "apart from me you can do nothing," said of Himself, "the Son can do nothing by himself," "by myself I can do nothing" (John 15:5; 5:19, 30; cf. John 7:17; 8:28; 14:10; Luke 22:39–44; Heb. 5:7–10).

10. Edward Heppenstall, 451: "The entrance of sin still left man face to face with God's requirements of obedience but with no power to obey. Even with his loss of freedom and his

ability to do what God commanded, he still possessed a strong desire to be justified by his own efforts."

11. How could an Old Testament believer have faith in Christ before Jesus actually came in the flesh? While they recognized or addressed their spiritual empowerer, sustainer, and provider as "God" (Hebrew, *elohim*) and LORD (Hebrew, *Yahweh*), nonetheless "they all ate the same spiritual food and drank the same spiritual drink; for they drank from the spiritual rock that accompanied them, and that rock was Christ" (1 Cor. 10:3–4). Faith in God and reliance on His righteousness was counted to them as faith in Christ and His righteousness. The examples presented in Hebrews 11 make this clear. By faith in God the Old Testament believer "became heir of the righteousness that comes by faith" (11:7). Centuries before Jesus came in the flesh, "By faith Moses…regarded disgrace for the sake of Christ as of greater value than the treasures of Egypt" (11:24, 26). As believers offered the proscribed animal sacrifices, they thereby demonstrated their faith in the substitutionary provision God would one day send to be "led like a lamb to the slaughter"—"pierced for our transgressions…crushed for our iniquities"—thereby making atonement for sin (Isa. 53:5, 7). John the Baptist recognized Jesus as the One sent by God to fulfill the promise—"Look, the Lamb of God, who takes away the sin of the world" (John 1:29). In due time Christ "died as a ransom to set them free from the sins committed under the first covenant" (Heb. 9:15)—the grace-based, gospel-bearing, faith-inducing, mission-directed covenant God provided His people during the Old Testament historical period (see chapter 4, "New Covenant DNA in the Old Covenant," for a further development of this theme). A case can be made that the Old Testament covenant God, *Yahweh*, was none other than Jesus Himself, and that when the Old Testament believers put their faith in *Yahweh*, they were putting their faith in Christ. See also note 1 on page 232 of this book for a futher discussion of the relationship between *Yahweh* and Jesus.

# Appendix C: Scholars' Comments on Colossians 2:16–17

The following commentary statements on Colossians 2:16–17 are representative of those scholars who believe that Paul never intended this passage as an abolishment of the Sabbath God Himself instituted at creation.

### Colossae Christians should not be intimidated by those who judge them for observing the Sabbath.

Troy Martin of Xavier University in Chicago points out that "the Colossian author warns his readers not to permit anyone to *criticize* or *judge* them in regard to eating or drinking or in respect to a festival, a new moon, or Sabbaths" (italics added). He further notes that "the critics may condemn the Colossian Christians for engaging, not engaging, or engaging incorrectly in these practices. The function is ambiguous." In other words, it is possible that the Colossian Christians were observing these holy days with Paul's approval, and that Paul was admonishing them not to be deterred by those who were criticizing them for doing so. Indeed, Martin concludes that "the Pauline community at Colossae, not the opponents, practices the temporal scheme outlined by Col 2.16....The Colossian Christians, not their critics, participate in a religious calendar that includes festivals, new moons, and Sabbaths." (Troy Martin, "Pagan and Judeo-Christian Time-Keeping Schemes in Gal 4:10 and Col 21:16," *New Testament Studies*, vol. 42:1 [January, 1996], 107ff.)

### Paul warns against observing sacred days with a legalistic motivation.

"Paul is not condemning the use of sacred days and seasons....What moves him here is the wrong motive involved when the observance of holy festivals is made a badge of separation and an attempted means of securing salvation out of fear and superstition. It is bad religion that

Paul attacks." (Ralph P. Martin, *Colossians: The Church's Lord and the Christian's Liberty* [Exeter: The Paternoster Press, 1972], 90.)

"Paul's objection is not to religious celebration per se, and probably not even to a congregation's public expression of worship that borrows from the traditions of Judaism. Rather, Paul's primary concern here is any observance that does not concentrate the celebrants' attention upon Christ's importance for salvation." (Robert W. Wall, *The InterVarsity Press New Testament Commentary* on *Colossians & Philemon* [Downers Grove, IL: InterVarsity Press, 1993], 122.)

Thurston likewise concludes that Paul is contending with judgmentalism and legalism, rather than with observance of religious days. "As a good Jew, Paul would not object in principle to sacred days and seasons.…The problem is not with religious holidays *per se*. The problem arises when one is judged on the basis of observing or ignoring those days, which, in any case, are 'shadow' and not 'reality' (2:17). For Paul, the Christian religion is not a matter of legalisms with regard to practices of any sort." (Bonnie Thurston, *Reading Colossians, Ephesians, and 2 Thessalonians: A Literary and Theological Commentary* [New York: Crossroad, 1995], 41.)

## Don't judge others based on their outward observances.

Trentham contends that in Colossians 2:16 Paul first condemns judging others based on outward observance of any kind, and secondly warns against all outward observances (both Jewish and Christian, which would include our modern observance of Christmas and Easter), no matter how good in themselves, that usurp the place of Christ, the reality they were intended to represent. "Only in Christ is there the substance of religion. The outward ceremonies and regulations are but shadows." (Charles A. Trentham, The *Shepherd of the Stars* [Nashville, TN: Broadman Press, 1962], 120.)

## The Sabbath(s) of Colossians 2:16–17 is/are ceremonial while the Sabbath of Creation is permanent.

"The Sabbath is something infinitely greater than a merely Jewish institution, for it was made 'for man' and dates from creation. There is scarcely anything more significant than the fact that just as the Jewish institution was being brought to an end Christ called himself 'the Lord of the Sabbath.' Thus Christ's canceling of the bond set aside the Sabbath as Jewish, but at the same time because we are 'under the law to Christ,' we have the Sabbath, or Lord's Day, as a divine institution dating from the beginning and intended for permanent observance." (W. H. Griffith Thomas, *Christ Pre Eminent: Studies in the Epistle to the Colossians* [Chicago: The Bible Institute Colportage Association, 1923], 83.)

"*Shadow...reality.* The ceremonial laws of the OT are here referred to as shadows (cf. Heb 8:5; 10:1) because they symbolically depicted the coming of Christ; so any insistence on the observance of such ceremonies is a failure to recognize that their fulfillment has already taken place." (Scholarly note on Colossians 2:17, *The NIV Study Bible: New International Version* [Grand Rapids, MI: Zondervan Bible Publishers, 1985], 1815.)

"The Sabbath—Omit 'THE,' which is not in the *Greek*.... 'SABBATHS' (not 'the Sabbaths') of the day of atonement and feast of tabernacles have come to an end with the Jewish services to which they belonged (Leviticus 23. 32, 37–39). The weekly sabbath rests on a more permanent foundation, having been instituted in Paradise to commemorate the completion of creation in six days. Leviticus 23. 38 expressly distinguishes 'the sabbath of the Lord' from the other sabbaths. A *positive* precept is *right because it is commanded*, and ceases to be obligatory when abrogated; a moral precept is *commanded* eternally, *because it is* eternally *right*....Even Adam, in innocence, needed one amidst his earthly employments; therefore the sabbath is still needed, and is therefore still linked with the other nine commandments, as obligatory in the spirit, though the letter of the law has been superseded by that higher spirit of love which is the essence of law and Gospel alike (Romans 13:8–10)." (Robert Jamieson, A. R. Fausset, and David Brown, *A Commentary, Critical and Explanatory, on the Old and New Testaments*, vol. 2 [Hartford: The S. S. Scranton Company, n.d.], 378.)

"'*Or of the Sabbath days.*' Greek, 'of the Sabbaths.' The word Sabbath in the Old Testament is applied not only to the seventh day but to all the days of holy rest that were observed by the Hebrews, and particularly to the beginning and close of their great festivals. There is, doubtless, reference to those days in this place, as the word is used in the plural number, and the apostle does not refer particularly to *the Sabbath* properly so called. There is no evidence from this passage that he would teach that there was no obligation to observe *any* holy time, for there is not the slightest reason to believe that he meant to teach that one of the ten commandments had ceased to be binding on mankind.... The use of the term in the plural number, and the connection, show that he had his eye on the great number of days which were observed by the Hebrews as festivals, as part of their ceremonial and typical law, and not to the *moral* law, or the ten commandments. No part of the moral law—no one of the ten commandments could be spoken of as 'a shadow of good things to come.' These commandments are, from the nature of moral law, of perpetual and universal obligation." (Albert Barnes, *Notes, Explanatory and Practical, on the Epistles of Paul to the Ephesians, Philippians, and Colossians* [New York: Harper & Brothers Publishers, 1873], 252–253.)

The following extended statement by Gordon Clark has in mind several of the above-stated themes: "The context [of Col. 2:16–17] speaks of food and drink, feasts, and new moons. All this is ceremonial. Then are not the Sabbaths, here condemned, ceremonial Sabbaths, and not the creation ordinance?...Given the Jewish milieu and Paul's training, he could have written these words on the reasonable assumption that no one would ever have thought of an attack on the Ten Commandments....

"What needs emphasis, however, in our contemporary unfamiliarity with ancient Jewish customs, is their celebration of Sabbaths on various days of the week. That these special celebrations were now prohibited, but that the weekly Sabbath is still required, the following argument aims to show.

"First, the Sabbath is a creation ordinance: it is not a Mosaic innovation. God not only rested from his work of creation, he blessed the day and sanctified it (Gen. 2:3). This is such an obvious and tremendous consideration that the reduction of the Sabbath to nothing more than a Mosaic ceremony is incredible. What can antisabbaterians make of Genesis 2:3?

"It is often said that there is no mention of the Sabbath before the Exodus from Egypt. Note, however, that before the time of Abraham the account is sparse on all points. For example, the law of monogamous marriage is not mentioned, though Christ referred to it as imposed at creation. Also, there is no mention of sacrifices from the time of Abel to Noah, nor from Genesis 47:1 till after the Exodus, a period of four hundred years. There is no mention of the Sabbath from Joshua to 1 Kings inclusive; and yet this was a post-Mosaic period. Even Psalms and Proverbs do not mention the Sabbath with any frequency. Hence sparcity, with reference to sacrifice, marriage, and the Sabbath, does not prove their non-existence.

"Sparcity, furthermore, is not silence. There are passages in Genesis which can be explained only on the basis of a previous Sabbath law. The word itself may not be used, but note the seven-day divisions in Genesis 7:4, 10 and 8:10, 12…17:12 and 21:4…29:27–28….

"Incidentally the division of time into weeks and so observed by the heathen nations, must be, since it cannot be justified astronomically, a reminiscence of creation.

"That the weekly Sabbath was not first instituted by the Ten Commandments, Moses himself makes clear. Exodus 16—the Decalogue comes in Exodus 20—without any mention of inaugurating a new custom, but rather giving the impression of something already known, indicates that the Sabbath is a day of rest.…Had it been a new law, the wording would have had to be different. Furthermore, the Mosaic law itself, the Ten Commandments, indeed the Fourth Commandment, says, 'Remember.' During the slavery in Egypt, the people had probably been forced to work every day. It is not likely that the Egyptians were Sabbatarians. Over the centuries the Israelites had perhaps half forgotten the Law. Now, on Mt. Sinai, God says, 'Remember.'

"The opponents no doubt reply, 'God at Sinai promulgated a new law and told them to remember it henceforth.' But the division of time into weeks, and the revelation in Genesis 2:3, are ruinous to such a reply.

"If the Fourth Commandment was newly instituted in the desert, how can one avoid inconsistency without regarding the other nine also as new? Now, there is no mention of any law against murder in the first four chapters of Genesis. Yet Cain clearly knew that murder was forbidden. He also knew that God had sanctified the Sabbath.

"For this reason the Ten Commandments must be regarded as the moral law, in the words of the [Presbyterian] Catechism, 'summarily comprehended.' Is it not utterly incongruous to think of a temporary ceremonial regulation embedded in the Decalogue? If all mankind, not the Jews only, are obligated to worship the one true God, to avoid images and profanity, are they not also obligated to sanctify the Sabbath forever? A negative answer is utter absurdity." (Gordon H. Clark, *Colossians: Another Commentary on an Inexhaustible Message* [Phillipsburg, NJ: Presbyterian and Reformed Publishing Co., 1979], 94–97.)

# Appendix D: Tables and Charts

## Table 1: The Covenant(s)

### The Everlasting Covenant

- The covenant love and commitment that exists within the Trinity—God everlasting.
- God's everlasting grace (favor), love, and commitment extended to and embracing the whole of His creation.
- The basis of all covenants God initiated with humankind.
- The ultimate covenant/relationship that is violated by sin—breaking trust with God leading to disobedience.
- Revealed/manifested/demonstrated most fully in Jesus Christ and His atoning sacrifice for the reconciliation of sinful human beings and the entire universe to God.
  (1 John 4:8; Matt. 7:9–12; Ps. 103:17–22; Gen. 9:16; Isa. 24:5; 42:6–7; 49:4–6; Col. 1:19–20; Heb. 13:20)

### The Covenant of Creation

- God's everlasting covenant love extended to and embracing our own world order, especially Adam and Eve, at creation, before their fall into sin.
- Everything created very good, including humankind in God's image, with no taint of sin.
- Three promises/provisions of the new covenant operative at creation, and the fourth provisionally so, for Adam and Eve.
- God's initial relationship with humankind one of trust and obedience on humanity's part, and the potential of eternal life if that relationship were maintained untainted by sin (distrust and disobedience).
  (Gen. 1:26–27, 31; 2:15–22; Jer. 33:20–26; Hos. 6:7; Titus 1:1–2; Rev. 13:8)

## The Covenant of Redemption / Covenant of Grace

- God's everlasting covenant graciously extended to sinners and especially adapted to meet human beings in their sinful state.
- The overarching, unified, gracious purpose of God operating in all covenants He has made with humankind from the fall of Adam to the Second Coming.
- "The everlasting gospel" bridge that spans from Paradise lost to Paradise restored.
- Purpose: to restore humanity to a right relationship with God, and thus ultimately to everything that humankind had lost through sin.
- God's means for reconciling all things to Himself, things in heaven (healing and resolving the primordial disruption Lucifer's rebellion caused in heaven) as well as things on earth (providing salvation to all who believe).
- Represented in God's covenants with Adam after the fall, Noah, Abraham, Israel, David, and the historical new covenant. (Gen. 3:15; Isa. 45:22; Eph. 2:1–10; Col. 1:19–20; Rev. 12:7–9; 14:6)

## The Historical Old and New Covenants—Old and New Testament Periods

- The two historical periods or dispensations of God's covenant(s) with humanity divided by the coming of Jesus Christ into the world—all things before He came being considered "old" and all things after He came "new."
- Characteristics of the historical old covenant:
    - A bearer of the everlasting gospel
    - A system of moral and civil laws based on love and the Ten Commandments
    - An elaborate ceremonial system eventually focused in a localized sanctuary
    - Administered by imperfect priests and centered on animal sacrifices which could never take away sin but served as an

anticipatory type and shadow of the atoning ministry of the Messiah who was yet to come
- Marked by redeeming acts of God
- Ratified by the blood of animals
- Characteristics of the historical new covenant:
  - A bearer of the everlasting gospel
  - An intensification of moral expectations based on the fuller revelation of love and the Ten Commandments as seen lived out in the life of Jesus Christ
  - A different ceremonial system consisting of baptism and the holy communion
  - Administered by the perfect priest, Jesus Christ, who ministers in the heavenly sanctuary to make intercession for humanity to save us completely
  - Centered on Jesus's atoning sacrifice, once for all, which provides forgiveness for sins committed in both historical dispensations
  - Marked by the redemptive act of God in Jesus Christ for the salvation of the world and the reconciliation of all things to Himself
  - Ratified by the blood of Jesus

(Exod. 19:4; 20:10; 25:8–9; Deuteronomy; Neh. 9:4–33; Isa. 52:7; Jer. 31:31–33; John 1:29; Rom. 10:14–17; Gal. 1:6–9; 3:8; Heb. 4:2, 6; 7–10; Rev. 14:6)

## Table 2: Historical Old and New Covenants

| Historical Old Covenant | Historical New Covenant |
| --- | --- |
| • Spans the period of spiritual history extending from Creation to the incarnation of Christ (i.e., the entire Old Testament period)—"when the old covenant [i.e., Old Testament] is read" (2 Cor. 3:14). | • Spans the period of spiritual history extending from the incarnation to the second coming of Christ (i.e., the entire New Testament period)—everything after Jesus came being considered "new," even if it had existed earlier (cf. 1 John 2:7–8). |
| • Purpose: To save people living in the Old Testament era through the initial covenant God made with fallen Adam and then expanded through covenants with Noah, Abraham, Moses/Israel, David, etc., and to groom them into a kingdom of priests, a holy nation, which would take God's message of salvation to the whole world (Gen. 3:15; Gen. 6:17–18; 9:8–17; 12:1–3; 15:1–18; 17:1–16; Exod. 19ff.; Deut.; 2 Sam. 23:5; Ps. 67; Isa. 45:22; 49:3, 6; 55:3; 56). | • Purpose: To save people living in the New Testament era through a "new covenant [God made] with the house of Israel and with the house of Judah," and to groom them into a kingdom of priests, a holy nation, which would take God's message of salvation to the whole world (Heb. 8:8–12; Matt. 28:19–20; 1 Pet. 2:5, 9). |
| • Characterized by the preaching of the gospel (Rom. 10:6–16; Deut. 30:11–14; Gal. 3:8; Heb. 4:2). | • Characterized by the preaching of the gospel (Heb. 4:2). |
| • Characterized by miraculous and redeeming acts of God on behalf of His people (Neh. 9; Ps. 78; 104–106; Acts 7). | • Characterized by the redemptive act of God in Jesus Christ for the salvation of the world and the reconciliation to Himself of all things in heaven and earth (2 Cor. 5:19; Col. 1:19–20). |

| Historical Old Covenant | Historical New Covenant |
|---|---|
| • Characterized by a system of moral and civil laws based on love and the Ten Commandments, expectations which everyone in this era fell short of—"there is no one who does not sin" (1 Kings 8:40; Exod. 20–24; Lev. 19:18; Deut. 5:6). | • Characterized by an intensification of moral expectations based on the fuller revelation of love and Ten Commandments as seen lived out in the life of Jesus Christ, expectations which everyone in this era has fallen short of—"all have sinned and fall short of the glory of God" (Rom. 3:23, 10–18; Matt. 5:17–30; 19:16–21; 22:35–40; James 2:10–11). |
| • Characterized by an elaborate ceremonial system eventually focused in a localized sanctuary which represented both God's presence among them and His greater sanctuary in heaven from which He ministered to them (Exod. 25:8–9; Heb. 9:1–7). | • Characterized by a simpler ceremonial system consisting of baptism and the holy communion which represented the finished work and atoning sacrifice of Jesus who continues His ministry on our behalf from His sanctuary in heaven (Luke 22:19–20; Col. 2:11–12; Heb. 8:1–2). |
| • Characterized by a human priesthood from the tribe of Levi who administered the sanctuary services, ministered imperfectly to the people, and represented God to the people and the people to God (Num. 3:5–9; Zech. 3:1–7; Heb. 7:11, 28). | • Characterized by Christ as our perfect high priest in heaven, having represented God to us through His ministry among us, and now representing us before the Father (John 7:39; Heb. 7:23–28; 8:1–2). |
| • Characterized by animal sacrifices which could never take away sin but served as an anticipatory type and shadow of the atoning ministry of the Messiah who was yet to come (Lev. 4:27–35; Isa. 53:1–7; Heb. 10:4, 11). | • Characterized by the once for all atoning sacrifice of Christ through which all believers in both historical eras were granted forgiveness of sins and the righteousness of God by which we obtain access to eternal life (John 1:29; Heb. 9:12–15, 23–28). |

| Historical Old Covenant | Historical New Covenant |
| --- | --- |
| • Characterized by the convicting, converting, sanctifying work of the Holy Spirit to save and empower for ministry (Gen. 6:3; Exod. 31:1–3; Ps. 51:9–12; 1 Sam. 10:6–10; Ezek. 36:25–27; 37:1–14). | • Characterized by a greater understanding of the multifaceted ministry of the Holy Spirit than was available to believers in the Old Testament era and a new phase of the Spirit's ministry based on the accomplished sacrifice and resurrection of Christ (John 7:39; 16:7; Rom. 8:4–17; 1 Cor. 12). |
| • Means by which the Holy Spirit birthed in many living during the Old Testament era a new covenant experience with an eternal hope assured (Heb. 11). | • Means by which the Holy Spirit birthed in many living during the New Testament era a new covenant experience with an eternal hope assured (1 Pet. 1:3–9). |
| • An old covenant experience with no eternal hope realized by many living during the Old Testament era due to unbelief and rejection of the everlasting gospel (Rom. 10:16; Heb. 4:2). | • An old covenant experience with no eternal hope realized by many living during the New Testament era due to unbelief and rejection of the everlasting gospel (Matt. 7:13–14; Luke 18:8; Gal. 3:10; 4:21–26; 5:4; Heb. 10:26–31). |
| • Ratified by the blood of animals (Exod. 24:8; Heb. 9:22). | • Ratified by the blood of Jesus (Luke 22:20; Heb. 9:22–28). |

# Table 3: Old and New Covenant Experiences

| Old Covenant Experience | New Covenant Experience |
| --- | --- |
| • Sin's counterpart of God's four provisions of the new covenant experience—*the gospel externalized* (Isa. 29:13; Matt. 15:8–9; 7:21–23; 25:1–12; John 17:25; Isa. 26:18; 52:5; Rom. 2:23–24; Luke 18:9–14): | • The four provisions of a new covenant experience—*the gospel internalized* (Jer 31:32–33; Heb. 8:10–12; 2 Cor. 2:14): |
| · "The Lord says: 'These people come near to me with their mouth and honor me with their lips, but their hearts are far from me. Their worship of me is made up only of rules taught by men.'" | · "I will put my laws in their minds and write them on their hearts." (*Sanctification*) |
| · "Many will say to me on that day, 'Lord, Lord,...' Then I will tell them plainly, 'I never knew you. Away from me, you evildoers!'" "Later the others came. 'Sir! Sir!' they said. 'Open the door for us!' But he replied, 'I tell you the truth, I don't know you.'" | · "I will be their God and they will be my people." (*Reconciliation*) |
| · "The world does not know you." "You who brag about the law, do you dishonor God by breaking the law? As it is written: 'God's name is blasphemed among the Gentiles because of you.'" "We have not brought salvation to the earth; we have not given birth to the people of the world." | · "No longer will a man teach his neighbor or a man his brother, saying, 'Know the Lord, because they will all know me, from the least of them to the greatest.'" "God... through us spreads everywhere the fragrance of the knowledge of him." (*Mission*) |

| Old Covenant Experience | New Covenant Experience |
|---|---|
| • "Some…were confident of their own righteousness and looked down on everybody else.…'God, I thank you that I am not like other men.'…But the tax collector …beat his breast and said, 'God, be merciful to me a sinner.…This man, rather than *the other*, went home justified before God" (italics added). | • "I will forgive their wickedness and will remember their sins no more." (*Justification*) |
| • An experience with God and His law that God never intended—"they did not remain faithful to my covenant" (Heb. 8:9). | • The experience with God and His law that God intended—"if you…keep my covenant, then…you will be…a kingdom of priests and a holy nation" (Exod. 19:5–6; 1 Pet. 2:5, 9). |
| • An experience possessed by many in both the Old and New Testament/covenant historical eras (Rom. 9:31–32; 10:2–3, 16; Gal. 4:21–31; Heb. 4:1–2). | • An experience possessed by many in both the Old and New Testament/covenant historical periods (Hebrews 11). |
| • Sinful from birth—"there is no one who does good," even "our righteous acts are like filthy rags" (Ps. 51:5; Rom. 3:12; Isa. 64:6). | • Initiated at conversion—"whenever anyone turns to the Lord, the veil is taken away" (2 Cor. 3:16). |
| • Simultaneously both "dead in… transgressions and sins,…gratifying the cravings of our sinful nature," and "as for legalistic righteousness, faultless." As helpless to change this condition on our own as a leopard is to change his spots or an Ethiopian his skin (Eph. 2:1, 3; Phil. 3:6; Jer. 13:23). | • "Born again," "born of water and the Spirit." "…because of his mercy [God] saved us through the washing of rebirth and renewal by the Holy Spirit, whom he poured out on us generously through Jesus Christ our Savior, so that, having been justified by grace, we might become heirs having the hope of eternal life" (John 3:3–5; Titus 3:4–7). |

| Old Covenant Experience | New Covenant Experience |
| --- | --- |
| • Characterized by outward compliance to the law's requirements for the purpose of gaining entrance into God's covenant and eternal salvation—"a yoke that neither we nor our fathers have been able to bear," "rely on the law," "brag about the law," "merely outward and physical," "by the written code," pursuing righteousness "not by faith but as if it were by works," "sought to establish their own [righteousness]," "did not submit to God's righteousness," "written...on tablets of stone" not "on tablets of human hearts," "covenant... of the letter," "the letter [that] kills," "the ministry that brought death," "the ministry that condemns men," "rely on observing the law," "want to be under the law," "trying to be justified by the law," "as for legalistic righteousness, faultless" (Acts 15:10; Rom. 2:17, 23, 28–29; 9.31–32; 10:3; 2 Cor. 3:3, 6–7, 9; Gal. 3:10; 4:21; 5:4; Phil. 3:6). | • Characterized by an inner transformation by the Holy Spirit writing God's law in the heart of a born-again, converted believer, resulting in a loving "obedience that comes from faith"—"I desire to do your will...your law is within my heart," "circumcision of the heart, by the Spirit," "you wholeheartedly obeyed," "the righteous requirements of the law might be fully met in [those] who do not live according to the sinful nature but according to the Spirit," "obtained...a righteousness that is by faith," "covenant...of the Spirit," "the ministry of the Spirit," "the ministry that brings righteousness," "justified by faith in Christ," "by grace you have been saved, though faith...it is the gift of God," "not having a righteousness of my own...but that which is through faith in Christ" (Rom. 1:5; Ps. 40:8; Heb. 8:10; Rom. 2:29; 6:17; 8:4; 9:30; 2 Cor. 3:6, 8–9; Gal. 2:16; Eph. 2:8; Phil. 3:9). |
| • Those with this experience are "slaves to sin," slaves "to impurity and to ever-increasing wickedness," "free from the control of righteousness," "a prisoner of the law of sin," "a slave to the law of sin," "does not submit to God's law, nor can it do so," controlled by the sinful nature," "cannot please God," "burdened...by a yoke of slavery" (Rom. 6:6, 16–22; 7:23, 25; 8:7–8; Gal. 5:1). | • Those with this experience are "freed from sin," "slaves...to obedience," "set free from sin," "slaves to righteousness," "slaves to God," "in [their] inner being [they] delight in God's law," "slave[s] to God's law," "controlled...by the Spirit," "the Spirit of God lives in you," "by the Spirit you put to death the misdeeds of the body," "led by the Spirit," "Christ has set us free" (Rom. 6:7, 16–19, 22; 7:22, 25; 8:9–14; Gal. 5:1). |

| Old Covenant Experience | New Covenant Experience |
|---|---|
| • Relating to God's law through the influence of sin/Satan/sinful nature which misapplies God's holy law, transforming it into "a law of sin and death" (Rom. 8:2). | • Relating to God's law through the influence of the Holy Spirit who perfectly applies God's holy law so that it functions as God intended as "the law of the Spirit of life" (Rom. 8:2). |
| • This experience "leads to death," "result[s] in death," and is a "body of death" (Rom. 6:16, 21; 7:24). | • This experience "leads to righteousness" and "leads to holiness," and "the result is eternal life" (Rom. 6:16, 19, 22). |
| • The gospel rejected (Isa. 52:7; 53:1; Rom. 10:16; Heb. 4:1–2). | • The gospel accepted (Isa. 52:7ff.; Rom. 10:6–16; Heb. 4:2; 11). |

## Table 4: New Testament Commands

Commands concerning what to do in the following situations:

- specific steps to take to deal with a believer who sins against you (Matt. 18:15–17)
- what kinds of things to say and not to say (Matt. 5:34–37; cf. Eph. 4:29; 5:4–5; Col. 4:6; 2 Tim. 2:16; James 3:2–10; 5:12; 1 Pet. 3:10)
- obeying those in political office and civil legislation including paying taxes (Luke 20:25; Rom. 13:1–7)

Commands against the following practices:

- spiritual worship if you have not reconciled an estrangement (Matt. 5:23)
- loving our relatives more than Jesus (Matt. 10:37)
- eating meat that has any blood in it (Acts 15:20, 29)
- certain ways of dressing and fixing one's hair (1 Tim. 2:9–10; 1 Pet. 3:3–4)
- grumbling and complaining (1 Cor. 10:10; James 5:9; 1 Pet. 4:9)
- becoming weighed down with the anxieties of life (Luke 21:34)
- conceit (Gal. 5:26)
- comparing yourself spiritually to others (Gal. 6:4–5)
- unresolved anger (Matt. 5:22; Eph. 4:26–27)
- harboring bitterness (Eph. 4:31)
- having debt (Rom. 13:8)
- eating anything that would offend someone (Rom. 14:13, 15, 20)
- refusing to eat what an unbelieving host set before you (1 Cor. 10:27)
- jealousy and disharmony and selfish ambition (Gal. 5:20–21)
- discrimination of any kind (James 2:1–11)
- even a hint of sexual immorality of every kind including lust (Matt. 5:27–28; Gal. 5:19; cf. Eph. 5:3; 1 Thess. 4:3; Heb. 13:4)
- cowardice (Rev. 21:8)

Commands on how to relate to specific kinds of people:

- those who sue you (Matt. 5:25, 40)
- those who cause you grief (Matt. 5:39)
- those who want to borrow from you (Matt. 5:42)
- your enemies (Matt. 5:44; Rom. 12:19–21)
- those who sin against you (Matt. 6:14; 18:15–17, 21–35)
- those caught in a sin (Gal. 6:1)
- faithful spiritual leaders (Heb. 13:7)
- hypocritical spiritual leaders (Matt. 23:1–3; Luke 20:45–47)
- civil authorities (Rom. 13:1–7; 1 Pet. 2:13–17)
- those who are spiritually weak (Rom. 14:1–3; 15:1)
- divisive people (Rom. 15:18; Titus 3:10)
- children (Matt. 18:10; Luke 17:1–3)
- widows (1 Tim. 5:4–16)
- believers who refuse to accept godly counsel (2 Thess. 3:14–15)
- unbelievers and hypocrites who are unresponsive to spiritual appeals (2 Tim. 3:1–5)
- strangers (Heb. 13:2)
- prisoners (Heb. 13:3)
- the poor (Luke 3:11; 1 John 3:17–18)
- doubters (Jude 22–23)
- believers whose beliefs and lifestyles don't meet your understanding of how Christians should think and act (Rom. 14:1–5, 13, 15, 20; 1 Cor. 8:9–13)
- people who argue about the gospel (2 Tim. 2:23–26)

Commands addressed to the following groups of people:

- young men (Titus 2:2–6)
- elderly men (Titus 2:2)
- elderly women (Titus 2:3–5)
- husbands (1 Cor. 7:3, 5, 10–11; Eph. 5:25–26, 28, 33; 1 Pet. 3:7)
- wives (1 Cor. 7:3, 5, 10–11; Eph. 5:22, 33; 1 Pet. 2:1–4)

- believers married to unbelievers (1 Cor. 7:12–14)
- fathers (Eph. 6:4; Col. 3:21)
- children (Eph. 6:1–3)
- slaves/employees (Eph. 6:5–8; Col. 3:22; 1 Tim. 6:1–2; 1 Pet. 2:18)
- masters/employers (Eph. 6:9; Col. 4:1)
- the rich (Luke 14:12–14; 1 Tim. 6:17–18; James 1:10–11)
- the poor (James 1:9)
- able-bodied people who refuse to work when work is available (2 Thess. 3:10–12)
- elders (1 Tim. 3:2–7; Titus 1:6–10; 1 Pet. 5:1–3)
- deacons (1 Tim. 3:8–10, 12)
- wives of deacons (1 Tim. 3:11)
- the sick (James 5:13–16)

## Commands admonishing us to:

- "consider others better than yourselves" (Phil. 2:3)
- "become blameless and pure…without fault" (Phil. 2:14–16)
- "avoid every kind of evil" (1 Thess. 5:22)
- "be self-controlled" (1 Pet. 1:13)
- "keep your lives free from the love of money and be content with what you have" (Heb. 13:5)
- be joyful in trials (James 1:2–4; cf. Rom. 5:3–5) and in the assurance that our names are written in heaven (Luke 10:20)
- "grieve, mourn and wail" if you are not converted (James 4:8–10)
- have "the same [self-giving attitude] as that of Christ Jesus" (Phil. 2:5–8)
- "be imitators of God" (Eph. 5:1–2)
- "be holy, because I [your God] am holy" (1 Pet. 1:15–16; cf. 1 Thess. 4:3–8; Heb. 12:14)
- "be merciful just as your Father is merciful" (Luke 6:36)
- "aim for perfection" (2 Cor. 13:11)
- "be perfect…as your heavenly Father is perfect" (Matt. 5:48)

# Chart 1: The DNA of the Covenant(s)

| Covenant | Everlasting | Humanity at Creation | Adam after His Fall | Noah | Abraham | Sinai | David | Covenant Consciousness at Temple Dedication | Covenant Consciousness in Isaiah 51-54 (54:10 "Covenant of Peace") | Covenant Language in Ezekiel 36-37 | Messiah Jesus Isa. 42:6-7 Isa. 49:4-6 Mal. 3:1 | New Covenant | Eden Restored |
|---|---|---|---|---|---|---|---|---|---|---|---|---|---|
| **Made by God with** | Earth and universe Gen. 9:16 Isa. 24:5 Eph. 3:10 Col. 1:19-20 | Adam/humanity Gen. 1:26-27 Gen. 2:15-22 Hos. 6:6-7 | Adam/humanity Gen. 3:15 | All life through Noah Gen. 9:8-17 Isa. 54:9-10 2 Pet. 3:3-9 | Abraham and his promised seed Gen. 15:18 Gen. 17:1-22 | Israel and foreign converts Exod. 19-23 Deut. Isa. 56 | David and his descendants 2 Sam. 23:5 Isa. 55:3 | Israel and foreign converts 1 Kings 8:41-43 Isa. 56 | Israel and foreign converts Isa. 56 | Post-exilic Israel and converts | Israel, Gentiles, "The ends of the earth" Isa. 42:6-7; 49:6 | Israel and Judah Jer. 31:31 Heb. 8:8 | Overcomers |
| **"I will write my laws in your hearts": Sanctification** | Heb. 13:20-21 Rom. 2:14-16 | Gen. 1:26-27, 31 implied | Gen. 3:15 implied | Ezek. 14:14, 20 Heb. 11:7 implied | Gen. 26:5 with John 15:5 implied | Exod. 31:12-13 Lev. 20:7-8 Deut. 30:6, 11-14 | Ps. 40:8 | 1 Kings 8:61, 58 | Isa. 51:7, 15-16 with Deut. 30:6, 11-14 and Rom. 10:6-16 | Ezek. 36:26-27 | Heb. 10:7 with Ps. 40:8 | Jer. 31:33 Heb. 8:10 | Rev. 22:11 implied |
| **"I will be your God and you will be my people": Reconciliation** | Ps. 103:17-22 Isa. 19:25 Col. 1:19-20 | Gen. 1:26-27, 31 implied | Gen. 3:15, 21 implied | Ezek. 14:14, 20 Heb. 11:7 implied | Gen. 17:7 Deut. 29:12-13 | Exod. 6:7 Lev. 26:12 | 2 Sam. 7:5-16 Ps. 89:3-4, 20-29 | 1 Kings 8:59 (cf. vv. 16, 30, 33-36) | Isa. 51:15-16 | Ezek. 36:28 37:23, 27 | Matt. 1:23 Matt. 3:17 Heb. 1:1-5 | Jer. 31:33 Heb. 8:10 | Rev. 21:2-3, 7 |
| **"All will know Me": Mission** | Isa. 19:19-25 Isa. 45:22 Ps. 19:1-4 Rom. 1:20 John 17:3 Col. 1:19-20 | Hos. 6:6-7 Gen. 1:26-27 Gen. 2:15-22 implied | Gen. 3:15 implied | 2 Pet. 2:5 | Gen. 12:3 Gen. 28:14 | Exod. 19:5-6 with 1 Pet. 2:9 Ps. 67:1-2 Ezek. 36:22-23 | 2 Sam. 23:5 with 1 Chron. 16:7-33 Isa. 55:3-5 | 1 Kings 8:41-43 | Isa. 52:7-15 | Ezek. 36:23 37:28 | Matt. 1:21 John 17:25 John 14:7, 9 John 10:30 | Jer. 31:34 Heb. 8:11 2 Cor. 2:14-16 | Rev. 21:2-3 Hab. 2:14 John 17:3 1 Cor. 13:12 |
| **"I will forgive your sins": Justification** | Heb. 13:20 Matt. 26:26-28 Mark 14:24 | Not needed but provided for 1 Cor. 1:23-24 1 Cor. 2:2, 7 2 Tim. 1:8-9 1 Pet. 1:18-20 Rev. 13:8 Heb. 13:20 | Gen. 3:21 implied | 1 Kings 8:46 Ezek. 14:14, 20 Heb. 11:7 implied | Gen. 15:6 Rom. 4:1-4 | Exod. 34:6-10 Ps. 103:2-14 | Ps. 32:1-5 with Rom. 4:6-8 Isa. 55:3-7 | 1 Kings 8:30, 33-34 1 Kings 8:46-51 | Isa. 53:5-12 | Ezek. 36:25 37:23 | Eph. 1:3-8 Heb. 2:9, 14-17 Heb. 9:15 1 Pet. 2:22-24 1 Pet. 1:18-20 Rev. 1:5 Rev. 13:8 | Jer. 31:34 Heb. 8:12 | Rev. 7:9, 13-14 with Zech. 3:1-5 |

Covenant / Gospel Provisions

# Chart 2: Graphic Summary of the Covenant(s)

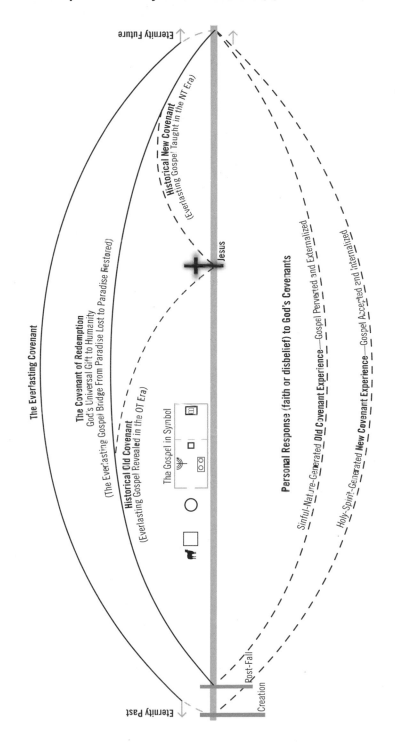

The Everlasting Covenant

The Covenant of Redemption
God's Universal Gift to Humanity
(The Everlasting Gospel Bridge From Paradise Lost to Paradise Restored)

Historical New Covenant
(Everlasting Gospel Taught in the NT Era)

Historical Old Covenant
(Everlasting Gospel Revealed in the OT Era)

Eternity Future

Eternity Past

Jesus

Creation

Post-Fall

The Gospel in Symbol

Personal Response (faith or disbelief) to God's Covenants

Sinful-Nature-Generated Old Covenant Experience——Gospel Perverted and Externalized

Holy-Spirit-Generated New Covenant Experience——Gospel Accepted and Internalized

# Scripture Index

# General Index

Abraham, covenant with, 16–17, 96–97, 172–78, 304

Adam, covenant with, 15, 25n5, 237–38, 242, 304

atonement. *See* justification; redemption, covenant of

Bacchiocchi, Samuele, 232n2

Badenas, Robert, 113

baptism, 63, 176–77

belief. *See* faith

born again. *See* conversion

Calvin, John, 102–4, 126, 179

ceremony, covenant and, 63–64, 91–92, 191–94, 255–60

Christ, Jesus the
    advent of, epicenter of history, 64
    advent of, makes the covenant new, 72–73
    everlasting covenant become flesh, 66–67
    law and, 50–53, 64–71, 113–15, 159–61
    magnified the law, 65–66
    new covenant and, 255–57, 263–65
    revealed righteousness apart from law, 160
    source of grace and truth, 50–53
    unifying agent of the covenants, 72
    Yahweh and, 232n1
    yoke of, 164

circumcision
    discarded as covenant sign, 176–78
    everlasting covenant sign, 177
    practiced in numerous nations, 207n4, 209n25
    replaced in New Testament with baptism, 63, 176–78
    ritual of Old Testament ceremonial system, 63, 177

sign of covenant with Abraham, 173
    spiritual meaning of, 173–76
    *See also* law, the

civil, law as, 102–3

commands. *See* law, the

common grace, 25n7

conversion, 240

covenant book
    Deuteronomy as, 37, 54n
    Exodus 20:22–23:33 as, 37

covenant, everlasting, 3–8, 291, 304–5

covenant(s)
    as term, 1n1, 6, 10
    core truths of, 7, 9, 48
    definition, 1, 10
    Jesus as God's, 66–67
    kinds of, 2
    likened to a will, 1, 185–87
    mission-directed purpose, 13–23
    nature of, 2–3
    of creation, 15, 25n4, 291
    of redemption/grace, 8–9, 19–20, 33, 48–49, 77, 79, 86, 238–39, 263, 292
    origins of, 9–10
    types of, 1–2, 10n1, 291–93
    universality of, 12–23
    with Abraham, 17, 86, 106
    with Adam, 15, 25nn4–5, 77, 86
    with David, 17
    with Israel, 17, 37–49, 85–86, 93–94
    with Noah, 15–16

Craigie, Peter, 63, 74n6

Cranfield, C. E. B., 107, 110, 141n28, 266n4, 282nn2–4

Creation, covenant of
    the cross and, 67–69
    nature of, 291
    Sabbath and, 178–81
    salvation history and, 19–22, 242, 304
    *See also* Adam, covenant with

Gane, Roy, 214n49
generations, covenant, 62–63, 73n6
Gentiles, Christian, 162–63, 197–99
golden rule, 5, 12n15, 73n3
Gospel
    different, 135
    embedded in Sinai covenant, 48–49
    encompasses the four new covenant
        promises, 260–61
    equated with covenant of redemption/
        grace, 10, 292
    everlasting, 8–10, 260–62, 281, 292
    of grace, 281
    only one true, 8–9, 238–39, 260–61,
        281
    preached throughout both Testaments,
        15–19, 261
    universal in application, 14
    veiled, 120, 123–25
    See also promises, covenant;
        redemption, covenant of
grace, 25n7, 107–8, 279–82, 292. See also
    experience, new covenant
grace, covenant of. See redemption,
    covenant of
great commission, Old Testament, 34, 44

Hasel, Gerhard F., 10n2, 25n5, 73n4
Hasel, Michael G., 10n2, 25n5, 73n4
Heppenstall, Edward, 62–63, 238n10
history. See new covenant, historical; old
    covenant, historical
Hittites, treaty form of, 54n4
holiness. See sanctification
holy days. See ceremony, covenant and
Holy Spirit
    conversion and, 240
    converting/sanctifying agent, 240–41,
        274–75
    flesh and, 94–96
    in the new covenant experience, 93–99
    law and, 109–10, 117–26, 141n28
    nature of new work in New Testament
        era, 70–71

operative in Old Testament era,
    69–70, 74–75n10, 274–75
relation to everlasting covenant, 4
salvation history and, 69–71, 74n10
vs. written code (letter), 109–10
See also experience, new covenant

imperative, law as, 104
individuals, covenant and, 62–63, 73n6
Israel, nation of, 183–85, 189–91
Israelites, covenant with. See law, the

Jerusalem council, 163, 197–99
Jesus. See Christ, Jesus the
justification, 32, 44–47, 238–40, 249–50,
    304

Kaiser, Walter C., Jr., 266n2
Kline, Meredith, 16–17, 54n4, 180

LaRondelle, Hans K., 73n4, 243n3
law, the
    apparent contradictions between two
        Testaments regarding, xi, 78
    as forgiveness, 44, 46
    as love, 146
    Calvin's/Reformers' three uses of,
        102–4, 283n7
    ceremony and, 91–92, 255–60
    Christ is the life of, 126
    dying to, 108–11
    end of, 113–15, 169n27
    faith and, 99–106, 111–13
    God's self-revelation in, 44–47
    gospel deeply embedded in, 113
    grace in, 39–49, 107–8, 143–45
    has no power of its own, 100–1
    Jesus and, 65–66, 160–61
    Jesus embodied, 160
    Jesus magnified, 65–66, 160
    letter vs. Spirit, 109–11
    love and, 145–52
    love as fulfillment of, 151

moral/ritual distinction, 259–60
new covenant and, 57–73, 152–60,
    301–3
of sin and death, 116
pure gospel, 48–49
required a faith response, 111, 113
Sabbath and, 192–93, 199–203
salvation history and, 17, 85–87,
    275–82, 304
shows how to live as God's friend, 144
sin and, 115–17, 126–28
suitable for all historical ages, 104
taught faith, 111
the Spirit and, 117–26, 141n28
transcript of Jesus's character, 65
under law vs. under grace, 107, 267–84
uses of, 102–4
written on the heart, 29–30, 39–41,
    132–33, 159, 164, 237, 240–41,
    259–60, 297
legalism
    a different gospel, 135
    a yoke none can bear, 163
    danger in New Testament era as in
        old, 134–36
    determined by motivation, 178
    Hebrews rescues true Sabbath from
        faithless, 227
    needs only one commandment, 153,
        164–65
    Sabbath designed by God to deliver
        from, 205
    See also experience, old covenant
letter, the, 110, 141n29. See also
    experience, old covenant
Lord, the. See Yahweh
Lord's Supper, the, 194–96
    replaced animal sacrifices, 63, 196
love, covenant, 4–7, 59–60, 73n3, 136,
    145–52
    basis of the law, 145–52
    first biblical reference to, 146
    first commanded in the law, 146
    for God inseparably linked with the
        Ten Commandments, 147–48

God's commandments and covenants
    rooted in, 147–52
God's, origin of everlasting covenant,
    4–7, 9–10, 291
magnified by Jesus, 80
motivation for obedience by Old
    Testament believers, 152

McComiskey, Thomas Edward, 11n8,
    40, 154
mission
    experience and, 241, 248–49
    salvation history and, 14–19, 30–32,
        42–44, 304
Moo, Douglas, xvn2, 88n1
Moses. See law, the
Murray, John, 1, 30n1, 265n1, 282n4,
    282n6

new covenant experience
    anticipates complete fulfillment at
        Second Coming, 239–42
    characteristics of, 82–84, 251, 297–
        300
    compared/contrasted with old
        covenant experience, 81–85, 235–36,
        251, 297–300
    differs from historical new covenant,
        80–84, 235–36, 294–300
    emphasis of Paul on the covenants, 92
    enjoyed by Adam at creation, 83, 237
    enjoyed by people of every era, 130–
        33, 237, 261
    experienced by many at Sinai, 251
    gained through operation of the Holy
        Spirit, 93–96, 237
    life in the Spirit, 83
    ministry of the Spirit, 117
    obedience from faith, 161
    of faith, 83
    of rest in God, 217–19, 226–29
    personally applied, 246–50
    prayers of, 87
    preceded the old covenant in time,
        83–84

new covenant, historical
    better covenant, 262–65
    characteristics of, 80–81, 293–96
    circumcision in, 176–78
    compared/contrasted with historical
        old covenant, 58–73, 79–81, 235–36,
        251–55, 294–96
    defined by God, 28
    differs from new covenant experience,
        80–84, 294–300
    DNA markers of, 28–32, 304
    dominant emphasis of Hebrews 7–10,
        91–92, 251–66
    equated with New Testament era, xiii
    faith-inducing, 59
    gospel-bearing, 33
    grace-based, 33
    law and, 133–35, 152–61
    made with Israel, 31
    mission and, 19
    mission directed, 19–20, 33
    old covenant and, 251–65
    Sabbath and, 182–206
    salvation history and, 305
    ultimate fulfillment at Second
        Coming, 30–32, 239–42
Noah, covenant with, 7–8, 15–16, 25n5,
    25n7, 171–72, 304
norm, law as, 103–4

obedience, 146–52, 161–62, 226. *See also*
    law, the
old covenant experience
    based on the flesh, 81, 93–96
    characteristics of, 81–82, 251, 297–300
    compared/contrasted with new
        covenant experience, 81–85, 235–36,
        251, 297–300
    differs from historical old covenant,
        79–82, 235–36, 294–300
    emphasis of Paul on the covenants, 92
    experienced by many at Sinai, 85–87
    legalistic obedience, 81
    lethal effect on spiritual life, 134
    ministry of death, 117

personally applied, 246–49
possible for people in New Testament
    era, 133–36
unbelieving, self-reliant response to
    gospel, 121–25
old covenant, historical
    characteristics of, 15–18, 79–80,
        292–96
    compared/contrasted with historical
        new covenant, 58–73, 79–81, 235–
        36, 251–55, 294–96
    designed for conversion and spiritual
        growth, 189
    differs from old covenant experience,
        80–82, 235–36, 294–300
    embedded with new covenant DNA
        markers, 38–47, 53, 235, 304
    emphasis of Hebrews 7–10, 91–92,
        251–66
    equated with Old Testament, xiii, 80,
        242n1
    equated with Sinai covenant, 49, 242n1
    equated with Ten Commandments, 37
    experience and, 85–87, 130–33
    faith-inducing, 49
    gospel-bearing, 48–49
    grace-based, 48–53, 55n22
    love in, 145–52
    mission-directed, 15–18, 42–44
    new covenant and, 91–92, 251–65
    not a different gospel, 106
    priesthood and ceremonial ritual of,
        260
    Sabbath and, 185–86, 198–99
    salvation history and, 161, 305

Paulien, Jon, 66, 157, 201
perfection, call to, 128–30
proclamation. *See* mission
prohibition, law as, 104
promises, covenant
    Jesus and, 66–67
    law as, 104
    salvation history and, 29–32, 39–47,
        242, 260–62, 304

provisions, covenant. *See* promises, covenant

punishment. *See* discipline, divine

rainbow, 7–8, 171–72, 180–81. *See also* gospel; Noah, covenant with

rapture, the, 207n3

Ratzlaff, Dale, 26n10, 54n10, 73n1, 74nn9–10, 166n1, 167nn14–16, 168n22, 213nn40–41

Rayburn, Robert, 1, 2n11, 12n18, 12n22, 34n3, 47, 84, 98, 100n4, 105, 122n27, 138n4, 139n6, 140n18, 141n29, 144, 158, 167n17

reconciliation
  experience and, 247–48
  relationship and, 30, 239
  salvation history and, 41–42, 304

redemption, covenant of
  characteristics of, 292
  creation and, 19–22
  promises of, 238–39, 242
  salvation history and, 79, 260–62, 275–82, 305

relationship, covenant as, 1–3, 30, 143–45, 239

rest, covenant, 217–23

Revelation, Book of, 199–203

revelation, progressive, 50–53, 60–62, 71–72

righteousness, 160–61

ritual, covenant and. *See* ceremony, covenant and

Robertson, O. Palmer, 34n3, 40, 54n8, 55n13, 70, 75n11, 79n3, 89n5, 105, 137n1, 138n3, 208n15

Sabbath, the, 39, 178–206, 217–23, 287–90.
  enduring covenant sign, 203
  in Revelation, 199–203
  instituted at creation, 178–79
  meaning of as sign, 181–82
  means "rest," 219

not a shadow, temporary ceremonial ritual, 192–93, 287–90

not for Israel only, 183–84

"residual glow" of creation, 179

seven-day week rooted in, 180

sign of covenant rest, 219–20, 227–29

sign of covenant with literal and spiritual Israel, 178, 184–85

sign of creation covenant, 180–81

*See also* law, the

sacrifice, animal. *See* ceremony, covenant and

sanctification
  experience and, 246–47
  of character, 54n7
  Sabbath and, 181–82
  salvation history and, 29–30, 39–41, 304
  the Spirit and, 240–41

saving grace, 25n7

schoolmaster, law as, 99–106

Shea, William, 33

sin
  Adam and, 237–38
  forgiveness of, 141n26
  law and, 107, 109–10, 115–17, 126–28
  *See also* experience, old covenant

Sinai covenant. *See* law, the

slavery, obedience and, 161–62

Stefanovic, Ranko, 145n6, 157, 158n25, 232n1

Stott, John, 139n10, 208n7, 242n2, 283n7

Strickland, Wayne, 40

Ten Commandments, 35n3, 44, 56n26, 58, 79–80, 91, 126, 143, 146–47, 155, 162, 166n7, 169n27, 191–92, 195–96, 198–205, 233nn2–3, 257–60, 265n1, 266n4, 283n7, 288–90, 292–93, 295
  as divine promises, 104
  "charter of freedom," 162
  equated with the old covenant, 37
  express essence of Sinai covenant, 37

forgiveness in, 44
God's love for people in, 146
in Revelation, 199–203
love as basis for obedience structured
    into, 147
magnified by Jesus, 80
New Testament authors and Jesus
    referred to, 143, 258
pit new covenant against, 108
prohibitive nature of, 104
second giving of, 124
unchanged, 257–60, 265n1, 288–90
universally applicable, 198
*See also* law, the
terminology, covenant, 1, 25n5
treaties, suzerainty, 54n4
Trinity, covenant within, 4–7
tutor, law as, 102–3, 159. *See also*
    schoolmaster, law as

unbelief. *See* faith
unity, covenant, 11n8

universality, covenant, 13–23
universe, the. *See* Creation, covenant of

veil, of Moses, 123–26
Vos, Geerhardus, 12n20, 43, 55n2, 89n5,
    180n17, 229n23, 242n1

Waggoner, Ellet J., 16, 89n4
Weinfeld, Moshe, 63, 73n6, 167n9
Westminster Confession of Faith,
    139n16
White, Ellen G., 79n2, 129n31, 233n4
will, covenant as, 1, 13–14, 185–89
Willard, Dallas, 14, 24n2, 35n3, 56n26,
    116n24, 165n30, 168n21, 260
works, 108. *See also* experience, old
    covenant

Yahweh, 232n1
yoke, the, 162–65